Policing Britain

Longman Criminology Series

Series Editor: Tim Newburn

Titles in the series:

Ian Brownlee, *Community Punishment: A Critical Introduction*
Adam Crawford, *Crime Prevention and Community Safety: Politics, Policies and Practices*
Philip Rawlings, *Crime and Power: A History of Criminal Justice 1688–1998*
Gary Slapper and Steve Tombs, *Corporate Crime*
Les Johnston, *Policing Britain: Risk, Security and Governance*

Policing Britain
Risk, Security and Governance

Les Johnston

 LONGMAN

An imprint of **PEARSON EDUCATION**

Harlow, England · London · New York · Reading, Massachusetts · San Francisco · Toronto · Don Mills, Ontario · Sydney
Tokyo · Singapore · Hong Kong · Seoul · Taipei · Cape Town · Madrid · Mexico City · Amsterdam · Munich · Paris · Milan

Pearson Education Limited
Edinburgh Gate
Harlow
Essex CM20 2JE
United Kingdom
and Associated Companies throughout the world

Visit us on the World Wide Web at:
http://www.pearsoned-ema.com

First published 2000

ISBN 0-582-29886-5   PPR

British Library Cataloguing-in-Publication Data

A catalogue record for this book is available from the British Library

Set by 35 in 10/12pt New Baskerville

Printed and bound in Malaysia, VVP

Contents

Series Editor's Preface

Our society appears to be increasingly preoccupied with crime and with criminal justice. Despite increasing general affluence in the post-war period, crime has continued to rise – often at an alarming rate. Moreover, the pace of general social change at the end of the twentieth century is extraordinary, leaving many feeling insecure. High rates of crime, high levels of fear of crime, and no simple solutions in sight, have helped to keep criminal justice high on the political agenda.

Partly reflecting this state of affairs, the study of crime and criminal justice is burgeoning. There are now a large number of well-established postgraduate courses, new ones starting all the time, and undergraduate criminology and criminal justice degrees are also now appearing regularly. Though increasing numbers of individual textbooks are being written and published, the breadth of criminology makes the subject difficult to encompass in a satisfactory manner within a single text.

The aim of this series is, as a whole, to provide a broad and thorough introduction to criminology. Each book covers a particular area of the subject, takes the reader through the key debates, considers both policy and politics and, where appropriate, also looks to likely future developments in the area. The aim is that each text should be theoretically-informed, accessibly written, attractively produced, competitively priced, with a full guide to further reading for students wishing to pursue the subject further. Whilst each book in the series is designed to be read as an introduction to one particular area, the Longman Criminology Series has also been designed with overall coherence in mind.

The subject of policing has received huge attention within criminology in recent years. In part this reflects the importance – symbolic and real – of the police to the character and order of our everyday world. It also reflects the extent to which policing, not just the police, is perceived to have changed and be changing. In this book, Les Johnston focuses on both state and commercial policing activities. In doing so, he reflects on how and why current policing arrangements take the shape they do, together with what the prospects for the future appear to be.

There is an array of complex structural changes affecting contemporary policing. Les Johnston examines the impact of globalisation and the concomitant pressures towards diversification and devolution, and centralisation and localisation, which appear to be pulling policing bodies in several different directions at once. As a consequence of such pressures the functions performed by policing bodies are also being transformed; such changes being characterised by Johnston as a move towards the 'policing of communities of risk'. The increasing diversification of policing involved in this transformation also raises a series of 'governmental problems'. These concern equity and justice, the relationship between different elements of the security network, and how such networks can and should be regulated.

In focusing on the future of policing, Johnston concentrates on the search for what he terms 'optimal policing': something that is neither 'quantitatively excessive' nor 'qualitatively invasive'. This involves embracing diversity. Networks that include both state and commercial policing are not only the precondition for many of our current policing problems, Johnston argues, but also a necessary means of their resolution – for the reimposition of a state monopoly over policing is impossible. This is a timely and provocative book, which will be of enormous value to students of criminology at all levels, as well as to practitioners looking for an informed guide to the most important debates in contemporary policing.

Tim Newburn
London, July 1999

Acknowledgements

Some of the arguments presented in this book first saw the light of day in earlier conference papers and seminar presentations. I am most grateful for the constructive feedback given by participants at the following venues: *Workshop On Evaluating Police Service Delivery* (jointly sponsored by the Ministry of the Solicitor General of Canada and the International Center for Comparative Criminology), University of Montreal (1994); *Globalisation and the Quest for Justice*, Law & Society Annual Meeting, University of Strathclyde (1996); Annual Conference of the Centre for Criminal Justice Studies, University of Northumbria (1996); Staff-Postgraduate Seminar, Centre for Criminal Justice, University of Leeds (1996); Annual Conference of the British Society of Criminology, Queen's University Belfast (1997); 49th Annual Meeting of the American Society of Criminology, San Diego (1997); Staff-Postgraduate Seminar, Scarman Centre, University of Leicester (1998).

While writing this book I have exchanged ideas with and/or received written material from a number of colleagues. I am particularly grateful to Ray Abrahams, Mike Brogden, Mark Button, Ray Coleman, Adam Crawford, Colin Dunnighan, Jaap de Waard, Peter Grabosky, Trevor Jones, Frank Leishman, Ian Loader (also for written comments), Barry Loveday, Peter Manning, Rob Mawby, Tim Newburn, Lesley Noaks, Clive Norris, Robert Reiner, Clifford Shearing, Jim Sheptycki, Joe Sim, Kevin Stenson, Neil Walker and David Wall. I am also grateful to the Research Policy Committee, School of Social Sciences, University of Teesside for financial support; to Tim Newburn, Series Editor, both for his general advice throughout, and for his constructive comments on the manuscript; to Les, Rob and Pearl for continuing to maintain a low profile; and to Reeth Amblers for a plentiful supply of quiet Tuesdays.

Introduction

The aim of this book is to examine late modern policing in Britain, drawing comparisons, where appropriate, with developments in North America and Europe. The book is organized around three themes: processes, functions and forms. Part One, comprising the first two chapters, is concerned with matters of process: specifically, the process of transition from modern to late modern society. After exploring the concept of policing, Chapter 1 considers the establishment of the new police in the context of the consolidation of the modern state. Chapter 2 focuses on the process of globalization as a core element in the restructuring of late modern society. Having outlined three dimensions of that process – economic restructuring, socio-cultural restructuring and governmental restructuring – the chapter makes some preliminary comments about the impact of globalization on policing and government. These issues are elaborated upon in later chapters and their implications considered more fully in the final chapter.

Part Two (Chapters 3 and 4) examines functional aspects of policing. Chapter 3 analyses the functions of modern police, considering both questions of 'what police do' and 'how they (should) do it'. During the course of this chapter a matrix of police action is constructed around two dichotomies: reactive versus proactive engagement; and minimal versus maximal scope. Chapter 4 considers how police functions are transformed under the impact of late modern change and relates some of these changes to the matrix of police action. Of particular significance here is the extent to which risk-based action signifies the functional integration or 'melding' of certain aspects of public and commercial police activity. The example of zero-tolerance policing is considered here in order to illustrate how risk-based techniques may be combined with disciplinary ones to produce new configurations of police action.

Part Three, which consists of five chapters, pursues the themes of governmental diversity and distanciation by examining the different forms of policing which may be found in contemporary Britain. Three of these chapters concentrate on different dimensions of public police organization. Chapter 5 considers the local dimension of public policing, a particularly important topic given the tendency for responsibility over matters of 'everyday' policing to be devolved to local levels. Among the issues considered here are police accountability, effectiveness and efficiency, community and problem-orientated ideologies, the relationship between local priorities and national objectives and the growth of consumerism in policing. Chapter 6 explores the fact that devolution and decentralization of policing appear to go hand in hand with its centralization. This chapter considers the extent to which key elements of police activity such as the policing of serious crime and public order are, effectively, nationalized or regionalized and explores the implications of such developments for accountability, effectiveness and justice. Chapter 7 looks at supranational and transnational developments in British and European policing and considers the significance of such developments for governance and the sovereignty of the nation state. By contrast, Chapter 8 analyses the structure and functions of the commercial security industry in Britain, paying particular attention to the impact its growth has on the delivery of just and accountable policing. Chapter 9 examines the local municipality and local civil society as loci for newly emergent forms of policing. After considering recent developments in municipal and civil policing, the chapter asks whether such initiatives can be integrated into local security networks in such a way as to enhance effective and responsive modes of policing at the local level.

Finally, Chapter 10 considers the future of late modern policing. Here, the aim is to speculate about the future while, simultaneously, discussing some of the normative issues which will have to be addressed if that future is to be a just and democratic one. In order to do this I reflect back upon a problem raised in Chapter 2: the fact that late modernity gives rise to both a fragmentation and a proliferation of policing. The former, if left unchecked, threatens us with unjust and ineffective policing. The latter, if left unchecked, threatens us with a 'maximum security society' (Marx, 1988). For that reason fragmentation and proliferation demand good government. The chapter first explores contemporary debates on the governance of diverse security networks, then focuses on issues of fragmentation and proliferation in the provision of security. Having reflected, once again, on the matrix of police action, it is suggested that what is required is neither the maximization nor the minimization of policing, but its optimization.

Part One:

Processes

Chapter 1

The Establishment and Consolidation of the Modern Police

Introduction

This book has three aims: to provide an analysis of the changing forms and functions of British policing; to consider the processes which have given rise to those changes; and to examine their implications for policing, society and governance. A unifying theme in addressing these three issues is the transition from 'modern' to 'late modern' systems of policing, a development which is increasingly apparent throughout Britain, Europe and North America. These transitional processes are considered in the first section of the book, the present chapter examining the establishment and consolidation of the modern police, the following one outlining some of the key features of late modern change and exploring their implications for policing. Since one of the central elements in the process of late modern transition is the fragmentation of policing into a diversity of forms (including municipal, commercial and civil modes) what follows, in subsequent chapters, is an analysis of *policing* rather than of the public police alone. For the same reason, the present chapter is concerned less with the detailed analysis of police history than with locating that history in the overall trajectory of change.

The present chapter consists of three sections. The first begins by considering the origins of organized police systems, then goes on to explore the concept of policing. Here it is argued that two terms – security and governance – are particularly fundamental to an understanding of modern policing. The second section examines the relationship between modernity and policing. Here a number of issues are considered: the problems of functionalism and teleology in modernist discourse; the significance of the diverse systems of policing which pre-existed the formation of the 'new police'; the impact of colonial policing on the development of modern policing systems; and the role of the modern police in the consolidation of national state sovereignty. A short concluding section reviews the implications of this analysis and outlines the structure of the remaining chapters.

Origins and definitions

Accounts of the transition to the formation of state police

Reiner suggests that modern societies exhibit what might be termed ' "police fetishism": the ideological assumption that the police are a functional prerequisite of social order, the thin blue line defending against chaos' (Reiner, 1997: 1003). However, as Reiner argues, many societies have maintained order without relying on the mobilization of a formal police system at all. Indeed, in a study of 51 pre-industrial societies, Schwartz and Miller (1964) found that only 29 contained specialized armed police forces deployed specifically for the enforcement of social norms. Schwartz and Miller (1964) contend that specialized police forces only emerged in relatively differentiated societies with a developed division of labour. By contrast, societies with simple structures enforced norms by alternative means. The level of complexity within Eskimo social structure, for example, was minimal, normative infractions being resolved by individualistic means: 'where homicide occurred, it was viewed as a private matter; consequently, private responses – the killing of the killer by the victim's kin – was condoned' (Mawby, 1990: 16). In those cases where such infractions threatened the wider social order – as in the case of repeated homicides – the group might agree to a collective response, such as a lynching. However, no permanent body existed to enforce group norms.

Schwartz and Miller's analysis draws upon certain teleological assumptions contained in the writings of Durkheim and Parsons about which I shall say more in the following section. Essentially, these writers link the emergence of specialized social institutions, such as the police, to the process of social differentiation. Indeed, for Parsons (1964; 1966) social differentiation is presumed to proceed along functional lines, social development being linked to the emergence of certain 'evolutionary universals' whose existence is central to effective social organization. However, as Reiner suggests, it is by no means necessary to link police forces exclusively to the emerging division of labour. They may also appear 'hand-in-hand with the development of social inequality and hierarchy' (Reiner, 1997: 1006). Those who adopt this second approach invariably link specialized police to the emergence of the state and class systems. Such a view – which also carries certain teleological assumptions – is central to the analysis of Robinson *et al.* (1994) whose aim is to link the emergence of police forces to the evolution of social control mechanisms in the transition from pre-state to state formations. Drawing upon anthropological evidence, the authors' central proposition is that 'a society dominated by a ruling class needs a coercive instrument to maintain its control over basic resources and over a labour force necessary to produce the surplus product to support and sustain the ruling class' (Robinson *et al.*, 1994: 3).

Robinson *et al.* (1994) suggest that while specialized police agencies are considered by many to be characteristic of societies organized as states, their origin can be traced to four transformations in kinship-based systems. 'Reciprocity' – a type characteristic of the Mbuti tribe of Zaire – involved a system of mutual aid in which there was no specialized division of labour other than that by sex, disputes being resolved within the group through processes of mediation and arbitration. Here there was no specialized police function since the control of basic resources was open to all. Under 'basic redistribution' tribal elders appropriated a surplus on the community's behalf for almost complete redistribution to group members. Usually, no police agency existed though, if one was present, it served the whole community. An example would have been the military societies of the Native Americans of the Great Plains, resources, such as, buffalo being protected for the benefit of all group members by police who held their powers on a temporary basis only. 'Complex redistribution' arose when tribal loyalty became subordinated to personal loyalty, the chief retaining enough of the surplus to attract retainers who enforced some of his orders. This process occurred with the Cheyennes, the Cherokees and other tribes, following their exposure to the values of white America. 'Complex chiefdom' arose when the chief's office became hereditary and the bureaucracy surrounding him increased, thereby providing the means for a transition to class society. In these last two cases the police function came to be concentrated more and more on the protection of particular, rather than communal, interests though no state apparatus and no class structure might have yet been present.

With the development of 'simple states' the chief's retainers became the nucleus of specialized police organizations, bodies which Robinson *et al.* argue 'must be maintained from the surplus labour appropriated by some central authority' (Robinson *et al.*, 1994: 52). Along with this process a state organization is formed, the incipient class structure turning the local kinship mode of production to its own ends. This process, it is said, occurred in a number of different ways. In the Gyaman society of West Africa, a slave-based economy replaced a largely kinship-based structure. By contrast, in Aztec society a centralized elite gained control over local lineage leaders who became alienated from kin-based communities.

Though the theoretical foundations of these two accounts are very different, one being grounded in functionalist sociology, the other in Marxist anthropology, they share a common view that the formation and consolidation of the state is inextricably linked to the establishment of organized police forces. I shall return to that issue in the following section where I also note some common problems arising from these accounts. For the moment, however, let us turn our attention to the concept of policing itself.

Policing and security

Elsewhere (Johnston, 1992a) I have suggested that one of the major shortcomings in the sociology of policing has been its tendency to conflate policing, a social function, with police, a specific body of personnel. Slippage between these two terms has, unfortunately, been commonplace. For example, Bittner's classic definition of the police role – 'a mechanism for the distribution of non-negotiably coercive force employed in accordance with the dictates of an intuitive grasp of situational exigencies' (Bittner, 1991: 46) – though perfectly adequate for that purpose, has frequently been interpreted as a definition of policing. This reduction of policing to the actions of a particular category of state agents is, however, both historically and substantively flawed. The fact is that the state's relative monopoly of policing was the product of governmental processes spanning the period from the early nineteenth century to the middle of the twentieth. The modern police's dominance of policing has been the historical exception rather than the rule, diversity rather than state monopoly being the normal pattern of provision.

Increasingly, the problems associated with this reduction have come to be recognized and there is a growing awareness of the need to consider patterns of historical and contemporary diversity. Reiner's recent analysis is emphatic on this point: '[p]olicing may be carried out by a diverse array of people and techniques of which the modern police is only one' (Reiner, 1997: 1005). These 'people and techniques', he points out, might include specialist state police forces ('the police'), state bodies whose main responsibilities may lie outside policing, contract security companies, in-house security personnel employed in commercial organizations, citizens engaged in civil policing initiatives and, increasingly, technological devices such as cameras and bugs. However, recognition of diversity poses new problems of definition. For, if policing is perceived as diverse and heterogeneous, rather than as singular and uniform, the temptation is to replace a reductive definition with an expansive one. It is for this reason that a common tendency has been to equate policing with social control.

The problem with this approach, as several writers point out (Johnston, 1992a; Bayley and Shearing, 1996; Reiner, 1997; Jones and Newburn, 1998), is that social control has ceased to have explanatory value because of the breadth of its definition. This produces particular difficulties in respect of policing, 'the unspoken assumption [being made] that policing (like capital punishment, education, potty-training, and imprisonment) are all manifestations of the same essential process' (Johnston, 1992a: 221). The result of this essentialist approach is a definition which explains everything and nothing, and it is for this reason that Cohen (1985) castigated those whose expansive use of the term social control had reduced it to a 'Mickey Mouse concept'. In order to resolve this problem and rescue the concept of social control from redundancy, Cohen argued that its use should be limited to describe 'organised ways in which society responds to behaviour and people it regards as deviant, problematic, worrying, threatening, troublesome or undesirable' (Cohen, 1985: 1–2). One obvious strength of this conception is that it defines social control as a purposive activity (something involving 'organised ways' of doing things) rather than merely one whose effect – whether intended or not – is to induce conformity.

Significantly, this purposive emphasis is also found in recent attempts to provide a more rigorous definition of the concept of policing. Reiner, whose definition owes much to Shearing (1992), sees policing as an attempt to produce security through 'the creation of systems of surveillance coupled with the threat of sanctions' (Reiner, 1997: 1005). Here, policing is defined as a purposive activity; though one whose ends are by no means guaranteed: '[p]olicing is the set of activities *directed* at preserving the security of a particular social order (although the effectiveness of any form of policing is a moot point)' (Reiner, 1997: 1005: emphasis in original). The most familiar system of policing, Reiner adds, is that associated with the modern police, comprising regular uniformed patrol of public space and *post hoc* investigation of crime and disorder. However, Reiner's definition also takes account of those policing activities undertaken by a wide range of public, commercial, military and civil agents.

Like Reiner, Jones and Newburn (1998) also distinguish policing from generalized social control and focus on its purposive character. However, unlike Reiner they exclude from consideration techniques of behavioural surveillance, such as observations made by neighbourhood watch groups. They also exclude from their analysis both informal social controls occurring in the community and formal controls administered by those in authority within organizations such as work places. Instead, their analysis addresses those 'organised forms of order maintenance, peacekeeping, crime investigation and prevention and other forms of investigation – which may involve a conscious exercise of coercive power' (Jones and Newburn, 1998: 18) where such activities are carried out by individuals or organisations regarding them as a central or defining part of their work. This definition has obvious strengths, emphasizing the purposive and organized element of policing and recognizing that policing is by no means the exclusive prerogative of those possessing coercive powers. However, its scope is narrower than Reiner's (1997), apparently excluding from consideration certain 'civil' modes of policing (see Chapter 9 below and Johnston 1996b), as well as those corporate modes of ordering, undertaken by bodies which, while not regarding policing as a central part of their activity, are fundamental to late modern governance (Shearing and Stenning, 1987; Shearing, 1992).

Bayley and Shearing define policing as a diverse, purposive activity and eschew all attempts to conceive it in the amorphous terms of social control: 'the scope of our discussion is bigger than the breadbox of the police but smaller than the elephant of social control. Our focus is on the self-conscious process whereby societies designate and authorize people to create public safety' (Bayley and Shearing, 1996: 586). This definition owes much to Shearing's earlier contention (1992) that policing is fundamentally about the establishment of security or peace. Security, he argues, always implies the preservation of some 'established order' against threat, the question of what constitutes a threat being conditional upon the particular order in question. The essence of security lies, however, less in the presence of protection than in the absence of risk. Here, Shearing affirms Spitzer's observation that security exists when 'something *does not* occur rather than when it does' (Spitzer, 1987: 47), a view which confirms the purposive element of policing: 'peace is seldom something that simply happens: it requires an *assurance* of security' (Shearing, 1992: 401).

This conception of policing as a purposive strategy involving the initiation of techniques which are intended to offer guarantees of security to subjects, provides a solid foundation for examining the diverse modes of policing considered in this book. Several things should be noted about this approach, however, all of which are addressed in later chapters. First, to conceive policing as an activity intended to provide guarantees of security to subjects does not, as Reiner (1997) observes, presuppose anything about the effectiveness of policing strategies. To offer guarantees of security is one thing. To assume that they are realized is another. Second, it cannot be assumed that policing is a singular, uniform, consensual activity. To define policing in terms of security says nothing about whose security is being put up for guarantee and it may be that the promotion of one person's security undermines another's. Third – and for our purposes most important of all – Shearing's (1992) approach defines policing as a governmental activity rather than just a criminological one. To say that policing is a governmental activity – that act of governance (or 'rule') directed towards the promotion of security – is not, however, to perceive it as an exclusive state function. On the contrary, one of the key features of late modernity is the dispersal of government to corporate, commercial and civil sites located outside, or on the periphery of, the state. Any understanding of late modern policing thus requires us to look beyond its criminological horizons towards those patterns of governmental restructuring which are characteristic of late modern societies.

Modernity and policing

The consolidation of the modern nation state was marked by the development of two bureaucratic institutions concerned with the matter of security: military organizations whose function was to secure national territorial boundaries against external threat; and police organizations whose function was to manage and secure internal boundaries and to protect the state and its citizens against internal threat (Dandeker, 1990). Prior to the formation of specialized police organizations for this latter purpose, policing was organized on an informal, private and localized basis, the locus of social order residing in the institutions of civil society (Johnston, 1992a). McMullan's (1987) account of crime control in London during the sixteenth and seventeenth centuries affirms the existence of such a diverse system of policing. Here, rising crime, coupled with the existence of various 'ungovernable' areas (Brewer and Styles, 1980) posed particular problems. Since enforcement agencies found it difficult to penetrate such areas, state rule was, in effect, 'an elaborate, negotiated and tenuous artifice' (McMullan, 1987: 123), order being maintained through a mixture of nepotism and patronage. In these circumstances policing was open to purchase, informants were encouraged by the authorities to spy on one another, victims were encouraged to seek out 'thief-takers' in order to recover their property, and the judiciary traded freely in warrants and pardons. Under these conditions, the state's authority was maintained through its involvement in various forms of 'commercial compromise' (South, 1987), government being, effectively, 'distanciated' (Giddens, 1990) or dispersed to agencies outside the state.

This example gives an insight into the pattern of policing which prevailed in England prior to – and to a significant degree after – the implementation of the early nineteenth century police reforms (Johnston, 1992a: ch. 1). This 'mixed economy of policing' (Mawby, 1990: 20) consisted of a variety of elements: thief-takers, spies and informants; associations for the prosecution of felons (cooperative bodies mobilized for the pursuit and prosecution of those engaged in burglary, sheep stealing and horse theft (Shubert, 1981; King, 1989; Philips, 1989); private police forces, such as the Bow Street Runners whose members offered, among other things, protection to brothels and inns in return for considerations (Bowden, 1978); and subscription and volunteer police forces set up by local authorities to undertake preventive patrols in the locality (Davey, 1983). Local circumstances added to that complexity. For example, early nineteenth century Portsmouth was policed by the navy, the military, customs officers and the yeomanry, as well as by borough police, municipal police, beadles, night watchmen and commercial security (Field, 1981).

Explanations for the emergence of the modern (or 'new') police have been dominated by the 'Anglo-American model'. Here, the emergence of public police forces is seen as a response to the problems of crime and disorder arising under capitalist industrialization and urbanization. Broadly speaking, the Anglo-American model may be divided into 'orthodox' (conservative) and 'revisionist' ('class-based') approaches (see, Reiner, 1992b; Brogden et al., 1988 for further elaboration of these terms). Orthodoxy (e.g. Reith, 1952; Critchley, 1978; Ascoli, 1979) explains the emergence of the new police in Britain in terms of the inability of an old, corrupt and disorganized system to cope with the escalating crime and disorder problems arising under rapid urbanization and industrialization. Peel's new police, it is claimed, introduced high standards of efficiency and integrity to policing without the degree of centralization that would threaten traditional liberties, thereby ensuring public support. For orthodoxy, the 'police solution' is also a reflection of 'Englishness'; as Reiner puts it, 'the irresistible force of industrialization and its control problems, meeting the immovable object of stubborn English commitment to liberty, could result in only one outcome – the British bobby' (Reiner, 1992b: 23–4).

For revisionists (e.g. Storch, 1975; 1976; Spitzer and Scull, 1977), by contrast, it is less the fear of crime than the need for a disciplined working class which precipitated the police solution. Capitalism's alienating tendencies gave rise to social tensions which demanded effective solution. The imposition of discipline on the working classes could not, however, be entrusted to the old parish constables whose allegiances were suspect. Moreover, reliance upon a patchwork system of protection funded from the coffers of private property owners could no longer be relied upon to ensure good order. Instead, a professional police force was recruited and paid for out of state funds. This solution was, itself, part of a wider process in which the costs of reproduction of labour power were socialized through the collective provision of health, welfare and protection. As Reiner puts it '[i]ntermittent, spasmodic law enforcement dependent on private initiative was replaced by continuous policing financed by the public purse' (Reiner, 1992b: 33). According to the revisionist view, the new police were concerned not merely with the problem of crime but also with the wider imposition of discipline on working class populations. For that reason the police officer was a 'domestic missionary' (Storch, 1976), subjecting the leisure and cultural pursuits of working class people to the same level of discipline which they experienced in the factory. Though beneficial to capitalism, those disciplinary techniques generated levels of resistance which persist until the present day and render police legitimacy permanently fragile.

The new police forces established under Peel's reforms were specialized public bureaucracies with responsibility for internal security. These organizations were staffed by salaried personnel, possessing full constabulary powers, and personifying, at street level, the state's monopoly of legitimate coercion. These three features of police organization – differentiation of function, rationalization of structure and location within the state – defined the police solution as a characteristically modern one. Yet, historical analyses of the new police – like the sociologies of modernity which influence them – have been unduly deterministic. In particular, they have been inclined to deploy concepts in a teleological fashion, seeing the police solution as the expression of some developmental force. Such teleological assumptions have also been combined with functionalist readings, the result being an analysis incapable of accounting for historical variations in police provision.

Many of these shortcomings are implicit in sociological accounts of modernity. Consider the concept of social differentiation – the emergence of specialized agencies for welfare, warfare, education, policing and the like. Though Durkheim (1964) saw social institutions as differentiated elements serving a socially integrative end, it was Parsons who developed a comprehensive theory of 'functional differentiation' – the process whereby particular social institutions evolved as the bearers of specialized 'functional prerequisites' on behalf of the societal system (Parsons and Smelser, 1957). Parsons contended that societies, social institutions and social practices could, in fact, be classified according to their degree of functional differentiation or, as he put it, their level of 'adaptive upgrading' (Parsons, 1966). More than that, he insisted that it was also possible to identify certain 'evolutionary universals': processes whose adaptive significance was so great that they constituted necessary conditions for the attainment of higher levels of social evolution.

Though Parson's analysis might seem of only marginal relevance to policing, the orthodox version of police history displays assumptions very similar to those contained in functionalist sociology. Reiner's (1992b) depiction of the orthodox account of the emergence of the 'British bobby', referred to earlier, describes a teleological cocktail of functionalism and evolutionism – stirred with a measure of cultural determinism – whose outcome ('the police solution') is, effectively, a form of 'adaptive upgrading'. Moreover, 'revisionist' accounts of the emergence of the new police, though based on different theoretical propositions and drawing substantively different conclusions, reproduce similar failings. In this case, the police institution arose as a functional corollary of the structural trajectory of capitalist industrialization. In both versions of police history – as well as in many mainstream accounts of modernization – the mode of explanation is both teleological and functionalist.

Such explanation gives rise to serious shortcomings. For one thing, it is clear that local studies of police history show a degree of variation in patterns of development which the dominant Anglo-American model is unable to explain (Johnston, 1992a: ch. 10). For example, Swift, suggests that revisionism's focus on the police's function vis-à-vis the capitalist state undermines the impact of local political considerations, 'since it was local rather than national considerations which underlay the organization, role and modus operandi of the new police' (Swift, 1988: 236). The same point is made by Davey (1983) whose study of the police in Horncastle, Lincolnshire – a body funded and controlled by the local authority to deal effectively with 'public morality offences' – casts doubt, both on the orthodox view that provincial police inefficiency was the norm prior to the new police and on its claim that fear of crime was the main catalyst in the development of police forces. Similar criticisms have been made about accounts of the police's development in the USA, one writer criticizing the functionalism of social historians for their tendency to treat the political realm as 'dependent' and 'epiphenomenal' (Ethington, 1987). It is hardly surprising for Mawby to claim, then, in respect of the both the USA and Britain, that 'no one set of conditions is common to even a majority of the situations within which the modern police became established' (Mawby, 1990: 22).

Brogden (1987) has argued that the Anglo-American model of police history is both narrow and ethnocentric, failing to consider a variety of alternative forms of policing which have appeared throughout modern history. In that respect, the dominant model not only ignores highly politicized forms, such as the 'high policing' of Fouchés France, but also both the 'administrative' and 'moral' forms which coexisted with the new police (Johnston, 1992a), and the contemporary commercial and civil forms which are discussed in later chapters. This suggests that what is required is an approach to police history which, being neither teleological nor functionalist, takes account of its unevenness and variability and places less emphasis on the supposedly rigid break between old and new forms. Such an approach would require us to take account of those private and informal modes of policing which continued to operate after the consolidation of the new police, thereby giving historical insight to our understanding of the present-day complex of public, commercial and civil policing (Johnston, 1992a).

To abandon the teleological reading of police history is to demand an analysis of those specific conditions which gave rise to particular policing systems. In the British case one of those conditions is Ireland, a particular failing of the Anglo-American model being that it 'typically overlooks the fact that modern police history on these islands began in Ireland' (Hillyard, 1997: 163). As Britain expanded its empire, a police model considered appropriate to colonial rule was put into place. This model 'was not, however, the Metropolitan Police Force but the Royal Irish Constabulary' (Mawby, 1990: 27). In 1786 the Dublin Police Act had established a new force in the city. (Ironically, similar legislation for London had been defeated in Parliament the year before amidst allegations of 'French despotism'). In 1814 Peel had established the Irish Peace Preservation Force, a highly militarized body which soon spread to ten counties. Eight years later the Irish Constabulary Act 1822 established the first regular rural police force, a body under centralized control, whose constables were accountable to the chief constable rather than to the law, and whose organization had a clear chain of command 'from the individual constable, through chief constable to inspector general and lord lieutenant' (Mawby, 1990: 28). The title 'Royal Irish Constabulary' was granted in 1867 following the Constabulary's deployment during the Fenian uprising.

As Bowden (1978) points out, the system of policing which the British established in Ireland bore little relationship to that obtaining elsewhere. While Britain had unarmed police forces responsible to local Watch Committees, Ireland had an armed, barracked and quasi-military force whose operation was more military than civil in character. A Sinn Fein pamphlet of the period noted that 'in Ireland no police force for the maintenance of the peace exists... as in other countries... The Irish police... are under the direct control of the English government', adding that a policeman would never be located in his native districts 'lest he should be on friendly terms with the people' (cited in Bowden, 1978: 168). Ireland was also policed more heavily than elsewhere. The number of police officers per head of population in 1836 stood at more than three times that for England and Wales and four times that for Scotland, and by 1897 Ireland still had 'over twice as many constables per capita than the rest of the United Kingdom' (Weitzer, 1995: 27).

Two issues are especially significant in respect of the history of Irish policing. First, there is the question of how far that history provides a basis for understanding later developments in British policing. One of the problems here is that analysis of the Irish situation has sometimes been used to justify the transfer of unsophisticated models of politics ('the strong state', 'the authoritarian state') to situations outside Northern Ireland (e.g. Ackroyd *et al.*, 1977). Nevertheless, that is not to deny the relevance of the Irish experience, Hillyard's (1997) analysis demonstrating that it is possible to gain a 'deeper structural understanding' of present-day security initiatives in the United Kingdom by a consideration of the past. Brogden (1987) makes a similar point regarding the long-term impact of Irish policing on contemporary operational tactics when he adds a corrective to those journalists who, mistakenly, traced the origins of public order tactics used during the mid-1980s to Hong Kong: 'The Hong Kong practices . . . derived initially from the same medley of experimentation that gave rise to both the Metropolitan Police and the Royal Irish Constabulary' (Brogden, 1987: 4).

A second issue concerns the relationship between the Irish model and colonial policing in general. Though Palmer (1988) takes the view that both the English and Irish models were exported during the nineteenth century, the former to towns, the latter to rural districts, he also subscribes to Jeffries's view that the Irish model was dominant in the colonies. Here a paramilitary organization, operating at the behest of metropolitan government, was well-suited to countries where 'the population was predominantly rural, communications were poor, social conditions were largely primitive, and the recourse to violence by members of the public who were "agin the government" was not infrequent' (Jeffries, 1952: cited in Hawkins, 1991: 18). However, it is now accepted that the pattern of influence was more complex than this analysis might suggest. Certainly, there were parallels between the Irish police and other colonial forces: central control by civil officials normally subordinated to the Governor; paramilitary organization; accommodation in barracks separate from the civil populations; recruitment of Irish officers by colonial forces; training of colonial officers in Dublin (Brogden, 1987; Hawkins, 1991). Nevertheless, there were also marked dissimilarities. As one commentator puts it: 'anyone who surveys the police forces of the empire . . . expecting to find so many replicas of the Irish constabulary will be disappointed . . .' (Hawkins, 1991: 19). Thus, while Ireland was heavily policed the colonies were not. While some colonial forces adopted Royal Irish Constabulary (and later Royal Ulster Constabulary) command structures, they did not necessarily follow their practices in training, method or development. And although some forces followed the Irish model, others were just as influenced by the Metropolitan one (Anderson and Killingray, 1991).

One thing which all colonial forces shared with their modern metropolitan counterparts, however, was a central role in the consolidation of national state sovereignty. Significantly, Bowden (1978) links the establishment of modern police to periods of crisis over the maintenance of public peace and security; crises which were 'ultimately about the continuance of governability' (Bowden, 1978: 21). Cain's (1996) analysis is consistent with this view. Police tasks in the colonies were wide ranging: maintaining external boundaries against other colonial powers; collecting customs duties; pacifying groups opposed to colonial expansion; collecting taxes; and so on. Yet, despite their breadth, most of these tasks concerned matters of governability and sovereignty. As Cain (1996) suggests, the colonial police's fundamental role – like that of the modern police of the metropolis – was not to control crime, but to produce order, a factor explaining the tardy development of many colonial CID departments (Cain, 1996). That connection between colonial policing and governance has continued to the present. Gaylord and Traver's (1995) analysis of the Royal Hong Kong Police confirms not only that the force's original organization as a gendarmerie related to the aim of deterring Chinese territorial ambitions, but also shows that in the recent period the force played a key role in the orderly transfer of sovereignty to China.

Conclusion

This book will argue that policing is a governmental issue. In this chapter it has been suggested that the development of the modern police, in both metropolitan and colonial locations, was linked to the consolidation of national state sovereignty. Moreover, as one commentator notes, the territorial integrity and internal stability of particular nation states was, itself, a precondition of meaningful relations between states: '[the modern police] became as indispensable for the functioning of the international state system as the standing armies and navies . . . No international treaty could be concluded unless all the signatory parties were reasonably secure at home' (Liang, 1992: 8). It must be remembered, of course, that state sovereignty is not only a historically specific concept connected with the rise of modernity, but also 'a highly distinctive political claim – to exclusive control of a definite territory' (Hirst and Thompson, 1995: 409). In the following chapter I shall suggest that social changes arising under late modernity have had significant impact on governance and policing, also altering the character of such claims to sovereignty. Subsequent chapters will explore the impact of these changes, suggesting that policing techniques orientated towards sovereignty are now combined with other disciplinary and risk-based techniques.

Before proceeding with that task, however, it is necessary to justify our use of the term 'late modernity' in the light of our earlier discussion of the hazards of teleological analysis. This issue can be illustrated by reference to one of the key features of late modernity, risk orientated action, a theme which is explored in several subsequent chapters. In the following chapter a distinction is drawn between two contemporary approaches to the analysis of risk: the sociological approach, associated with writers such as Beck (1992) and Giddens (1990); and the genealogical approach, associated with Foucault (1991) and others. One hazard of the sociological approach – common to the earlier sociologies of modernity associated with writers such as Parsons – has been to endow society, or in this context 'risk society' (Beck, 1992), with an unwarranted degree of sociological 'fate'. In order to avoid the teleological pitfalls of social determinism, many commentators choose, instead, to adopt the genealogical approach towards the analysis of risk, focusing on risk orientated action as the product of a particular style of thinking, rather than seeing it as the effect of mere external sociological forces. Accordingly, those inclined to this view prefer to describe the present risk orientated order as a period of 'post-Keynesianism' (O'Malley and Palmer, 1996) or 'advanced liberalism' (Rose, 1996), rather than as one of late modernity – arguably, a concept with teleological overtones. Though the analysis which follows is, itself, influenced by the genealogical approach, it has been decided to retain the concept of late modernity as a means of contextualizing changes in policing and governance. The reason for doing so is simple. Genealogical accounts, though rightly eschewing sociological determinism, invariably take account – sometimes only tacitly – of the social conditions of existence of risk orientated action. There seems little justification, then, for avoiding sociological definition of those conditions, provided that such definition avoids the pitfalls of teleology and social determinism. For that reason, two qualifications need to be made about our use of the term late modernity. First, there is no suggestion that the contemporary period marks the terminal stage of some unfolding, sequential process whose ends are predetermined by essential structural forces. Second, there is even less suggestion that some correspondence exists between that putative sequential process and particular forms of policing or governance, a view which is common to some historical accounts (see, for example, Robinson, *et al.*, 1994). On the contrary, the social conditions pertaining in late modernity are mediated by political factors which may alter outcomes significantly (O'Malley, 1992). Accordingly, the final chapter speculates about the future of late modern policing and discusses some of the normative issues which need to be addressed if that future is to be a just and democratic one.

Chapter 2

Globalization, Restructuring and Late Modern Policing

Introduction

A recent analysis of British policing suggests that police studies are increasingly 'going global' (Leishman *et al.*, 1996: 9). The purpose of this chapter is to explore the impact of globalization on policing, the assumption being that without an awareness of those global processes which are at the heart of late modernity it is increasingly difficult to make sense of contemporary developments. This does not mean that globalization produces predetermined outcomes. As Leishman *et al.* (1996) suggest, the British Conservative Party's reform agenda – itself a product of ideologies connected to globalization – has been partly resisted by the police in recent years. Nevertheless, fundamental changes in policing, such as the growing involvement of commercial and other non-state bodies in the provision of security, cannot be understood without reference to the globalization process. As the previous chapter suggested, the evolution and consolidation of modern policing was connected to the development of the state and the public sphere. What was new about the 'new police' was the fact that its constables personified state (public) authority at street level. Such a conception of policing was predicated upon the mainten- ance of some meaningful distinction between the state, the market and civil society. Globalization has undermined that distinction and, in so doing, has called into question the view that policing is an inherently public function.

Globalization is neither easy to define nor to explain. There is broad acceptance that it involves the growing transnational interdependence of societies and the reduction of temporal and geographical constraints on social processes (Waters, 1995). Yet there is less agreement on other matters: for instance, whether the process of globalization should be seen as linear or non-linear or whether it is a recent phenomenon or one with a long history. On this second issue some writers see globalization as a universal historical force, others link it to the process of capitalist modernization, while yet others relate it to the specific forms of post-industrialization characteristic of contemporary 'disorganized capitalism' (Lash and Urry, 1987). For the purposes of this chapter, however, globalization will be conceived as a multidimensional process (Held and McGrew, 1993) involving the simultaneous 'shrinking' and 'stretching' of space and time. Though more will be said on that in due course, 'shrinking' and 'stretching' in this context refers to the fact that social relations, economic transactions, cultural interactions and political exchanges become extruded, escaping the traditional parameters of locality, region or nation which previously contained them. Such spatial extrusion coincides with temporal extrusion, developments in information technology, electronic data processing, satellite communications and supersonic travel compressing time and minimizing its impact on human relations. At the same time, globalization should not be seen as something which integrates the world into a single 'world community' (Cope *et al.*, 1995), nor as something which eradicates nation states. Rather, globalization gives rise to inconsistent and sometimes contradictory patterns.

Globalization involves societal restructuring. The following section examines three dimensions of that process: economic restructuring, socio-cultural restructuring and governmental restructuring. The second section makes some preliminary comments about the impact of globalization on policing and on government. As to the former, the aim is to introduce themes which are discussed more fully in the next eight chapters. As to the latter, the aim is to introduce issues which are examined in the final chapter.

Dimensions of globalization

Economic restructuring

Globalization engenders two distinct but related forms of economic restructuring. First, there is the restructuring of production and the market. Essentially, this involves two processes: the internationalization of production and the globalization of financial transactions, both of which are related to the expansion of transnational corporations (Held and McGrew, 1993). By their very nature the national subsidiaries of transnational corporations operate according to overriding corporate strategies. To that extent, investment and production decisions may sit uneasily with local, regional and national concerns. This has led to the suggestion that during the last two decades the interdependence of capitalist economies is such that national governments no longer have the capacity to pursue independent economic policies on the grounds that it is 'exceedingly difficult to "buck" global markets' (Held and McGrew, 1993: 270). This state of affairs is compounded by the transformation of the financial sector, through technological means, into a twenty-four hour global market place. As Held and McGrew (1993) suggest, the effect is to shorten the chain of connections between global economic processes and the direct experiences of consumers: not only do sudden movements in international financial markets impact directly on governmental policy, they rapidly filter down to affect the lives of individual citizens.

Waters (1995) suggests that these developments indicate a transition from multinational capitalism to globalizing capitalism, the latter involving a shift to 'spatial optimization of production of profit opportunities; growth of European and Japanese sourced FDI [foreign direct investment]; increased FDI in the European ex-state socialist societies; [and] expansion of inter-firm alliances and joint ventures' (Waters, 1995: 78). A dominant form of transnational enterprise is now the 'alliance' through which allied corporations engage in technology transfers, production licensing, market sharing and the 're-badging' of each other's products – as in the marketing of British made Honda cars as 'Rover' (Waters, 1995). Though some have suggested that these processes are indicative of a transnational corporate hegemony whose power erodes the sovereignty of nation states, the reality is rather more complex. Indeed, it might be argued that the governance of international markets involves nation states in a critical new role – less as 'sovereign' bodies than as components of an international 'polity' in which their function is that of 'distributing and rendering accountable powers of governance, upwards towards international agencies . . . and downwards towards regional and sub-national agencies of economic coordination and regulation' (Hirst and Thompson, 1995: 408). The existence of shifting alliances between corporations simultaneously involved in competition and cooperation with one another, suggests that corporate power is variegated and rumours of the death of the nation state, as yet, exaggerated. For not only is the erosion of national sovereignty unevenly spread, the development of regional strategies by groups of nation states – notably in Europe – aims to handle some of the consequences of global competition. In addition to that, it is clear that the nation state still retains a key role in matters, such as the control of labour migration (Waters, 1995) and the general regulation of populations (Hirst and Thompson, 1995), both of which are also central to debates about the future of policing. For these reasons, it is more accurate to see economic and political sovereignty as diverse and fractured, rather than as eroded.

A second form of economic restructuring applies at the organizational level. The most significant shift here has been from Fordist to post-Fordist systems of organization. Fordism, named after the practices initiated by the Ford Motor Company in the USA, produced standardized items for mass markets using intensive mechanization in order to maximize economies of scale and reduce costs. During the post-war period Fordism became a global productive system covering both the capitalist west and the socialist east. As Waters (1995) points out, however, Fordism was an incomplete paradigm, leaving untouched the question of who makes decisions and by what means. In consequence, economic decision making in Fordist enterprises varied from country to country, some being centralized others decentralized, some being dominated by managers others by state managed bureaucracies. Post-Fordism has subsumed some of these cultural differences, proposing a 'single idealization of appropriate organizational behaviour' (Waters, 1995: 81).

First and foremost, post-Fordism is preoccupied with developing flexible structures and practices to deal with the exigencies of uncertain market conditions. Accordingly, where Fordism is characterized by mass production and top-down organizational hierarchies, post-Fordism emphasizes 'innovation, quality, customised products and the flexible machinery that such customisation requires' (Murray, 1991: 25). In order to meet these demands emphasis is placed upon the inculcation of customer-orientated work cultures, the decentralization of organizational structures and the maximization of labour flexibility. Though initiated by private sector companies, these organizational reforms soon spread to public sector organizations like hospitals, universities, prisons and the police. Bagguley *et al.* (1990) identify some of the key components of post-Fordist organizational ideology, all of which are now prevalent in public sector organizations: the development of flexible 'dual' labour markets in which a distinction is drawn between highly rewarded 'core' and poorly rewarded 'peripheral' work; the commodification of services which come to be bought and sold like any other commercial product; encouraging people to engage in 'do-it-yourself' forms of self-provisioning; sub-contracting parts of the service to cheaper providers; encouraging managers to manage their resources more intensively in pursuit of organizational objectives; devolving responsibility for service delivery to the lowest appropriate organizational level while, simultaneously, ensuring that relevant ministers remain able to control the most operationally sensitive areas. It is the paradoxical connection between these last two elements – 'the *centralisation* of the planning of production . . . [and] the *decentralisation* of the units of production (Bagguley *et al.*, 1990: 20) – which is at the centre of debate about the impact of post-Fordism on governmental power. Does post-Fordist organization indicate a real decline in state-governmental authority or does it merely obscure the surreptitious consolidation of rule?

Socio-cultural restructuring

Globalization in general and economic restructuring in particular add complexity, diversity and contradiction to societal structures and processes. Not only are the effects of restructuring uncertain – governmental power is, arguably, both decentralized and recentralized – the terminology by which we understand these processes is, itself, called into question. Restructuring at the socio-cultural level produces similarly diverse effects. Consider the example of social stratification. During the post-war period conventional sociological understanding has declared that Britain has moved from a society dominated by economic class divisions to one in which such divisions are far less salient. Proponents of that view would maintain that while economic class remains a significant element of social division, differentiation by religion, race, gender, region, nationality, ethnicity and age have grown in significance. For much of the post-war period it has been argued that such changes have been associated with a shift in political behaviour, culminating in the decline of class-based voting and the demise of political ideologies based upon class divisions (Drucker *et al.*, 1979; Lipset, 1960; Dunleavy, 1980). Though these arguments are sometimes based upon an over-reductive reading of the political efficacy of class (Johnston, 1986), it is undoubtedly the case that social divisions – and the conflicts associated with them – are, nowadays, distributed along plural lines. If that is true, of course, it poses obvious problems for British policing. Can a system of state-centred policing, historically engineered – at least in part – to manage the disorders arising from a society with relatively simple class divisions, handle the problems associated with a more complex and less predictable system of social divisions?

Contemporary analyses of the social plurality characteristic of late modern societies, such as Britain, have focused on two key dimensions: mass consumption and risk. Though consumption of commodities is a defining characteristic of all capitalist societies, mass consumption proper was built upon the economic growth of the post-war period. During this time two features of mass consumption stood out as particularly significant: the television set and the automobile (Therborn, 1995). The expansion of mass consumption was, of course, US led, self-service shops and supermarkets spreading across Europe in the early post-war years. Later, during the 1970s, American corporations such as Coca-Cola and McDonald's opened outlets in Europe, Australia and Japan, finally expanding into Eastern Europe and China during the 1980s. As Therborn suggests, although consumption patterns retain a 'class imprint' they also make possible the reorientation of behaviour around 'chosen life-styles and chosen consumption identities' (Therborn, 1995: 145). For that reason it is important to make a distinction between mere consumption and the development of a mass consumer culture (Featherstone, 1991). In a mass consumer culture, products possess not merely a material value but a symbolic one: 'consumption becomes the main form of self-expression and the chief source of identity . . . both material and non-material items, including kinship, affection, art and intellect become commodified' (Waters, 1995: 140).

A particularly significant development in this regard is the commodification of security. The expansion of private security during the post-war period may be traced, in part, to the need for consumption locations, such as supermarkets and shopping malls, to be policed. It is these sites of 'mass private property' – areas of private ownership whose profitability is contingent upon relatively unrestricted public access – which are closely linked to the growth of private policing (Shearing and Stenning, 1981). It is not merely that private policing grew in order to secure the conditions of profitable consumption, however. During the post-war period, security itself became more and more commodified, the industry's expansion being linked to its capacity to persuade consumers to demand higher levels of protection. The problem is, however, that the success of consumer capitalism is based upon the indefinite expansion of demand rather than the satisfaction of need. As Spitzer (1987) points out, the objective consumption of security – through the provision of bars, bolts, alarms, static and mobile guards, CCTV cameras and razor wire – is unlikely to satiate the demand for subjective security. Indeed, such are the contradictions of consumption that the more security we consume, the less secure we may feel.

Security is, of course, closely connected to risk. The ubiquity of risk has become a dominant theme of contemporary life, virtually every item of human conduct seeming to have a risk associated with it. Work is stressful but unemployment is more so. Walking the streets is risky (muggers, robbers, stalkers) but so is staying at home (burglars, domestic accidents, domestic violence). Increasingly, society is organized to manage and minimize risks, battalions of experts being deployed to gain the trust of clients at fear of risk: counsellors, therapists, commercial risk managers, dieticians, ecologists and the like. Additionally, state insurance against risk is supplemented by the activities of a private sector willing to offer protection against virtually any insurable hazard. Yet, paradoxically, the resolution of risks may create new dangers, a point well demonstrated by the pathologies and side effects associated with medical intervention (Illich, 1975). In consequence, public demand for the knowledge of experts is often accompanied by a fundamental lack of trust in the solutions they invoke to manage risks.

There are two dominant explanations for our contemporary preoccupation with matters of risk. The first has its roots in the sociology of modernity. Giddens (1990) has a particular interest in the relationship between risk, trust and security under conditions of 'high modernity', seeing risk as both globalized (distributed on a global rather than a local scale) and personalized (built into people's subjective concerns about their identity). For Beck (1992; 1996) the 'risk society' is a distinct stage of modernity, superseding the 'class society' of the industrial era. Risks in class society, such as occupationally induced diseases, are, he suggests, the inevitable cost of industrial growth. Moreover, politics in class society is concerned, not with risk, but with the equitable distribution of the products of growth. By contrast, risk society is a stage of development in which the thrust of technical innovation generates global risks (nuclear war, pollution) which are beyond effective control. Risk society is a society of 'fate', the salience of class divisions being overridden by the similarity of destinies which unites offenders with victims. After all, those who perpetrate acts of nuclear war will share the same fate as their victims since risk is undiscriminating. For Beck, those living in risk societies are no longer concerned with the attainment of 'good' normative ends such as justice, equality or equity. Their sole preoccupation is with 'preventing the worst' (Beck, 1992). The risk society is a society obsessed with security.

An alternative, genealogical account, prefers to analyse risk as 'part of *a particular style of thinking* born during the nineteenth century' (Rose, 1996: 341). This explanation is particularly concerned with the historical development of the statistical and human sciences and with the deployment of social scientific techniques for the management of aggregate populations through health, welfare and social security reforms. According to this view government during the twentieth century has become increasingly preoccupied with the management of aggregate risks through the application of actuarial and insurential techniques (Ewald, 1991; Castel, 1991). In the contemporary period such techniques have been accompanied by the growth of a wide variety of risk-based technologies. In the field of policing, for example, these include designing out crime, offender profiling and situational crime prevention. In the view of some writers these techniques represent a decisive shift from disciplinary to actuarial and risk-orientated modes of government (Feeley and Simon, 1994).

Whether one focuses on the sociological preconditions of risk or on the modes of thinking deployed to manage it, risk is a central feature of contemporary life. This is particularly important when considered alongside the issue of security. If, in a consumer culture, personal identity is a product of the life-style associated with the purchase of given commodities, and freedom from risk constitutes a major personal preoccupation, then '[p]rotection against risk through investment in security becomes part of the responsibilities of each active individual' (Rose, 1996: 342). This new definition of civil responsibilities has several implications for policing and for the role of the state in the provision of security on an authoritative basis. First, it confirms that a rising demand for policing and security services is likely to be associated with conditions of globalization. Second, it suggests that there is a changing relationship between those who provide such services and those who consume them. Far from being the mere 'clients' of state-delivered police services, those who purchase commercial security will enjoy the status of 'sovereign' consumers. Others may choose – or be obliged through lack of income – to engage in various forms of 'self-provisioning' in order to ensure their own security and satisfy the requirements of responsible citizenship. Finally, it changes the character of the community to be policed. One of the main problems for policing under conditions of globalization is how to achieve the 'civic' virtues of public accountability and social justice in communities composed of atomized consumers. That problem is not restricted to the local level. The globalization of consumption means that the reconstruction of civil society is a global problem as well as a local one (Lipschutz, 1992).

The state and governmental restructuring

The complex and contradictory effect of globalization is seen no more clearly than in the restructuring of government and the state. Here, three processes are at work. First, the policy of privatization alters both the balance and the relationship between the public and private spheres (Edgell *et al.*, 1994). In referring to privatization at this point, it should be emphasized that I am referring only to an economic policy. Elsewhere (Johnston, 1992a), I have suggested that privatization should be seen in broadly sociological, rather than narrowly economic terms. This broader definition will be used later when we consider the different dimensions of the privatization of policing. The economic privatizations of the 1980s and 1990s had their derivation in the governmental crises of the 1970s. During that time recession, industrial unrest, high unemployment and soaring inflation had led some to consider whether Britain was 'ungovernable' (Rose, 1979) and others to argue that western states were experiencing 'fiscal crisis' (O'Connor, 1973). The governmental response in Britain – as in many other countries – was to try and shrink the public sector by a process of 'rolling back the state'. Privatization took many forms including the selling of nationalized assets, the introduction of compulsory competitive tendering in the public sector, the deregulation of public services and the application of private sector management techniques to public bodies. The aim of such policies was to introduce market-based forms of service delivery into the public sector or, at the very least, to subject public sector organizations to the effects of quasi-markets. By the 1990s much of the Civil Service had been reorganized into agencies, all of them having business plans and clear statements of their contractual responsibilities. As Rhodes points out the effect of such reorganization was to 'distance ministers and top civil servants from operational matters, leaving them free to concentrate on policy' (Rhodes, 1994: 141).

It is worth making two observations about these reforms. First, they constituted an attempt to 'reinvent government' (Osborne and Gaebler, 1993) and, in so doing, blurred many of the conventional distinctions between levels of governmental responsibility. In Britain, for instance, the Head of the Prison Service now bears responsibility for those operational failings which would, hitherto, have been borne by the Home Secretary. Second, it is important to recognize that 'rolling back the state' was an uneven process. The Thatcherite rhetoric of public expenditure cuts was not met by a significant reduction in total levels of spending due to the expanding social security budget, an ageing population and high levels of unemployment (Savage and Charman, 1996). All that was achieved after 1979 was a small reduction in the percentage of gross domestic product expended by government relative to previous administrations. However, that reduction was not evenly distributed. Certain public services, such as housing, were net losers in this process. Others, such as the police, were not. In 1982 police expenditure stood at £2,780m. By

1993 it had risen to £7,685m (Savage and Charman, 1996). However, as Savage and Charman point out, the relative success of the police in expenditure terms has also to be put into context. Not only was the bulk of police expenditure absorbed by pay, police organizations had already begun to be subjected to managerial efficiency reforms during the early 1980s. By the 1990s it was clear that politicians were no longer willing to treat the police as a special case. One other factor should be taken into account here. The commercial security sector had experienced significant levels of growth since the 1960s and 1970s. Thus, while policing was expanding in absolute terms, the relative balance between the state and commercial sectors of provision was undergoing its own process of restructuring.

Second, government and the state are affected by developments occurring at European and international levels. As Cope *et al.* (1995) suggest, globalization has diminished the capacity of government to manage their economies independently, thus encouraging them to cooperate within regional forums such as the European Union. For Rhodes (1994) this is symptomatic of 'the Europeanization of everything'. According to this view, Europeanization transforms British government, eroding national sovereignty and instigating a new transnational policy network in which professional-bureaucratic interests, accountable to nobody, gain increasing influence. Whether that view is indicative of some future European super state or merely suggestive of a policy process with a 'hollow core' (Dyson, 1994), there is common agreement that the future is one of complexity and uncertainty. This is no more clear than in respect of the issue of sovereignty: 'any conception of sovereignty which assumes it is an indivisible, illimitable, exclusive and perpetual form of public power – embodied within an individual state – is defunct' (Held and McGrew, 1993: 273).

Those complications are by no means limited to Europe, Held and McGrew pointing to a wider internationalization of the liberal democratic state. During the post-war period states have engaged, increasingly, in international and multinational forms of governance through intergovernmental organizations, transnational pressure groups and international non-governmental organizations. In addition, organizations such as the World Bank, the International Monetary Fund and the General Agreement on Tariffs and Trade, along with the United Nations itself, have addressed issues of international resource allocation in a highly political forum. By their very nature such organizations place constraints on national sovereignty. Thus, the North Atlantic Treaty Organization is able to impose constraints upon the military autonomy of member states, thereby demonstrating the internationalization of security. Some of the issues which these developments raise are well illustrated in respect of non-military security and policing matters. While the International Criminal Police Organization (Interpol) has functioned only as a global intelligence network between autonomous national members, it is less clear whether such a limited role will apply to Europol. Though legal, jurisdictional and police organizational factors at the national level create obstacles to effective operational coordination, some writers have speculated that there will be a transnational melding of internal and external security organizations (Anderson *et al.*, 1995), one effect of which may be the greater integration of 'high' and 'low' police functions (Brodeur, 1983). That possibility begs the question of whether key dimensions of policing and security – internal and external, civil and military, public and commercial – might, in future, become more integrated along transnational lines. Whatever the prospects, we should also remember that security is, by no means, an exclusively public function. Indeed, leading commercial security corporations, such as Securicor, Pinkerton, and Wackenhut, have long operated in a transnational arena (Johnston, forthcoming).

The third area of governmental restructuring has occurred through the application of the so-called New Public Management (NPM). NPM applies post-Fordist organizational principles to the public sector and has several components: the professionalization of public sector management; the introduction of explicit standards and measures of performance; the introduction of a greater emphasis on output controls; the disaggregation and decentralization of work units; the initiation of competition; the importation of private sector management practices into the public sector; and the inculcation of an overriding emphasis on discipline and economy in resource use (Hood, 1991). NPM provides the managerial philosophy which lies behind many of the privatization policies instigated during the last two decades. Leishman *et al.* (1996) draw particular attention to the paradoxical effects of the philosophy: centralization, decentralization and fragmentation. First, as was suggested earlier, policy is placed in the hands of a governmental executive represented by senior ministers and officials. Thus, for example, key aspects of policing, penal and judicial policy are, increasingly, defined by the Home Secretary and senior civil servants. At the same time the delivery of such policy is decentralized to agencies, quangos, voluntary bodies, commercial contractors and disparate groups of citizens. (Though one is speaking here about policy delivery within nation states, it is clear that similar issues are at stake in the European Union with respect to 'subsidiarity': the principle that responsibility for carrying out tasks should be held at the lowest level of government competent to take them.) The paradox of centralization and decentralization is further accompanied by various forms of fragmentation. Thus, the process of compulsory competitive tendering splits the client (the elected body) from the contractor (the local authority or private contractor), stripping local government of many functions and redistributing them among a plethora of non-elected quangos (Leishman *et al.*, 1996).

Fragmentation and diversity of service provision is further underlined by two other influences. The first of these is the rhetorical appeal to community as a site of government, a view which has spread across Europe and North America in recent decades. That rhetoric is not peculiar to (community) policing, also being prevalent in penal policy (punishment in the community), justice policy (community mediation), schools policy (community education) and health policy (care in the community). Alongside community there is the accompanying rhetoric of partnership and the call to establish interagency and multiagency networks for the effective delivery of services. In Britain, governmental initiatives such as the Urban Programme, City Challenge and the Single Regeneration Budget have focused on the development of partnerships between public, commercial and voluntary bodies. These twin rhetorics constitute an attempt to address a governmental problem: how to establish coherence in a governmental system which is, increasingly, fragmented. Both are, however, predicated on simplistic notions of social homogeneity. The multiagency model assumes that the common interests of partners will override the centrifugal tendencies inherent in the partnership model. Proponents of community, likewise, hark back to a mythical past in which the collective sentiments of communal life are expected to provide insulation against the forces of fragmentation and difference. The irony of community is that, far from being a solution to the problem of fragmented government, it constitutes – along with privatization, internationalization and the new managerialism – a locus of that fragmentation.

Globalization, rule and policing

Fragmentation and images of rule

The paradoxes of globalization call into doubt traditional conceptions of governmental authority. The conventional view that states govern through the exercise of authority, backed by the capacity to exert their monopoly of legitimate coercion through bodies such as the police (Weber, 1964), has given way to a rather more uncertain definition of government. In recent years this uncertainty has been expressed in a complex imagery of government, rule and the state. Here, the state has been conceived as 'stretched' (Bottoms and Wiles, 1996); as 'lean' (Cope et al., 1995); as subject to the processes of 'unravelling' (Crook et al., 1993), and 'hollowing out' (Jessop, 1993; Rhodes, 1994); and as engaged in strategies of 'rule at a distance' (Shearing, 1996) through its adoption of 'steering', rather than 'rowing', functions (Osborne and Gaebler, 1993). Though these matters are discussed more fully later, it is worth making a few preliminary comments on some of the issues at stake.

Rhodes has argued that the British state is undergoing a process of 'hollowing out' in which government is 'eroded' by the various developments described throughout this chapter. Rhodes does not believe that the era of the 'hollow state' has yet arrived in Britain, though he considers that the processes which lead to its hollowing are potentially dangerous ones. In particular, he believes that the loss of central and local governmental functions to agencies and to the European Union, coupled with the impact of the new managerialism, gives rise to 'fragmentation and diminished accountability' and 'enlarges the potential for catastrophe' (Rhodes, 1994: 151). Yet, this account endows the process of restructuring with a degree of singularity it does not possess. Certainly, part of the logic of globalization is a logic of uniformity. National identity is eroded by the internationalization of capital. Space and time are compressed by supersonic travel and satellite communications. Yet, globalization is also a contradictory process giving rise to counter-tendencies. Despite Europe's development of supranational organizations during the post-war period, we have also witnessed a dramatic rise in nationalist political movements. Despite the influence of global consumerism, regional and local cultural variations remain important. To that extent, globalization is perfectly compatible with regionalization and localization and may, indeed, provoke their very development. The result of globalization is not uniformity but an unstable combination of tendencies: centralization and decentralization; internationalization and nationalism; homogeneity and diversity; fragmentation and consolidation.

Jessop's analysis of the 'hollowing out' process takes account of some of these contradictions. He suggests that although the nation state retains important areas of sovereignty, its capacity to exercise rule is limited by the triple displacement of powers 'upward, downward and outward' as evidenced by the processes of Europeanization, decentralization and privatization. However, he also notes that this complex of tendencies produces diverse effects: 'the national state's tendential loss of autonomy creates both the need for supranational coordination and the space for sub-national resurgence' (Jessop, 1993: 10). Jessop's conception of 'hollowing out' is analogous to the 'hollow corporation' in which transnational companies have headquarters in one country while pursuing operations elsewhere. This analogy suggests that the nation state retains certain headquarters executive functions, having some of its powers displaced. As Cope *et al.* (1995) point out, this indicates not that the state is being 'eroded or eaten away' (Rhodes, 1994: 138) but that its 'hollowing' involves the separation of core and peripheral functions, the former being carried out at the centre, the latter at the periphery. On that basis, they insist that while some parts of the state are 'hollowed out', others are 'filled in' (Cope *et al.*, 1995). Accordingly, the decentralization of certain state functions is perfectly compatible with the centralization of others.

This debate raises a number of issues, three of which are particularly important. First, there is the question of 'who (or 'what') rules'? Rhodes argues that, as a result of the processes associated with global restructuring, 'government is smaller' (Rhodes, 1994: 151). Whether this is true, of course, depends on one's meaning of government. Yet, even if we accept the claim at face value, it is clear that the shrinkage of government does not imply any minimization of the governmental function ('rule'). Indeed, in a later work, Rhodes himself refers to the process of 'governing without government' (Rhodes, 1995). One of the implications of restructuring, therefore, is that rule may be located outside the formal agencies of government and the state. This begs not only the question of 'who may rule'? In a world of expanded corporate economic and political power – a power which is not reducible to the capacities of any given individuals (Johnston, 1986) – one has also to address the question of 'what may rule'?

Second, there is the matter of how rule is exercised. One answer to that question is given by Osborne and Gaebler (1993) who suggest that an element of differentiation has emerged within rule, the state retaining certain 'steering' functions while devolving the responsibility for 'rowing' to external agencies, commercial organizations, voluntary bodies, the community and groups of active citizens. Drawing upon that image, Shearing (1996) suggests that what we are presently witnessing is 'state rule at a distance': the re-emergence of those 'distanciated' (cf. Giddens, 1990) modes of governance which were prevalent in Europe before the eighteenth century. This image raises a number of issues, not least whether effective state rule can be maintained over those outposts of governance which are in the hands of bodies with substantial powers, such as business corporations; and, if it cannot, what this implies for the concept of – albeit distanciated – 'state rule'. An alternative answer to the question of how rule is exercised is given by Cope et al. (1995). Whereas Osborne and Gaebler (1993) and Shearing (1996) argue that there is a differentiation within the *practice* of rule, Cope et al. (1995) suggest that the differentiation occurs along *functional* lines, the 'lean state' taking on core tasks and devolving responsibility for peripheral ones to alternative domains of rule. Obviously, this image of rule assumes two things: first, that a distinction can be made between core and peripheral governmental functions; and, second, – by implication – that the former are more essential to the 'lean state's' maintenance of rule than the latter.

So far, two issues have been raised: who (or what) rules, and how? There is also a third question. How do particular governmental functions relate to particular domains of rule? Or, to put it another way, which societal functions are subjected to which modes of rule? Is it the case, for instance, that policing remains a core function of the state under conditions of late modernity? Or, may the 'distanciation' of the state's rule over policing proceed to a point at which this view can no longer be sustained?

Globalization and policing

At this point it is useful to make some observations about the impact of globalization on policing. For the moment, the aim is a very limited one: to make some preliminary comments on matters which are discussed more fully in the next eight chapters. To that extent, these comments serve only to link the substantive matters discussed in these chapters to the theoretical focus of the present one. The objective is merely to provide some clues to the direction of future arguments by referring to earlier ones.

Consider, first, the issue which is raised in the following two chapters: the functional characteristics of modern and late modern policing. In the previous chapter I discussed the establishment and consolidation of the new police, relating its formation to key elements of the modernization process and to its role in the consolidation of the nation state. The establishment of the new police was confirmation of governmental investment in the application of what one might call 'a state police solution' to the problems of crime and disorder arising in industrial capitalist societies such as Britain. Subsequently, much of the history of state policing has been preoccupied with resolving how to strike an appropriate balance between the 'crime control' and 'order maintenance' functions of policing. These matters are discussed in detail in the following chapter. Further complexity is added to these debates by the social changes emanating from the globalization process. Two, in particular, have repercussions for debates about the functional characteristics of contemporary policing. First, as was suggested earlier, the growing salience of plural social divisions during the contemporary period begs the question of whether there is a discrepancy between modern police organisations and the policing problems they are required to face. Second, there is the question of how risk-based forms of thinking impact on policing practice. In Chapter 4 it is suggested that the traditional functional priorities of the police are now undercut by alternative ones whose impact, though uncertain, derives from a preoccupation with the management of risk. One implication of this is that public police practice mimics practices associated with the private policing sector.

Whereas Chapters 3 and 4 consider how policing functions are constructed and transformed through the modernization process, Chapters 5 to 9 concentrate on the different policing forms. Here I examine both the characteristics of, and the changing connections between, public, commercial and civil forms of policing under global conditions. Clearly, many of the developments described in the present chapter have implications for an understanding of these issues. For example, the commodification of security and the consequent escalation in public demand for enhanced safety, owes much to the marketing practices of commercial security organizations. Yet it also has a major impact on public police organizations (discussed in Chapters 5 to 7) in two respects. On the one hand, public demand for increased safety does not discriminate between the public and private sectors. In other words, security commodification leads not only to an increase in demand for private security products, it also increases demand for public police services. On the other hand, the escalation of public demand for policing, in circumstances where governments are committed to the philosophy of privatization, transforms the consumer of public police services from a client into a customer. In turn, this transformation demands new forms of vetting and assessment of services. When the philosophy of NPM is stirred into the porridge of 'customerization', the effect is a revolution in the discourse of public police accountability. The most striking factor in British police governance during the last decade has been the extent to which the formal apparatuses of local police accountability have been denuded of political content: for 'political accountability' now read 'balanced budgets', 'financial propriety', 'quality of service', 'customer satisfaction' and 'consumer sovereignty'. That model of accountability is, of course, predicated on post-Fordist organizational structures and on service-based models of delivery and it is for these reasons that police forces are now devolved and decentralized at local levels. Yet two other processes are at work, both of them contradictory to this one – and, indeed, to each other. First, devolution notwithstanding, the centre reconsolidates its authority through the imposition of Home Office power in key areas of police policy and practice. Second, the expansion of commercial security (see Chapter 8) indicates a sphere of policing relatively immune from government control. Not only that, the emergence of experiments in civil and municipal policing (discussed in Chapter 9) provide a similarly 'distanciated' sphere of policing, relatively detached from central government authority.

These developments suggest a system in which increasingly diverse forms of policing are subject to complex forms of rule. Public policing at the local level is, increasingly, depoliticized, giving rise to what might be termed 'governance without (party) politics'. Conversely, enhanced Home Office control over key operational areas indicates that despite such depoliticization, some areas of policing remain firmly within the sphere of government control: what one might term 'governance by government'. In addition to that, however, both civil and commercial modes of policing at the local level and commercial and public modes of policing at the supranational level signify the emergence of 'governance without government': in other words, 'distanciated' spheres of rule which are relatively immune from formal governmental control, either by virtue of being market-based, or by virtue of being uncoupled from the formal state apparatus. These three modes of governance are illustrated in Chapters 5 to 8.

Part Two:

Functions

Chapter 3

The Functions of Modern Police

Introduction

This chapter and Chapter 4 are concerned with the complex theme of continuity and change in police functions. In a recent analysis, Bayley and Shearing suggest that democratic systems of policing have reached a watershed: 'Future generations will look back on our era as a time when one system of policing ended and another took its place' (Bayley and Shearing, 1996: 585). Two developments define that change: the emergence of plural policing networks, an issue discussed in Part Three of this book; and the public police's search for an appropriate role, something which is inextricably connected to debates about the police function. Bayley and Shearing (1996) suggest that the police's uncertainty about their role is connected to processes of functional restructuring which are, themselves, related to wider social changes – some of which have been discussed in Chapter 2. Yet, the dynamics of functional change have also to be considered alongside police organizational structures which have, in the past, exhibited continuity and uniformity. Bayley, despite his recognition of police restructuring, has also emphasized the capacity of police organizations to resist the impact of exogenous factors:

> Police forces around the world are organised to do the same sorts of work regardless of the social circumstances they confront. They do not adapt to the work they must do, rather the work they must do is adapted to the police organization (Bayley, 1996: 30).

Undoubtedly this point is a valid one, the sociology of police work demonstrating time and time again the similarity of police structures, cultures and practices within and between jurisdictions. Yet, similarity is not incompatible with change, and in Chapter 4 I suggest that late modernity has a transforming impact on police functions.

This chapter consists of two sections. The first addresses the question of what modern police do, paying particular attention to debates about the police's role in crime control, service provision and order maintenance. The second section focuses on the question of 'how police do what they do' and whether they should do it differently. Here, particular attention is paid to the relationship between two elements of policing: the extent to which police practice is (or should be) reactive or proactive; and the extent to which police practice is (or should be) maximal or minimal. Combination of those two dimensions produces a four cell matrix. This matrix enables us both to consider the normative aspects of police practice and to identify concerns about particular aspects of the police function.

What do police do?

The implementation of the 'new police' reforms of 1829 confirmed the British state's reluctance to organize domestic policing on the absolutist lines of continental Europe. However, that decision was a paradoxical one. For while a centralized national police force was resisted on mainland Britain, precisely such a system was considered necessary to control the Irish. While 'high policing' was initiated in Ireland, 'low policing' was instituted in England, Scotland and Wales, its primary concern being with routine matters of security and protection. As Sir Richard Mayne's instructions to the new police put it, the function of the police was 'the prevention of crime . . . the protection of life and property [and] the preservation of public tranquillity' (cited in Newburn, 1995: 200). This task incorporated a wide range of responsibilities. Not only were the police concerned with crime prevention, order maintenance and the protection and punishment of offenders, they undertook a wide variety of service and administrative functions and were also involved in matters relating to the general regulation of populations (Donzelot, 1979). A similar pattern of service activity was present in the USA where the police 'maintained soup kitchens, ran shelters [and] surveilled the community for fire and other public safety hazards' (Greene and Klockars, 1991: 275). In Britain the scope of such work increased after the 1856 County and Borough Police Act and the 1858 Local Government Act (Steedman, 1984), with a wide range of social and administrative functions being devolved to the police: inspection of lodging houses, inspection of weights and measures; collection of the county rate, surveying of roads and bridges, supervision of market trading, regulation of contagious diseases, and a plethora of other activities supportive of the Victorian 'administrative state' (Johnston, 1992a).

It is against this historical background that one has to understand current debates about the police function. A view commonly expressed by police is that their role has expanded dramatically during the twentieth century. In many ways this claim is fully justified. Escalating public demand has generated a massive increase in the absolute quantity of police provision. At the same time social changes have altered the relative balance of police services. For example, developments in transport have meant that significant proportions of police time are now devoted to traffic duties. That relative balance has also been altered by organizational reforms, the growth of specialist units – child protection teams, drugs squads, domestic violence units and the like – ensuring that the scope of the police function has expanded into new areas. Yet, that scope has also been restricted by the police's withdrawal from some of their earlier regulatory and administrative responsibilities. All in all, the police's role – as in Rowan and Mayne's day – remains a complex and dynamic one:

> The purpose of the police service is to uphold the law fairly and firmly; to prevent crimes; to pursue and bring to justice those who break the law; to keep the Queen's Peace; to protect, help and reassure the community; and to be seen to do this with integrity, common sense and sound judgement (ACPO [Association of Chief Police Officers], 1990).

ACPO's statement confirms what history tells us: that the police are concerned with the provision of security – in its broadest sense – through a variety of different means. However, this pluralistic view is not universally shared. The Conservative Government's White Paper on Police Reform was unequivocal about the essence of the police's role: 'The main job of the police is to catch criminals' (Home Office, 1993, para. 2.3). While acknowledging that the police undertake a broad range of duties, the White Paper was emphatic that none was as important as the responsibility to reduce levels of crime. Significantly, the performance targets established under the Police and Magistrates' Courts Act 1994 (PMCA) as a basis for measuring police effectiveness and efficiency have been skewed towards matters of crime control.

This perception of the police as a specialized crime-fighting force is linked to the historic emergence of a professional criminal justice system which took the responsibility for justice out of the hands of communities (Rawlings, 1995). Accordingly, the state claimed a monopoly over the supply of police and criminal justice services. Faced with rising rates of recorded crime in the mid-twentieth century, senior police managers saw it as their professional duty to take responsibility for its reduction. Their message to government was simple: 'we are the experts, give us the resources and we will deliver the goods'. Nor was that perspective exclusive to police managers. The view that the police are a specialized body of experts dedicated to crime control remains, after all, the image held by the vast majority of rank and file officers. Yet, rank and file views are not always consistent with the public's attitudes about the police services they require. For one thing, the public consistently demand service functions which rank and file police officers dismiss as 'rubbish work'. For another, while sharing the police's preoccupation with crime control, the public may have different views about how best to achieve it. A survey of police officers and members of the public undertaken by *Which?* in 1996 found that although both groups rated burglary as the priority offence from a list of fifteen others, they had very different views about how best to tackle crime. Whereas almost 70 per cent of the public favoured increased foot patrols, police officers argued strongly for increased use of CCTV and the deployment of specialist squads for targeting specific crimes. In addition to that, while both groups saw drug dealing and street robbery as priority crimes, the public also wanted the police to deal with matters which police respondents saw as low priority: notably vandalism and dangerous or drunk driving (*Police Review*, 2 August 1996).

The earliest empirical studies of police work were carried out in the USA during the 1960s. Typically these studies measured workload according to one or more of four criteria: citizen calls to the police, dispatch records, self-reporting by officers and observational studies of police work (Greene and Klockars, 1991). Within a short time they had begun to challenge the conventional wisdom that police work was, primarily a 'crime-fighting' activity. One of the earliest and most influential studies was Wilson's (1968) analysis of citizen calls to the Syracuse Police Department, New York. During one week in June 1966 Wilson examined a 20 per cent sample of citizen calls relayed to police vehicles, concluding that only 10.3 per cent related to crime and law enforcement, the remainder concerning information gathering (22.1 per cent), service (37.5 per cent) and order maintenance (30.1 per cent). Wilson concluded that the principal function of the patrol officer was not to enforce the criminal law but to 'handle his beat' (Wilson, 1968: 31) using the law as one resource among others for this purpose. Though contemporary studies produced slightly different estimates of the volume of calls in different categories, they confirmed that a relatively minor proportion of police time was devoted to enforcement. In addition to that they showed that 'at least one-half of the officers' patrol time [was] not accounted for in the dispatching system' (Greene and Klockars, 1991: 276). Self-report and observational studies of the period confirmed these conclusions. Cordner's (1978) observational study of police in a Midwestern city (cited in Greene and Klockars, 1991) found that 55 per cent of patrol time was uncommitted, 39 per cent of that time being spent in taking breaks and 39 per cent in patrol activity of some sort. Overall, as much as 44 per cent of a patrol officer's time was 'downtime', only 13 per cent of work time being devoted to crime related activities.

Subsequent research has tended to confirm the results of these early studies. In Britain it has been suggested that by the mid-1980s a consensus was emerging among police researchers about the disparity between the realities of police work and the perceptions of it held by the police and the public (Jones and Newburn, 1997). Hough's (1985) analysis of the workload of uniformed patrol officers provided confirmation of this view. He suggested that the chances of a patrol officer intercepting a crime in progress were small, adding 'this is not surprising when one recognises that even in a busy sub-division only ten crimes per day will be reported to the police and many of these will occur in places inaccessible to police patrols' (Hough, 1985: 9). Hough's analysis of 1,944 incidents attended by patrols in the research division suggested that only about one-third (36 per cent) involved crime incidents, the remainder being related to accidents (14 per cent), public order (19 per cent) and social service (31 per cent) (Hough, 1985: Table 2.3: 11). Other studies had suggested that the proportion of service calls was not only higher than that estimated in previous studies, but varied according to the nature of the location policed. Punch and Naylor's (1973) analysis of calls made to the police in three Essex towns over a two week period demonstrated that the proportion of service calls was lower in the 'new town' (49 per cent) than in either the 'old town' (61 per cent) or the 'country town' (73 per cent). On that basis it was maintained that the police constituted not so much a crime-fighting force as a 'secret social service' (Punch and Naylor, 1973).

Many of these earlier findings are confirmed in Bayley's (1994; 1996) research on 28 police forces in five countries carried out between 1989 and 1993. Bayley argues that '[what] the police do is strikingly similar around the world . . . about 60 per cent of police personnel patrol and respond to requests from the public, 15 per cent investigate crime, 9 per cent regulate traffic and 9 per cent administer' (Bayley, 1996: 29). As for patrol work, most of it is entirely reactive to public demand and little of it is crime related, British and US studies having 'consistently shown that not more than 25 per cent of all calls to the police are about crime' (Bayley, 1996: 31). Moreover, such crime as the police deal with is, largely, of a minor nature, and by the time they arrive at the scene 'the trail is almost always cold' (Bayley, 1996: 32). Like Wilson before him, Bayley insists that patrol officers spend most of their time restoring order and providing general assistance. However, they rarely invoke their full legal powers in doing this, police officers in the USA during 1990 making an average of only 19 arrests per year: one arrest per officer for every fifteen working days. All in all, Bayley confirms what the sociology of police work has told us repeatedly: that most patrol work is boring, routine and undramatic, rather than dominated by the thrill of the chase.

Detailed studies of police patrol have also pointed to its limited efficacy as a means of crime control. The Kansas City Preventive Patrol Experiment (Kelling *et al.*, 1974) used quasi-experimental methods to assess the effect of varying the quantity of motor patrol on different beats. The study found that increasing or decreasing patrol levels had no significant effect on crime, fear of crime or public satisfaction with the police. Studies have also cast doubt on claims that the speed of motorized response, in itself, provides an effective measure against crime. Research in both Britain and America found that few calls for police help relate to crimes in progress and that even where this is the case 'offenders required seconds rather than minutes to make good their escape' (Hough, 1996: 65). In any case, as Reiner (1992) points out, most offences are discovered some time after the event and most victims do not call the police immediately.

The limited effects and potential dysfunctions of motor patrol – not least its tendency to insulate the police from routine public contact – raises the question of whether other forms of patrol might better facilitate the control of crime. The most famous study of foot patrol, the Newark (New Jersey) Foot Patrol Experiment (Police Foundation, 1981) involved an examination of the effects of varying the levels of foot patrol on a number of matched beats. On four beats, previously without foot patrol, it was initiated for the first time. On four pairs of beats where patrols had been present, they were either continued or discontinued. Though the results of the experiment showed that crime levels were unaffected by these variations, foot patrol appeared to have some beneficial effects, members of the public evaluating police services more highly, and experiencing reduced levels of fear of crime.

The limited efficacy of routine mobile and foot patrol in preventing crime has led some writers to suggest that aggressive patrols, combined with 'crackdowns' in which 'hot spots' are targeted for vigorous policing, can be more effective. Sherman (1991), having reviewed a number of American crackdowns, concludes that some succeed in creating initial deterrence, or at least displacement, of some kinds of offending. However, he notes that it is difficult for these initiatives to be sustained for any significant length of time due either to implementation problems or to a decline in offenders' perceptions of risk of apprehension. Sherman (1991) suggests that crackdowns might be more effective if used on a short-term basis, being shifted from area to area or from problem to problem. Such an approach might confront the problem that in the USA 'less than 3 per cent of street addresses and 3 per cent of the population in a city produce over half the crime and arrests' (Sherman, 1992: 159).

Applying Sherman's analysis to Britain, Waddington (1996c) has argued that the stop and search powers contained within the Prevention of Terrorism (Provisional Powers) Act could provide an effective means of combating crime. Under the Act senior police officers are empowered to define locations which are vulnerable to terrorist attack as 'designated areas' where constables may stop and search pedestrians and vehicles. Waddington sees this power as closely connected to Sherman's analysis of crackdowns: 'Sherman's prescription is remarkably similar to the provisions of the recent anti-terrorist legislation. The "hot spot" becomes the "designated area"' (Waddington, 1996c: 17). Under such conditions, Waddington argues, extended stop and search might make a modest contribution to combating crime and securing 'the liberty of ordinary decent people'. While stop and search may have a modest impact, however, it is an ineffective means of detection. Moreover, American and British research suggests that the price of using it is a 'considerable increase in public hostility' (Reiner, 1992b: 154). In Britain the aggressive use of stop and search both precipitated major incidents of public disorder (as in the Brixton riots) and led to repeated allegations of racial discrimination by police officers against young black males.

Three points arise from this brief review of research evidence. First, the popular crime-fighting model of police work gives an inaccurate account of what police do. This model is not only a poor description of uniformed police work, it is equally inapplicable to detection. Bayley (1996) puts it succinctly: 'Detectives know they are unlikely to be able to find the perpetrators of crimes unless they are identified by the victims or by people at the scene. As a result most crime, especially property crime, goes unsolved' (Bayley, 1996: 29). The main factor in detection is, therefore, information provided by members of the public – more often than not the victim – to detectives or uniformed officers at the crime-scene. In addition to that, around one-quarter of offences are cleared up by offenders admitting other offences to be 'taken into consideration'. This means that rather less than one-quarter are cleared up by anything resembling 'classic' detection (Reiner, 1992b). As for the limited efficacy of uniform patrol in crime prevention, one other factor should be borne in mind. The fact is that once allowance is made for headquarters and management staff, specialist personnel, and officers absent from operational duties because of sickness, training, or court appearances – and once further allowance is made for the effects of the shift system – no more than about ten per cent of officers are available for patrol work at any one time. Since those officers will also spend about half of their time on duties within the police station, 'the number . . . actually on patrol at any one time is only about 5 per cent of strength' (Morgan and Newburn, 1997: 126). For that reason officers are unlikely to discover crimes in progress. Moreover, such is the thinness of police on the ground that forces will find it difficult to increase strengths sufficiently to make the public notice a major difference in officer numbers at street level. Furthermore, though recent initiatives in New York – to be discussed in the following chapter – indicate that police visibility can be increased, such increases may pose financial and social costs which politicians and the public may be unwilling to accept.

Second, though popular imagery has over-emphasized the crime-fighting role of the police, recent analysis has added qualifications to the findings of workload studies. In a study of the Wilmington Police Department, Greene and Klockars (1991) stated that the availability of more technically sophisticated recording systems revealed crime-related police work to be two or three times greater than was previously believed. Other writers have cast doubt on the classifications used in previous research. Kinsey *et al.* (1986) suggested that Wilson's (1968) research systematically underestimated the police's involvement in crime by classifying criminal acts (such as cases of domestic violence) as examples of 'order mainten-ance'. Left-realist criminologists have also argued that local victimization studies undertaken in urban areas reveal higher rates of crime related police–public contact than is revealed by national victim studies (Jones *et al.*, 1986). It has also been pointed out that the categorization of incidents as 'service', 'crime' or 'order maintenance' takes place *post hoc*. Much police work involves incidents of 'potential crime' – many of them emergencies – where a member of the public has asserted, rightly or wrongly, that a crime has taken place. Shapland and Vagg's (1988) analysis of messages received by the police showed 53 per cent to involve such cases of 'potential crime'.

Third, those qualifications notwithstanding, crime work – however defined – is a relatively minor part of police activity and the police's capacity to control crime remains a limited one. As Loveday (1996b) suggests this means that attempts to wage an aggressive 'war on crime' are doomed to fail. Rather, the police should confront the fact that they will, on average, be able to effect only between about six per cent and eight per cent primary detections per annum and educate the public to this fact. Such limited capacity as the police have to respond to crime depends, largely, upon the public's willingness to communicate information to those engaged in patrol. (Whether those engaged in such patrol need, invariably, to be sworn police officers is an issue to which I shall return in later chapters.) To that extent, efficacy in relation to crime control is contingent upon peace-keeping styles of policing rather than upon aggressive techniques which alienate the public. This view stands in marked contrast to Home Office attempts to measure police performance by crude crime control targets, something which is likely to lead to greater 'professional obfuscation' and a temptation to fabricate crime statistics (Loveday, 1996b).

Faced with the evidence discussed in this chapter, Bayley and Shearing suggest that the 'scarecrow' function of the police – their deterrent capacity – has grown tattered in relation to the prevalence of crime' (Bayley and Shearing, 1996: 588). Limited preventive capacity, coupled with increased competition from the commercial security sector, has led the police to adopt three strategies. First, they have tried to salvage crime-orientated policing by encouraging 'smarter enforcement' tactics: targeting career criminals, destabilising criminal markets, etc. (I suggest, however, in the following chapter that some of these tactics are singularly lacking in concern for enforcement.) Second, they have invested in community policing, a tactic discussed in the following section. Third, they have instigated a particular form of order maintenance policing: what one might call 'order maintenance as crime control'. In part, this third strategy has arisen from the research discussed earlier. The results of the Newark experiment – particularly in regard to the impact of police patrol on reduced fear of crime – were especially influential during the 1980s when police forces increasingly focused on fear reduction as an objective in its own right, distinct from crime prevention and control. Ironically, as Hough (1996) notes, this development came about at the very time when criminologists were, more and more, disinclined to draw a rigid distinction between the two. By the mid-1990s, Wilson and Kelling's (1982) 'broken windows' thesis – an argument predicated upon the indivisibility of crime and fear of crime – was being translated into the concrete policing strategy of Zero Tolerance Policing (ZTP). Here, it is contended that order maintenance is a precondition of minimizing the fear of crime which, if left untreated, precipitates increases in real crime. ZTP is discussed further in Chapter 4.

How police (should) do what they do

The previous section concentrated on the characteristic functions undertaken by police. However, some analysts prefer to concentrate less on the nature of police functions themselves, and more on the manner in which they are undertaken. This view is associated particularly with Egon Bittner for whom incidents become matters for police attention, not because they are illegal, but because they usually require an emergency response. In Bittner's view policing involves dealing with an infinite range of problems, many of which require instant action. According to this view the defining characteristic of the police is their capacity to engage in decisive action. Action is decisive where it is authoritative, the police's authority deriving from their capacity to exercise legitimate force where it is required. Police action is authoritative not because force is used – more often than not the police will resolve matters without recourse to coercion – but because the public have a reasonable expectation that its use will be appropriate to the situation at hand. Accordingly, for Bittner, 'the role of the police is best understood as a mechanism for the distribution of non-negotiably coercive force employed in accordance with the dictates of an intuitive grasp of situational exigencies' (Bittner, 1991: 46).

For Bittner the essence of the police role lies in the means deployed (the 'how') rather than in the functions undertaken ('the what'). According to this view it is the state's delegation of coercive capacity to police officers which is decisive in their definition. However, the capacity to coerce is only one aspect – albeit a critical one – of 'how police do what they do'. In the past there has also been debate about the form which police action should take. In this section I shall examine two dimensions of that debate: the extent to which police action is (or should be) maximal or minimal; and the extent to which it is (or should be) proactive or reactive. Past discussion of these questions has been partial and somewhat narrow – as, for example, in debates about whether the police are, primarily, a 'reactive force', a 'proactive service', or some combination of the two. In what follows I suggest that the question of 'how police do what they do?' can best be considered by constructing a four cell matrix out of these two dimensions of police action. By these means it is possible both to move outside the narrow confines of the 'force versus service' debate, and to consider forms of police action in their wider social context.

Figure 3.1 comprises a four-cell matrix of the different forms of police action. Though these forms are not mutually exclusive, and in practice will inevitably overlap with one another, they provide a useful way of thinking about 'how police do what they do' and, for that matter, 'how they might do it in the future'. The horizontal axis in the matrix consists of a distinction between reactive and proactive engagement. Reactive engagement involves those circumstances in which the police – either collectively or individually – respond reactively to public demand. Clearly, the bulk of police work is – and will continue to be – reactively driven, something which can constitute an obstacle both to internal management reform and to external mechanisms of control and accountability (Johnston, 1988). Proactive engagement involves situations where the police take pre-emptive action in order to achieve a given end – as, for example, with crime prevention initiatives and with policies to divert juveniles from the criminal justice system. Proactive engagement involves forward planning, rather than mere reaction to events, and has been a dominant ethos in late twentieth-century police thinking. The vertical axis of the matrix relates to the scope of police intervention. Maximal scope occurs where there are few limits on the police's capacity for action. For example, Bittner (1991) believes that the scope of the police role is a maximal one since the multifarious character of demand makes it virtually impossible to delimit what police are called upon to do. Minimal scope, by contrast, occurs when the police's capacity for action is restricted in some way. For instance, left-realist criminologists have argued that the legitimate scope of police intervention should be limited strictly to the prevention and detection of crime (Kinsey *et al.*, 1986).

Combination of the horizontal and vertical axes in the table produces four cells, three of which (Cells A, B and C) are considered below. The first two of these (Cells A and B) describe existing mainstream police practice. Maximal-reactive policing (Cell A) is an enforcement-based model sometimes referred to as 'fire-brigade policing'. Maximal-proactive policing (Cell B) is the form characteristically associated with 'community' and 'problem-orientated' modes of policing, proaction having become a dominant theme in contemporary police discourse. Minimal-reactive policing (Cell C) is a methodology of police practice proposed by left-realist criminologists, critical of the lack of democracy and effectiveness contained in the previous two models. Cell D is different from the others in that it appears to constitute a contradiction in terms – how can one have a system of policing which is both minimal *and* subject to the invasive and expansive tendencies associated with proaction? For this reason Cell D remains vacant. However, the question posed by Cell D (can one have a system of policing which is both proactive and minimal?) is a particularly important one, given the growth of risk-based forms of police practice (Chapter 4) and the expansion of commercial and civil policing (Chapters 8 and 9) – developments which are characterized by their proactive focus. As a result further reference to Cell D is reserved for Chapter 4, in which I consider risk-based policing practices and for Chapter 10, where matters of policing and security are linked to more general questions of governance.

Figure 3.1   Forms of Police action

Scope \ Engagement	Reactive	Proactive
Maximal	**A** 'Fire-Brigade' or Enforcement-Led Policing	**B** Community Policing
Minimal	**C** Minimal Policing	**D**

At this point it should be emphasised that the purpose of the matrix is not to provide a detailed analysis of the complexities of the police function. Its aim is, merely, a heuristic one: to map out some of the dynamics of police practice and to identify concerns which have been expressed about particular combinations of scope and engagement. In the course of doing this it will become clear that one of the effects of late modern change is to expose tensions in the matrix, calling into question the adequacy of some of its categories. In Chapter 4 I suggest that the matrix requires some modification if it is to be relevant to the dynamics of late modern policing.

Cell A: Maximal-reactive policing: ('fire brigade' or enforcement-led policing)

The maximal-reactive model is an enforcement-led style of policing whose claim to authority is grounded in law. As such, it confirms Fielding's (1996) observation that 'what matters most in understanding everyday police work is that the lower ranks believe . . . their mission is law enforcement' (Fielding, 1996: 43). Yet, it is obvious that the police are unable to implement all laws. In practice, everyday police work involves a varying balance of enforcement, coupled with the judicious exercise of discretion. Maximal-reactive policing aims to push that balance in the former direction in two ways: first, by ensuring that what police do is determined, largely, by public demand; second, by reacting to that demand with an enforcement-led response. It is this style of policing which is sometimes referred to as the 'fire-brigade' model, the emphasis being on reaction times and clear up rates (Fielding, 1996), rather than on the individual discretion of officers. 'Fire-brigade' policing is heavily crime-orientated, tending to encourage a 'stop-watch' attitude to performance measurement and a quantitative, rather than a qualitative, view of police service (Fielding, 1996). In practice, its effect is to encourage attending officers to resolve problems as quickly as possible in order to free themselves for the next service call.

A more controversial – and increasingly influential – form of maximal-reactive policing occurs when that model is applied not just to individual officers but to specific operations and strategies. One well-known example occurred when the Metropolitan Police implemented 'Operation Swamp' in the Brixton area of London during April 1981. 'Swamp '81' was targeted at mugging and street crime and involved the saturation policing of a black inner city area. During its course 943 people were stopped, Lord Scarman's inquiry into the subsequent riots declaring the operation to have been 'a serious mistake' (Scarman, 1981). Another example is the recent implementation of ZTP strategies in a number of British towns and cities. Though ZTP is more complex than it might first appear – an issue discussed further in the following chapter – its stated purpose is to apply maximum enforcement techniques against 'quality of life' offences (begging, drunkenness, and other routine incivilities), thus confirming the public's 'zero tolerance' of minor crime and disorder in public places. Both of these examples differ from the (routine) maximal law enforcement described earlier, the police responding not merely to *individual* service calls (as in the 'fire-brigade' model) but reacting, also, to what they perceive as a *generalized* public demand for police action. In practice, of course, there is a slippage between the police's mere 'reaction' to that generalized demand and their 'proactive' manufacturing of it.

In general, maximal-reactive policing is criticized for its lack of accountability to those whom it polices. Placed in the specific context of late modernity, however, the model has further serious failings. For one thing, enforcement-led policing is based upon a bureaucratic-militaristic organizational structure (Fielding, 1996) which is out of step with the organizational changes – devolution, decentralization, de-layering – described in Chapter 2. For another, it is predicated upon a universalistic conception of law and a unitary view of social order, both of which are difficult to sustain. The fragility of those views is exposed by the Brixton example, 'Swamp '81' having precipitated social division and riot rather than social consensus and stability. Undoubtedly Scarman (1981) was correct to suggest that excessive enforcement may generate disorder. He might have added that with the growing social diversity associated with late modernity, disorder is the normal, rather than the exceptional, product of maximum enforcement. As I suggest in the following chapter, ZTP attempts to square that circle by mobilizing popular (majority) support for enforcement-led policies on crime and disorder. Yet, that 'majoritarian' policy assumes the very social unity which late modernity denies. At best, ZTP is a strategy in which the law is invoked on behalf of some community interests against others. It propounds the universality of law in theory, while denying it in practice.

Cell B: Maximal-proactive policing: (community policing)

Community and problem-orientated modes of policing have become increasingly influential in recent decades. Problem-Orientated Policing (POP), usually appearing in the guise of 'sector policing' in Britain, is premised on the idea that 'conventional policing is overly reactive, and fails to tackle the roots of the problems to which uniformed patrols are deployed (often with monotonous regularity)' (Hough, 1996: 67). Under this model dedicated patrol officers are allocated to particular areas with a view to developing long-term proactive solutions to problems. Goldstein's (1979) original formulation of POP emphasized that police should concentrate less on the means of policing and more on its ends, aiming not to eliminate problems – an unrealistic objective – but to initiate rational and systematic policies for minimizing their volume and effects. Subsequently, POP initiatives have been implemented widely in the USA (Eck and Spelman, 1987) and, more recently, in a number of British police forces including Thames Valley (Pollard, 1997), Leicestershire (Gibbons, 1996c; Tilley and Brooks, 1996) and Cleveland (Romeanes, 1996).

POP is a logical extension of the community policing model (Alderson, 1979). In this model emphasis is placed upon the development of proactive crime prevention policies informed by an understanding of the social context of crime. Community policing encourages the formation of local, regional and national 'partnerships' between police and other agencies, the aim being to further crime prevention and enhance community safety. Bennett (1994) notes that, surprisingly, there is as yet no standard or accepted definition of community policing. However, on the basis of existing evidence he suggests that community policing programmes usually contain at least some of the following components: community constables; community liaison officers; schools liaison schemes; youth programmes; police consultative communities; local crime prevention initiatives; neighbourhood watch schemes; decentralized command structures; commitment to foot patrols; police–public partnerships; and an emphasis on non-crime problem-solving.

The community policing model has been subjected to two types of criticism. First, some radical writers have expressed concern about the invasive impact of maximal-proactive policing on local communities, fearing the emergence of a 'local police state' (Gordon, 1984). Alderson (1982), himself, accepted that community policing could, under certain social and political conditions, mutate into pathological forms – as, he suggests, occurred in Nazi Germany and Communist China. At its most extreme the radical view regards community policing as the 'velvet glove' surrounding the 'iron fist' of police power, policing being conceived as an integrated totality of repressive and ideological components. While this view of the state police is seriously flawed (Johnston, 1986), it is undoubtedly true that Gordon's (1984) view of community policing – a multi-agency framework connecting the central state with the local state in a coordinated network – is a surprisingly accurate description of the official conception of multi-agency crime prevention (Home Office, 1984).

However, this qualification has to be squared with a second type of criticism concerning empirical studies of the efficacy of community policing. Reiner (1992b: 154–5) sums up these research findings in the phrase 'nothing works', a view which is substantially validated in Bennett's (1994) review of research evidence. Here Bennett (1994) draws attention to a number of problematical areas: rank and file police resistance to community policing programmes; management shortcomings; implementation failures; problems in establishing partnerships between the police and the community; and tensions between the police and other 'partner' agencies. This view has been substantiated, time and again, in British studies during the last twenty years (Jones, 1980; Gill and Thrasher, 1985; Fielding, Kemp and Norris, 1989). The fact is that, on the basis of existing evidence regarding repeated implementation failure, it is impossible to maintain that community policing comprises one element in a cohesive system of authoritarian state police control. Nevertheless, this does not negate the valid concerns of those who fear the invasive potential of maximal-proactive policing, a potential which is further enhanced by contemporary developments in surveillance technology. I return to some of these issues in the following chapter. One thing which I also suggest is that if community policing is to have any relevance to late modern conditions, it must embrace the diversity of *communities*, rather than the singularity of *community* (Rose, 1996). This would imply a very different and more complex conception of community policing from that which has dominated current debate. In particular, it would make no assumption that community policing has to operate under the leadership of public police.

Cell C: Minimal-reactive policing: (left-realism's 'minimal policing' model)

The previous two models have been castigated as inflammatory (Cell A), invasive (Cell B), and as both ineffective and unaccountable (Cells A and B). Minimal-reactive policing is an attempt to construct a model of police action which avoids these problems. This model (called 'minimal policing' by its proponents: Kinsey *et al.*, 1986), is part of a wider left-realist criminology. Left-realists argue that, since criminal victimization is a real problem for working class communities, criminologists have to 'take crime seriously'. This suggests that 'the issue is to get a police force that will deal properly with [crime]' (Lea and Young, 1984: 259). To that extent, left-realists cast doubt on those who 'let the police off the hook' (Kinsey *et al.*, 1986) by over-emphasizing their limited efficacy in crime control. The fact that the police do not respond effectively to crime, they suggest, does not mean that they cannot. Effectiveness can, it is argued, be enhanced in two ways. First, the police should focus exclusively on crime, rather than on the multifarious social service functions associated with the community policing model. Social service policing both deflects the police from their real job (crime control) and makes it more likely that they will engage in dangerous and unaccountable forms of community penetration. Second, the establishment of a genuinely accountable police force will win the trust of the community, thereby increasing the information flow upon which the police depend for an effective response to crime. Accountable policing, in this context, is both minimal and reactive. Rather than allowing the police to exercise discretion as to how and when they carry out their functions, minimal-reactive policing restricts police intervention *only* to those situations where there has been an infraction of the criminal law *and* where such intervention is initiated by some public demand (either through an individual complaint or through a request for action by some representative body such as a police committee). Unless both of these conditions pertain there is no legitimate foundation for police action.

Minimal-reactive policing poses an important question about the extent to which, and the manner by which, police discretion can be minimized so as to enhance accountability and effectiveness. However, the solution proposed by left-realists raises a number of problems. For one thing, by focusing exclusively on crime as the essence of the police role, attention is drawn away from those 'peace-keeping' activities which are central to conceptions of policing grounded in security. For another, there is a serious conflict between minimalist principles and the common-sense practicalities of police work, a conflict to which realism is forced to make significant concessions. Take, for instance, the case of a domestic dispute (Johnston, 1988). According to the criteria laid down in the model, police intervention (say, to prevent violence) would be illegitimate unless a legal infraction had already occurred. Since this seems to conflict with common sense – an officer might reasonably want to intervene if, on the basis of his or her judgement, domestic violence was *likely* to occur – it is hardly surprising that the writers are obliged, ultimately, to broaden the 'illegality' criterion to include *potential* legal infractions: 'The appropriate criterion of police action is whether a crime has been *or is about to be* committed, and whether the public deems it worthy of police intervention' (Kinsey *et al.*, 1986: 205: emphasis added). Unfortunately, what this does is resuscitate the very police discretion (who, after all, but a police officer defines a 'potential' infraction?) which the minimal-reactive model had sought to eradicate in order to maximize accountability. Ironically, then, left-realism produces a decidedly unrealistic model of police action. Moreover, in opting for 'a Procrustean bed of legalism untempered by discretion' (Reiner, 1992b: 145) left-realists deploy the same universalistic conception of law as advocates of the maximal-enforcement model. Yet, as I have already suggested, that conception of law is increasingly undermined by the diversifying effects of late modern social change.

Concluding comments

This chapter has considered the questions of 'what police do'? and 'how they do it'? (or 'how they might do it in the future'?). Empirical analysis of what police do confirms that they undertake a broad range of security and peace-keeping functions, devoting a relatively small proportion of their overall time – though rather more than, previously, was considered to be the case – to the control of crime. Of course, evidence about how police *do* spend their time tells us little about how they *should* spend it. In particular, studies of police workloads do not, by themselves, indicate whether more or less time should be devoted to crime work. That question is a particularly important one under conditions of late modernity. In later chapters I consider the police's function relative to other agencies which undertake policing roles and speculate on how the policing division of labour might develop in years to come.

The question of 'how police do what they do' was addressed by constructing a four cell matrix of police action derived from two cross-cutting dimensions: reactive-proactive engagement; and maximal-minimal scope. The aim of this matrix was to map out some of the dynamics of police practice focusing, in particular, on its normative dimensions. Analysis of three of these cells – two (Cells A and B) being models of current police practice, the third (Cell C) a hypothetical model of future possible practice – raised various concerns: about the negative implications of maximal-reactive policing for public peace; about the invasive potential of maximal-proactive policing; and, paradoxically, about the impossibility of minimizing such invasive potential by reducing policing to a purely reactive practice. It was also suggested that Cell D (minimal-proactive policing) while, apparently, an impossible combination in the context of police organization, raises an important question: if the future trajectory is towards increasingly proactive means of policing, to what extent can the negative effects of proaction be minimized? Analysis of the matrix also suggested that it needs to be re-worked to take account of late modern change. The following chapter considers the impact of late modernity on police practice by examining risk-based modes of policing. Here, I suggest that risk-based policing occupies an ambiguous position within the cellular structure, having both 'maximal-proactive' and 'minimalist' tendencies. This combination draws attention to the limits of the matrix and poses some governmental problems which are addressed in the final chapter.

Chapter 4

The Functions of Late Modern Police

Introduction

The previous chapter considered some of the main functions undertaken by the police. The present one examines how these functions are being transformed under the impact of late modern change. In this chapter I suggest that a degree of functional integration or 'melding' is occurring between public and commercial police organizations due to the impact of risk-based modes of thinking and acting. This does not mean that public and commercial police are indistinguishable: merely that the risk-based philosophies of the commercial sector have begun to penetrate public policing in significant ways. For that reason transformations in *police* function can only be understood as a corollary of wider changes in the character of *policing*. The chapter is divided into three sections The first examines the impact of risk on policing. One of the things suggested here is that popular imagery gives a misleading view of policing: late modernity is characterized less by 'community policing' than by 'policing communities of risk'. Late modern policing should not, however, be seen as the mere reflection of some overbearing risk-based rationale for, in practice, 'risk-based' approaches are combined with 'disciplinary' ones. This distinction between risk-based (or 'actuarial') and disciplinary modes of policing provides a basis for the remaining discussion. The second section provides an analysis of some of the main risk-based police practices to have emerged in recent years. The third focuses on a single example – what has been termed 'zero-tolerance policing' – in order to illustrate how these are combined with disciplinary techniques. Finally, a short conclusion reflects back on how the arguments presented here relate to the cellular model of police action outlined in the previous chapter.

Risk and policing: from 'community policing' to 'policing communities of risk'

In Chapter 2 it was argued that risk is a central feature of the global restructuring which characterizes late modern societies. One of the most striking features of recent times has been the extent to which police and criminal justice agencies have adopted policies based on assumptions and techniques derived from commercial risk management. Consider an obvious example. Over a decade ago, Cohen (1985) observed that situational crime prevention, far from being concerned with the causal explanation of crime, was interested solely in its spatial and temporal manipulation through techniques such as defensible space and target hardening. This fundamental lack of concern about the causal preconditions of risk is confirmed in Broder's classic definition: '[r]isk management is the anticipation, recognition and appraisal of a risk and the initiation of some action to remove the risk or reduce the potential loss from it to an acceptable level' (Broder, cited in Nalla and Newman, 1990: 92).

A number of writers regard the risk-based model of crime management as one aspect of the supersession of 'disciplinary' techniques of policing – forms which seek to deter criminality through enforcement – by 'actuarial' ones (e.g. Castel, 1991; Ewald, 1991; Simon, 1988). Simon suggests that while disciplinary techniques aimed to alter individual behaviour and motivation, actuarial ones merely seek to manipulate the physical and social structures within which individuals behave. The aim of these latter strategies is 'not to intervene in individuals' lives for the purpose of ascertaining responsibility, making the guilty "pay for their crime", or changing them. Rather it [is] to regulate groups as part of a strategy of managing danger' (Feeley and Simon, 1994: 173). Under actuarial principles risk is attached to everybody. As Hudson (1996) puts it, the risk that the criminal justice system seeks to manage is the risk of victimization and the target of criminal justice is no longer the offender 'but the community of potential victims' (Hudson, 1996: 154). This view not only 'takes crime for granted' (Feeley and Simon, 1994: 173), it underpins a criminology from which *particular* offenders are expunged. In situational crime prevention the offender is seen, not as a specific agent, but as an abstract, calculating, subject. This subject is capable of 'weighing up the risks, potential gains and potential costs, and then committing an offence only when the benefits are perceived to outweigh the losses' (O'Malley, 1992: 264). In short, the offender is the bearer of the generic subjective capacity of rational choice.

It is useful to consider this view in the context of community crime prevention. Up until the1970s professionals experts, such as social workers and police, were deployed to inject social values into declining communities. Today community crime prevention is, primarily, about external agencies working in partnership with empowered communities to minimize the risk posed by rational – and, thereby, culpable – offenders. Some of the implications of these developments are discussed in Hebenton and Thomas's (1996) analysis of sexual offenders in the community, two of their observations being especially worthy of note. First, risk-based crime prevention places considerable emphasis on the collection, compilation and dissemination of information. For that reason, effective communication between participating agencies is paramount. According to HM Inspectorate of Probation (Hebenton and Thomas, 1996), public protection from victimization by sexual offenders requires the effective marriage of risk assessment (evaluations as to whether a subject is likely to cause harm to others) and risk management (actions taken to monitor a subject's attitudes and behaviours in order to minimize the risk of such harm occurring). One of the main preconditions of that marriage is effective information exchange between participating agencies including 'common computerized and integrated recording systems for cases' (Association of Chief Officers of Probation Guidance cited in Hebenton and Thomas, 1996: 434). Such developments have profound implications for police organizations, a point to which I return in the following section.

Second, there is the matter of the paradoxical relationship between security and risk already mentioned in Chapter 2. As Hebenton and Thomas's (1996) analysis implies, it is not just a question of whether risk-based initiatives work – the problem of effective inter-agency implementation is, after all, a long-standing one. Rather, the strategies are, themselves, paradoxical. Statutes recently implemented in the USA guaranteeing communities the right to be notified of the presence of sexual offenders in the vicinity doubtless empower communities, but they also breed further insecurity: insecurity about the reliability of available information; insecurity about the trustworthiness of the expert knowledge upon which it is based; and insecurity about the capacity of rational-calculating offenders to evade disclosure.

Preventive strategies such as that described by Hebenton and Thomas (1996) are part of the general ethos of community policing and crime prevention. But what, precisely, is the communal basis upon which these strategies are grounded? Elsewhere (Johnston, 1997b), I have suggested that the discourse of community policing needs to be subjected to critical scrutiny. The conventional model of community policing is predicated upon a conception of community as the embodiment, or potential embodiment, of collective sentiments. This invariably evokes an imagined past in which society was less impersonal and less prone to conflict than at present. It is because community, in this sense, is assumed to embody in-built stabilizing forces that community policing is able to promise 'a government that acts to advance the "natural" mechanisms of social control peculiar to a locale' (Mastrofski, 1991: 515–16). The problem is, of course, that that image of community is both a poor representation of the past and a poor predictor of the future. As Mastrofski confirms communities – whose structure is, in any case, more often heterogeneous than homogeneous – rarely express shared norms about crime. Social conflicts are, moreover, far from exclusive to low income neighbourhoods, division, distrust and lack of participation also being the norm in many middle class communities.

Of course, the police are well aware of these problems, few of them seeing contemporary community as the living embodiment of common sentiments. Yet, for all that, the rhetoric of community policing is nothing without the reforming potential assumed to reside within collective communal organization. That is the paradox of conventional community policing. On the one hand, its discursive thrust concentrates on the need to reconstitute collective communities. On the other, the substantive obstacles facing that project make even definition of the term 'community policing' problematical (Bennett, 1994). This commitment to an impossible project has dangerous consequences for the police: '[a]s long as community-as-consensus is perceived as a prerequisite for governance, police will be burdened with the necessity of fabricating one where it does not exist' (Mastrofski, 1991: 527). In practice, such manipulation of consensual images reduces community policing to little more than a cosy rhetoric. Like tourism and heritage, conventional community policing is preoccupied with the reconstruction of nostalgia.

The other paradox of community policing is, that for all its invocation of self-regulating communities, the initiative remains state-led. The effects of this are easy to see. Rosenbaum (1995), a keen but critical advocate of community policing, rightly insists that crime control and social order cannot be the exclusive function of the police, concurring with Jacobs's (1961) view that public peace is the product of informal networks of voluntary controls located within neighbourhoods. Yet, his conclusion is ambivalent. On the one hand, he deems police to be 'supplemental' to the community. On the other hand, he insists that the police must take a 'lead role' in community change (Rosenbaum, 1995). This begs an obvious question. Are self-regulated communities compatible with police leadership? Or does the concept of self-regulated community demand a fundamental rethink about the government of policing?

What I am suggesting here is that the conventional model of police-led community policing is flawed. It is not merely that its implementation is problematical (Bennett, 1994; 1995), the very concept is undermined by the characteristics of late modern change. It was suggested in Chapter 2 that the processes of globalization, localization, privatization and commodification undermine traditional assumptions about state-rule, leading to its increased distanciation. Rose (1996) argues that 'government through society' – the state-led project of the past – is being supplanted by 'government through community', a much more diverse and distanciated undertaking. However, the community of which Rose speaks is far from the homogeneous entity beloved by proponents of community policing. Nowadays, the singularity of 'community' has given way to the plurality of communities: moral communities (religious, ecological, gendered); life style communities (of taste and fashion); communities of commitment (to personal and non-personal issues); contractual communities (composed of subscribing consumers); virtual communities (joined together in cyberspace); and so on. Such communities, far from being homogeneous, are diverse, overlapping, pragmatic, temporary and, frequently, divided from one another.

With the expansion of 'government through community' – rather than mere government by the state – community policing will be the norm for the future. Rather than being based upon 'communities of collective sentiment', however, it will be focused upon risk. Furthermore, late modern communities are not merely 'at risk' from some external threat – the model implied in the traditional model of community policing – they are increasingly defined, orientated, organized and governed around matters of security and risk. Community policing, in this context, will not be about organizing and mobilizing 'communities of collective sentiment', it will be about 'policing communities of risk' (Johnston, 1997b). Though communities of risk are made up of members who share some significant behavioural or attitudinal similarity, this neither implies that they share common interests and collective sentiments, nor that they embody a community spirit. It cannot be assumed that members of such diverse communities will share common perceptions of, and interests in, risk. Communities of risk may be 'at risk', but they may also constitute a risk for other communities.

One of the implications of this view – that, in the future, diverse communities of risk will be policed diversely – is considered in later chapters. For the moment, however, let us return to another aspect of risk. In Chapter 2, I referred to the sociological and genealogical accounts of risk, the former having its roots in the analysis of modernity, the latter in particular styles of thinking arising during the nineteenth century. Though both of these explanations give useful insights into matters of risk, it is the latter which is most pertinent to the present discussion. In order to understand the significance of the genealogical account it is necessary to draw upon Foucault's (1991) distinction between the three dimensions of rule (or governance): sovereignty, discipline and governmentality. Sovereignty consists of strategies exercised by an authority claiming the legitimate monopoly of coercion over a given territory. Disciplinary modes of rule are, by contrast, concerned with attempts to control the human body. During pre-modern times disciplinary power was exercised through corporal and capital punishment, serfdom, compulsory conscription and other forms of physical domination. In modern times, the formal freedoms associated with the rise of citizenship have underpinned a system of disciplinary power based upon the deprivation of liberty and the surveillance of subjects in factories, asylums, schools and prisons (Foucault, 1977). Foucault's third category of rule, governmentality (or 'government rationality') emerges during the nineteenth century when 'population comes to appear, above all else, as the ultimate end of government' (Foucault,

1991: 100). The techniques of governmentality are concerned with the management of aggregate populations, twentieth century government becoming increasingly preoccupied with the management of aggregate risks through the application of actuarial and insurential techniques.

As I suggested earlier, some writers maintain that the expansion of such risk-based, actuarial techniques of policing and government coincide with the decline of disciplinary methods. Simon (1988) contends that during the last fifty years government has moved away from disciplinary techniques 'and toward actuarial practices that are, in turn, more efficient in the use of resources and less dangerous in the political resistances they generate' (Simon, 1988: 773). The claim that actuarial techniques have become dominant because of their effectiveness – a claim which is both teleological and functionalist in character – is, however, highly questionable. O'Malley (1992) is particularly keen to emphasize the political context in which ruling technologies operate, suggesting that their place and form is 'largely determined by the nature and fortunes of political programmes with which they are aligned' (O'Malley, 1992: 252). Thus, while neo-liberal ideology in Britain has encouraged a wide variety of risk-based policing techniques during the last twenty years, neo-Conservative political programmes have modified, and in some cases, curtailed these risk-based interventions, focusing instead on the increased application of disciplinary-based methods. O'Malley's (1992) analysis confirms that while governmentality is a key mode of rule in the current period, particular configurations of policing involve determinate combinations of risk-based and disciplinary techniques. It is this issue which provides a basis for the remaining discussion. The following section examines the character and impact of risk-based policing practices on police organizations. The third section considers the relationship between those risk-based practices and disciplinary ones by looking at the particular example of zero tolerance policing.

Risk-based police practices

Commercial risk management has a number of prime objectives: to anticipate risks by proactive means; to appraise the character of risks and assess the probability of their occurrence; to calculate the losses or pathologies arising from such occurrence; to balance the probability of risks occurring with any anticipated losses or pathologies arising from their occurrence; and to control risks through direct intervention or, where this is considered inappropriate, to displace or transfer them elsewhere (cf. Nalla and Newman, 1990). In short, risk management is actuarial, proactive and anticipatory, the application of those principles requiring the collation and analysis of information obtained through the systematic surveillance of those at risk or likely to cause risk.

The public police's growing orientation towards information gathering, anticipatory engagement, proactive intervention, systematic surveillance, and rational calculation of results demonstrates an ethos comparable to that found in the commercial security sector. The growing influence of this ethos may be seen in a number of developments. Consider the case of crime management. Here, the Audit Commission has played a particularly important role in shaping police practice, its 1993 document, *Helping With Enquiries: Tackling Crime Effectively* (Audit Commission, 1993), having urged forces to set up 'crime management desks' in order to allocate resources more efficiently; to target prolific offenders; to make better use of informants; and to develop integrated systems for compiling and interrogating databases. Though some remain sceptical about the novelty of these developments – one *Police Review* editorial insisting that these 'most basic of skills have been practised since the time of the Bow Street Runners' (*Police Review*, 6 September 1996) – it is undoubtedly true that they reflect a qualitative change in police practice. The Head of the National Crime Faculty at Bramshill has recently stated that criminal investigation is undergoing a fundamental shift 'from an emphasis on resource allocation to [one on] detectability' (Pyke cited in Gibbons, 1996a: 4). In effect, the present system of categorizing crimes (A, B or C) according to offence type and resource availability will be replaced by a system which defines detectability according to available skills (personnel) and data quality (intelligence). By these means some assessment can be made of the costs and benefits associated with deploying a given investigative technique and, indeed, whether the particular level of detectability justifies an investigation being undertaken at all.

Of course, such practices depend upon the systematic production of high quality intelligence. One key element of intelligence-led policing involves the cultivation of informants, the Audit Commission, the Home Office, ACPO and Her Majesty's Inspectorate of Constabulary (HMIC) all having given support to this tactic in recent years. Such is the unanimity of support among official bodies, it has been said that 'we have a de facto national policy to facilitate and encourage the use of informers' (Dunnighan and Norris, 1997: 3). Drawing upon the McDonald Commission Enquiry ('Concerning Certain Activities of the Royal Canadian Mounted Police'), Gill (1994) identifies four characteristic types of informant: the volunteer citizen offering information on a one-off basis; the 'undeveloped casual source' who is encouraged to pass on information gained during the normal course of their work (e.g. the taxi driver or telephone company employee); the 'developed casual source' who is both paid for such information and given specific information-gathering tasks to undertake; and the 'long term deep cover operative' who may, for instance, be the 'turned' member of a target organization. In Norris's (1996) study of British police informants very few were volunteers, 85 per cent of contacts being initiated by detectives in the first instance. Most informants had a long history of criminality, 55 per cent having been convicted of more than six offences. Money was found to be only one of several forms of inducement, others including revenge, the desire to be released from custody and the wish to have charges against them dropped.

However, the cultivation of informers may give rise to problems. First, there is the question of their effectiveness and efficiency. In Norris's (1996) study the attrition rate was high: in one force studied, out of 82 per cent of informers registered in one year, only 21 per cent remained active a year later. In addition to that, Norris (1996) argues that once the costs of recruiting, maintaining contact and supervising informants are taken into account, their efficiency becomes questionable. As for matters of effectiveness, the critical question is the quality of the information produced. Gill (1994) points out that since informers are giving information in exchange for money or immunity from prosecution, like all private entrepreneurs they will overestimate its value. Thus, in comparison with information gained through purely technical means, that produced by informers poses serious problems of validity. It is for these reasons that Norris (1996) is also sceptical of official claims about the increasing contribution informers make to improvements in the clear-up rate.

Problems may also arise at the organizational level. The most extreme of these occurs when 'the informer [comes] to control the sworn agent rather than the reverse' (Marx, 1988: 152). As one of Marx's police respondents put it 'I worry when I hear things like "there are good crooks and bad crooks" and so-and-so is really a pretty good guy' (Marx, 1988: 157). Lack of effective supervision is, however, only one element of organizational dysfunction. Gill (1994) suggests that the close relationship which sometimes develops between informer and officer engenders a tendency to secretiveness which 'may well have a negative effect on the co-ordination of operations within an agency, and even more so between different agencies' (Gill, 1994: 157). At its most extreme this can produce conflict between individual officers. Dunnighan and Norris (1997) describe the case of one officer stealing items of information from another: 'this cop had started to dip into my tray ... to see if there was anything ... I was getting from Polly [the informant] ... I started locking all my stuff away' (Dunnighan and Norris, 1997: 13).

A third set of problems relate to matters of ethics and accountability. Marx (1988) observes that undercover police work, in general, and the use of informants in particular, can give rise both to the amplification of deviance and to the facilitation of criminal activity. Gill (1994) refers to the case of Kenneth Lennon who, having infiltrated an IRA team in Luton on behalf of Special Branch during the early 1970s, claimed to have been coerced into acting as an *agent provocateur*. Three days after making this claim Lennon was found shot, dead, apparently by the IRA. The subsequent enquiry found no support for Lennon's allegation, though Geoffrey Robertson (cited in Gill, 1994) maintains not only that Special Branch absolved Lennon of the serious crimes he had previously committed, but also incited others to commit offences they would not otherwise have contemplated. A more recent example occurred in 1996 when Eaton Green, a Metropolitan Police informer, arranged – with the approval of his handlers – for two Jamaican criminals to enter the country. Subsequently, Green and one of these men took part in an armed robbery.

Dunnighan and Norris (1997) point out that whereas some forms of conduct – such as officers gaining financial benefit from corrupt dealings with informers – are universally condemned by police, matters of 'noble cause corruption' are the subject of more varied responses. ACPO Guidelines specify that participating informers (those actively involved in crimes about which they may be informing) have to be authorized by a senior officer, but official authorizations are rarely requested. In practice, 'there is no . . . unanimity . . . as to the line between legitimate participation [by those taking part in crimes about which they are, simultaneously, informing] and the illegitimate use of an agent provocateur' (Dunnighan and Norris, 1997: 7). In lieu of this, officers fall back on their own sense of morality to inform any decisions which they make and, by so doing, may breach formal rules. This informal solution, though normalized throughout the organization is, however, problematic. For in the event of things going wrong, the officer concerned will be held accountable to those same formal rules which are routinely breached.

Although informers are central to information-led policing, the available evidence would seem to indicate that their cultivation and deployment may raise problems both for the public (ethics, accountability) and for the police (the quality and reliability of information). However, in respect of the latter, Gill (1994) reminds us that the productivity of informers cannot be measured solely in terms of their information-gathering potential. One key function of informers – particularly those employed by state security services – is that 'their presence, or even the suspicion of their presence may be highly disruptive' (Gill, 1994: 155). Indeed, for Brodeur (1983) one of the defining features of 'high policing' is that it uses informers not merely to collect information but to create disruption. This factor is a particularly pertinent one in the light of recent legislative changes in Britain.

One significant development in the drive towards intelligence-led policing has been the decision to marshal the security services in the fight against serious crime. The Security Services Act came into effect in October 1996. Under its provisions MI5 agents will work alongside police officers, the Director General of the National Criminal Intelligence Service (NCIS) having overall responsibility for the coordination of their activities. Initially, it is anticipated that some seventeen or eighteen MI5 agents will be seconded to NCIS to help the police tackle organized – especially drug-related – crime and terrorism. This development has raised questions about the powers of security personnel. (As Gill (1994) points out, this issue has also been debated in other jurisdictions, the Australian Security Intelligence Organisation Act 1979 stipulating that ASIO is not a police force and has no powers to arrest, detain or interrogate people.) Prior to the enactment of the British legislation both senior police officers and the Committee of Local Police Authorities (CoLPA) insisted that the security services should not have an operational policing role. As a spokesperson for CoLPA put it: 'The proper role for the security services is to augment and assist the work of the police in intelligence gathering to prevent and solve crime . . . MI5 should not be involved in operational matters' (*Police Review*, 24 November 1996: 12).

Subsequent to these claims, an amendment to the Security Services Bill confirmed that the police would retain primacy in operations involving MI5, the function of the latter being 'to act in support of the activities of police forces and other law enforcement agencies' (cited in *Police Review*, 2 February 1996: 4). The principle invoked here is that of the 'civil primacy' of chief constables over other agencies (such as the military, special police forces or, in this instance, MI5) with which they interact on public space. Although there is insufficient room to analyse this issue here, I have suggested elsewhere that the concept of civil primacy is flawed in a number of respects. For example, there are convincing grounds for arguing that in the event of a serious military (Johnston, 1992b) or nuclear (Johnston, 1994) incident, the civil primacy of chief constables would be overturned in the name of national security. Moreover, in the case of MI5, the situation is complicated by the necessarily secretive nature of the security function. Not only are we unlikely to know whether the security services have restricted their activity to non-operational matters, the very distinction between mere intelligence-gathering and operational activity is a very hazy one.

This point is confirmed by the Australian example. As Gill (1994) points out, although ASIO possesses no police powers it may 'take suitable lawful steps to discourage or inhibit . . . activity [considered prejudicial to security]' (ASIO Report to Parliament 1987–8 cited in Gill, 1994: 137). In Britain also, it is clear that the implementation of 'suitable lawful steps' by the security services will be a key factor in the fight against organized crime. What is being proposed is the systematic deployment of what one might call 'techniques of disorganization', strategies equivalent to the 'countering' tactics routinely used by state security services. Just as counterintelligence programmes use tactics of misinformation and demoralization to destabilize the coherence of targeted political groups, so techniques of disorganization are used to undermine the activities of criminal groups. A recent comment from a 'Home Office source' regarding the enhanced role of MI5 suggested that '[d]isrupting the activities of organised criminals may be a desirable role if MI5 is unable to bring them to justice' (cited in Gibbons and Hyder, 1996: 5). Here, contrary to the stipulations of civil primacy, it is clear that the role of the security services is a decidedly operational one, the object being to 'make life difficult' for those whom conventional law enforcement agencies cannot reach. Thus, in one recently reported incident, the security services 'managed to identify a drug runner's bank account and remove all the funds from it' (Palmer, 1997: 17). What is at stake here is not merely the conflation of civil policing and state security, however. The use of (informal) techniques of disorganization is strikingly similar in character to the application of 'informal justice' by those engaged in private security and commercial risk management. In both cases the rationale is to circumvent the formal justice system in order, more easily, to effect the speedy closure of a given problem. Such solutions pose obvious ethical questions. How are standards of public justice to be maintained? How can one ensure that those subjected to informal sanctions are 'deserving', rather than 'undeserving' targets?

The cement which binds together the various risk-based strategies so far described is surveillance. Surveillance is fundamental to the intelligence-gathering functions of the state security service. Equally, however, it is central to the activities of commercial security. As Shearing and Stenning (1981) suggest, 'the feature uniting the diverse activities undertaken by private security under the heading of prevention is surveillance' (Shearing and Stenning, 1981: 213). Some senior police officers would maintain, of course, that surveillance is nothing new. Commenting on the controversy surrounding the recent Police Bill, ACPO spokesman Sir James Sharples insisted that 'the police service has been using surveillance tactics to combat serious crime since 1829' (cited in Gibbons, 1997b: 25). Yet, technical developments have produced a qualitative change in surveillance. Concern about the increasingly invasive potential of electronic surveillance was reflected in the controversy about proposals in the Police Bill giving chief constables a statutory authority to plant bugs in the prevention and detection of serious crime. Opposition amendments in the House of Lords rejected these proposals, favouring instead a system where chief constables would seek authorization from a commissioner. Particular concern arose that the nebulous definition of a serious crime – which included activities by 'a large number of persons in pursuit of a common purpose' – combined with the technical sophistication of bugs, would encourage police deviance. As an editorial in the *New Law Journal* put it, the police 'have shown many times that they have not behaved well enough to allow them this additional right' (cited in *Police Review*, 24 January 1997: 5).

As Shearing and Stenning (1981) suggest, then, the essence of the security function lies in surveillance. Increasingly, however, that core function cannot be separated from its wider role in providing information for risk analysis. Potential for information gathering and processing is further enhanced by sophisticated security technologies. In Britain the most striking manifestation of electronic surveillance has been the rapid growth of CCTV cameras in towns and cities. Sometimes this has had a direct impact on crime. In June 1996 more than 80 people were arrested after Northumbria Police released pictures of football fans rampaging through Newcastle city centre to a local newspaper. Though dramatic claims have been made about the capacity of CCTV systems to reduce levels of recorded crime, little is known about the long term impact of the technology. Despite this uncertainty the previous Conservative Government invested hugely in CCTV. In 1993 the CCTV market in Europe stood at £506m, the UK accounting for 25 per cent of that total. Projections to 1996 indicated that the total value of the market would stand at £697m with annual UK growth rates of some 12 per cemt (Narayan, 1994).

CCTV is the exemplar of actuarial technology since, under it, aggregate populations as well as particular offending groups, constitute the community of risk. Sometimes, this raises questions about privacy. In August 1996 Strathclyde Police decided to issue pictures from a Glasgow red-light district in order to aid the investigation into the murder of a prostitute. This decision was criticized on the grounds that it might damage the reputations of those caught on camera. By contrast, the police's view was that if witnesses did not voluntarily come forward, there was justification to release their photographs for publication. Though this example puts a new slant on the adage that 'only those who have done something wrong need fear CCTV surveillance', the issue of privacy is by no means the only problem. Coleman and Sim (1996) raise two other issues. First, there is the tendency of CCTV to circumvent due process by informal means. In the Liverpool CCTV system the targeting and banning of groups from the city centre is 'finely tuned' with facial recognition computer technology which 'matches facial images on camera to a local database of "known" or "potential" offenders' (Coleman and Sim, 1996: 16). The system operator is alerted to any threatening presence and informal intervention by private security staff occurs. In the USA some stores now operate 'what are effectively "store courts"' able to deal with offences without recourse to the formal justice system (Coleman and Sim, 1996). Second, there is the matter of risk itself. As Coleman and Sim (1996) suggest, the interests behind CCTV discourage all conceptions of risk which lie outside a traditional crime prevention framework. These might include, for example, sexual, homophobic and racial harassment or the hazards associated with homelessness and pollution.

So far I have considered the impact of risk-based practices on those subjected to them by police. However, there is also the question of how risk impacts on the police themselves. Ericson and his colleagues (Ericson, 1994; Ericson and Carriere, 1994; Ericson and Haggerty, 1996) suggest that orientation to risk alters the structure and practice of police organization. Police are, increasingly, preoccupied with the collation, collection and dissemination of information for risk management purposes. Police organizations become part of a network of information-based expert systems seeking to produce knowledge for – and to collect reciprocal knowledge from – other security agencies. Such risk-based methodologies, backed by information technology, define the parameters of risk-based policing, including the population to be policed: 'information technology has been employed by police organizations to construct the population of police' (Ericson and Haggerty, 1996: 4). Significantly, this population includes members of police organizations as well as outsiders, various risk-profiling mechanisms being applied to the internal management of risk within the organization: employment screening, work activity reports, competence ratings, drugs tests and other health and safety measures. (Here, one is reminded of Manning's (1979) observation that the main problem for police organizations is not the control of crime but the control of its own personnel.) Ericson and Haggerty's (1996) point is that information technology defines and manages risk more precisely than hitherto. Rank and file officers may resist expert systems but, in the long term, discretion 'is curtailed, taken away from the individual officer and dispersed into the embedded knowledge systems' (Ericson and Haggerty, 1996: 32). The effect is to muddy the issue of organizational accountability, making it difficult to know who is in control: hierarchical authority is replaced by transparency and self-regulation; working structures and cultures are transformed; and intraorganizational diversity flourishes. Alongside these internal changes, interorganizational diversity also grows. Since the police are, increasingly, enmeshed in multiagency information networks, they are, first and foremost, 'information-brokers'. For this reason, Ericson (1994) suggests that what is conventionally termed 'community policing' should, more accurately, be described as 'communications policing'.

'Zero-tolerance', discipline and risk

At first sight ZTP would seem to bear little relationship to the risk-based techniques described above. ZTP first came to public notice in 1994 when William Bratton was appointed Commissioner of the New York Police Department. Within a short time the developments in New York began to influence policy in a number of British police forces. Bratton based his policing strategy upon Wilson and Kelling's (1982) 'Broken Windows' thesis of a decade earlier. Here, it was argued that public toleration of routine, minor incivilities on the streets – window breaking, vandalism, aggressive begging, drunkenness, public urination – generated fear, encouraged a spiral of community decline and, ultimately, increased the risks of more serious crime occurring. For that reason ZTP required police officers to arrest peddlers, drunks, vandals and others committing so-called 'quality of life' offences. They were also told to run computer checks on offenders in order to determine whether they were associated with other, more serious, offences. This popular American image of ZTP as a robust, enforcement-led strategy directed against quality of life offences committed by young males in public places was reinforced by police, politicians and the media in Britain. That image was encapsulated in Jack Straw's call, during 1995, to 'reclaim the streets from the aggressive begging of winos, addicts and squeegee merchants'.

In terms of the categories contained in our matrix, ZTP comprises an example of maximal-reactive (enforcement-led) policing. This enforcement-led emphasis is visible in the Cleveland example. Here, Superintendent Ray Mallon, following his appointment as Head of Middlesbrough CID in 1996, declared that if crime did not fall by 20 per cent within 18 months he and his two detective inspectors would ask to be relieved of their duties. Within three months of the strategy being adopted in Middlesbrough it was claimed that rates of recorded crime had fallen by 22 per cent. In this case the initiative focuses on a small number of primary offences: anti-social behaviour by young people, house burglary and quality of life crimes. In Mallon's view the commission of minor offences predisposes offenders to engage in more serious ones. Thus, the burglar begins offending at a young age, not by burgling but by 'hanging round on street corners . . . [doing] anti-social things . . . [Then] he allows himself to be carried in a [stolen car]. Next time he steals the car himself. Then he does his first break-in' (Mallon cited in Dean, 1997a: 17).

However, ZTP is not only concerned with using enforcement to halt the progression of criminal careers. It is also a disciplinary technique for reimposing civility on the streets. To that extent, it contains the implicit assumption that the police have a 'civilising mission'. Yet, the imposition of civility through enforcement is fraught with dangers. During the 1980s the over-robust policing of street crime gave rise to serious incidents of public disorder, Lord Scarman's Report on the Brixton Riots (Scarman, 1981) drawing attention to the problematic relationship between the police's enforcement and order maintenance roles. ZTP is, in part, an attempt to resolve these earlier difficulties. The essence of its rhetoric lies in the attempt to win popular support for the imposition of civility on 'dangerous' and 'marginal' populations, thereby avoiding a community backlash against the police. For that reason police action against incivility has a major symbolic function attached to it. As Mallon puts it, if a youth rides his bike on a pavement or drops litter in front of a police officer, 'that officer must do something about it there and then' (Mallon cited in Dean, 1997a: 18) or risk losing his or her authority and, with it, public confidence. By imposing immediate discipline over unruly youths officers may restore public confidence in the police and halt the spiral of anti-social behaviour which pervades the streets. More importantly, the diligent policing of routine public concerns – minor incivility and mundane disorder – will, it is believed, mobilize the support of ordinary 'decent' and 'respectable' citizens (Dennis and Mallon, 1997: 65) against those marginal groups which threaten them. For that reason, ZTP is much more than mere 'community policing with the gloves off' (Waddington, 1997). It is an attempt to win support for vigorous enforcement policies against an uncivil minority on behalf of a respectable majority. In that sense, it is more accurately described as 'utilitarian community policing' (Read, 1997): an attempt to achieve the greatest happiness for the greatest number.

In one sense ZTP is nothing new, being an enforcement-led strategy directed against those whom Reiner (1992b) describes as 'police property'. The allegation from academic circles that ZTP is a mechanism for 'rounding up the usual suspects' (Johnston, 1997a) has been accompanied by criticisms from senior police officers that it is likely to precipitate disorder rather than reduce it. Charles Pollard, Chief Constable of Thames Valley Police, alleges that the strategy 'seems to be concentrated on aggression: on ruthlessness in dealing with criminality and disorderliness; of "rapid response", "searches, sweeps and arrests" . . . and of the single-minded pursuit of short-term results' (Pollard, 1997: 44). Yet, it is important to emphasize that ZTP is far more complex than its popular image – one emphasizing the enforcement of laws against routine acts of incivility – would suggest. That much can be confirmed by considering two instances where ZTP-type programmes have been initiated.

In Cleveland the approach was first developed in Hartlepool in 1994, subsequently being implemented in Middlesbrough during 1996. Though, as I have indicated, the focus is on burglary, anti-social behaviour and quality of life offences, the broader objectives of the programme are to reduce all recorded crime (particularly within the categories of house burglary, violence and auto crime), to reduce fear of crime, to increase police performance and to increase public confidence in, and support for, the police. The police deal with burglary in three ways: through the use of informants; by instigating proactive and covert operations; and by the operation of stop checks. The other targeted offences – anti-social behaviour and quality of life crimes – are dealt with by the police asserting direct authority over offenders on the streets. The initiative features three other elements. First, monthly public meetings are held to increase confidence in the police. Second, the police aim to capitalize on all press opportunities to publicize their activities in a positive light. Third, police managers aim to motivate the workforce, offering support and feedback on their performance and undertaking constant analysis of crime patterns. By these means, it is claimed, the police can effect dramatic reductions in crime.

Two things are striking about the Cleveland initiative. First, there is ambiguity about the terminology by which it is described. It is clear that there is an official reluctance to use the term ZTP. Mallon prefers to call it either 'Here and Now Policing' or 'Confident Policing' (Dennis and Mallon, 1997) and, latterly, the force has also used the term 'Positive Policing'. However, confusion has arisen due to the continued use of the term ZTP by some senior officers and by Mallon's own willingness to participate in radio and television debates on that theme. Second, despite Mallon's continued engagement with the popular discourse of zero tolerance, it is clear that the reality of ZTP in Cleveland is more complex. Not only is it heavily orientated towards intelligence-led activities including 'the cultivation of informants . . . and . . . information-based police action' (Dennis and Mallon, 1997: 69–70), more recently it has been integrated on a force-wide basis with 'Problem-Orientated Policing'

(POP). Here, it seems, the enforcement and quality of life elements of ZTP comprise a short-term tactic for removing trouble-makers from the streets prior to the implementation of POP. As the Force Operations Adviser puts it, 'Zero tolerance clears the ground for problem-orientated policing . . . [and] . . . allows the officers to reimpose their authority in an area . . . When you get the streets back, it is a case of what you do with them' (Romeanes cited in Dean, 1997b: 23). Whether these two operational philosophies are compatible with one another remains to be seen. The significant point for present purposes, however, is that the philosophy of POP accords fully with the risk-orientated and intelligence-based modes of policing outlined earlier.

Similar conclusions can be drawn from the New York experience where ZTP consisted of five elements. First, post-Fordist organizational reforms led to the decentralization of management structures and to the downward devolution of responsibility and accountability to precinct commanders. Second, commanders were required to place a dual emphasis on quality of life crimes as well as on more serious ones. Those arrested for the former were always interviewed by detectives in order to collect intelligence towards the resolution of the latter. Third, in addition to quality of life crimes, the police adopted crime control strategies in seven other areas: drugs, guns, youth crime, auto theft, corruption, traffic and domestic violence. Fourth, Compstat (Comprehensive Computer Statistics) – a computerized process for measuring the success of crime goals – was instituted. Compstat meetings were held twice weekly, each command in rotation accounting for its monthly results set alongside its goals for that period (Griffiths, 1997; Read, 1997). Fifth, patrol officers, rather than specialists, were given the authority to make vice and drug-related arrests, something which they had been prevented from doing in the past because of fears about police corruption.

From this summary of the New York example two things are clear. First, the 'quality of life' focus, though prominent in media accounts of the initiative, played a relatively minor role: a role, moreover, which was, primarily aimed to facilitate the collection of intelligence in respect of more serious crimes. Second, although rigorous enforcement was a major component of the programme, it was merely one element in a wider (post-Fordist) reform of management structures, communication systems and intelligence-gathering practices. In the light of these observations, it is possible to appreciate the meaning of Bratton's startling declaration that what happened in New York was 'neither zero-tolerance policing nor quality of life policing' (Address to *Zero-Tolerance Policing Conference*, Institute of Economic Affairs, London, 12 June 1997).

It would be naïve to deny that, at one level, ZTP is a maximal-reactive mode of enforcement-led policing. Indeed, having borrowed ZTP from the USA, British police should take note of the American experience. For if, as critics of ZTP claim, aggressive enforcement by civil police increases the chances of civil disorder, the danger is an increased militarization of civil policing. The following comment from a local US police commander concerning the increased role of police paramilitary units in routine patrols, suggests that paramilitarism is perfectly compatible with ZTP and with what is euphemistically called 'community policing':

> We conduct a lot of saturation patrol . . . we're an elite fighting team . . . We focus on '*quality of life issues*' like illegal parking, loud music, bums, neighbourhood troubles . . . Our tactical enforcement team works nicely with our department's emphasis on community policing (Kraska and Kappeler, 1997: 13: emphasis in original).

However, ZTP is more than merely an enforcement-led disciplinary technique. It is also a discursive device for describing a wide range of actuarially-driven police practices orientated towards the management of risk and the resolution of more serious crimes. Among the most significant of these practices are the targeting and profiling of offenders, crime pattern analysis, the collection, collation, organization and dissemination of intelligence, the reform of organizational structures and communication systems, and the initiation of resource-sensitive models of police practice such as POP. In that respect, ZTP has more to do with risk-based policing than with addressing the problem of incivility.

Concluding comments

This chapter has examined the impact of risk on policing. In the first section it was argued that the image which dominates much of contemporary police discourse – that of community policing – is a misleading one. This image is based upon the view that communities are relatively homogeneous places whose members share common interests. According to that image, the object of community policing is to organize and mobilize people into 'communities of collective sentiment'. However, late modernity is better represented by the image of 'communities of risk'. Late modern communities are not merely homogeneous places which are 'at risk' from some external threat – the view implied by the traditional discourse of community policing – they are, more and more, defined, orientated, organized and governed around matters of security and risk. Though such communities may comprise members who share certain behavioural and attitudinal similarities, it should not be assumed that they embody common interests and sentiments which can be expressed through community policing. A more appropriate image for the current period is one of 'policing communities of risk'. This image suggests a diverse and disparate system of policing which reflects, fully, the plurality of late modern societies. It involves many agencies and may generate conflicts as well as resolve them. The first section also drew a distinction between disciplinary and risk-based policing. Here, it was argued that while late modernity is dominated by risk-based thinking, disciplinary techniques are likely to remain central to the policing of communities of risk. The second section looked at the impact of risk on police organizational practices and suggested that there was a functional overlap (or melding) between these and the practices of commercial and state security. This functional overlap was considered further in the third section which focused on the example of ZTP, an approach which – contrary to popular imagery – involves both disciplinary techniques (enforcement) and the risk-based practices described earlier (surveillance, intelligence processing and resource-sensitive crime management).

One question which remains is how this argument impacts on the matrix of police action outlined in the previous chapter. It will be recalled that the purpose of that matrix was to outline some of the ways in which police practice has been examined previously. In Chapter 3 the matrix served as a means of comparing enforcement-led (maximal-reactive) with community-based (maximal-proactive) policing. It also enabled us to consider one influential – if untenable – critique of the limits of each (minimal policing). It will also be recalled that the fourth cell of the matrix (minimal-proactive policing) was left empty on the grounds that it constituted an impossible form. After all, the more police organizations are proactive the less are they likely, of their own accord, to limit the scope of their actions.

It was also suggested in the previous chapter that the matrix would need to be adjusted to take account of the impact of late modernity. Accordingly, the present chapter examined *police* functions in the broader context of risk-induced transformations in *policing*. Though, in consequence, our focus was on the relationship between disciplinary and risk-based forms of policing, rather than on the categories contained in the matrix, those categories are by no means redundant. Indeed, it is our contention that the discipline-risk distinction cuts across these categories in ways which are increasingly significant. Just as there is a melding between police practices and those of commercial and state security, so the categories contained within our matrix are undercut by late modern change.

This point can be illustrated, once again, by reference to ZTP. Not only is ZTP a mode of policing which combines disciplinary and risk-based techniques, it is also, simultaneously a maximal-reactive (enforcement-orientated) practice and a maximal-proactive (surveillance-orientated) one. To that extent, ZTP would seem to occupy an ambiguous place in the matrix, being located in both Cell A and Cell B. Of course, two responses might be made about that observation. First, it might be said – with clear justification – that it is normal for specific cases of police action to breach cellular divisions. Enforcement-led police initiatives are often proactive and planned operations. Undoubtedly, this observation is true, though as I shall suggest in a moment, it misses the point of our argument. Second, it might be said that that ambiguous location is, in any case, implicit in the categories contained in the matrix. After all, is not discipline a reactive (enforcement-led) technique and surveillance a proactive, preventive one? In fact, this is by no means always the case under late modern conditions. In this chapter reference has been made to the growing significance of the police's use of those same 'techniques of disorganization' which have, hitherto, been the exclusive preserve of commercial security operatives and state intelligence agents. What is striking about this example is that it constitutes a form of disciplinary policing which is neither reactive nor, for that matter, concerned with enforcement. Its exclusive aim is the imposition of discipline by proactive, rather than reactive means, on those alleged to be involved in organized crime or in politically motivated activity.

It would seem, then, that a distinction has to be drawn between the location of practices in more than one cell of the matrix – something which, though interesting, is commonplace – and the existence of a slippage between the categories which define the cellular structure. It is this second point which is important since it would suggest that the risk-induced tendencies of late modernity require us to rethink the terms by which, conventionally, we understand police practice. In short, we can no longer equate 'discipline' with 'enforcement' and 'proaction' with 'prevention'. The view that policing comprises some, more or less complex, combination of 'force' and 'service' (Stephens and Becker, 1994) may still be true, but what those categories mean may demand careful reassessment.

Such reassessment will, necessarily, pose questions about the future governance of policing since, more than ever before, the interaction between risk-based and disciplinary-based techniques exposes issues of justice, effectiveness, and accountability. In Chapter 3 I suggested that the empty Cell D (minimal-proactive police action) posed an important question for governance. If, as is clearly the case under late modern conditions, the future trajectory is towards increasingly proactive forms of policing, to what extent can the pathological effects of proaction be minimized? This question is of pressing importance since one corollary of risk is an ever-escalating demand for more and more security. However, only by considering policing and security in the wider context of governance can one pose the question of its legitimate limits. Otherwise, consideration of the quantity and quality of security appropriate to a given community is left for resolution by market forces.

In the final chapter I shall address the problem of governance, suggesting that whilst 'minimal policing' (Kinsey *et al.*, 1986) is unfeasible under late modern conditions, 'optimal policing' is a necessary object for pursuit. Ironically, while late modernity and risk engender an apparently insatiable demand for security and, by so doing, raise the threat of a 'maximum security society' (Marx, 1988), they also provide the preconditions for rethinking the governance of policing. Where state policing has a relative monopoly, the maximization of security – whether expressed as a demand for 'more bobbies on the beat' or for faster reaction times – is considered a self-evident public good, worthy of satisfaction. Under those conditions it is impossible to begin to pose the question of the legitimate limits of security. However, risk is not merely associated with the expansion of security, it also correlates with social diversity and with the corresponding diversification of policing. It is that diversity which opens up new possibilities in the governance of policing. The paradox of risk is that it maximizes security while making its optimization thinkable.

Part Three:

Forms

Chapter 5

Public Policing: Devolution, Decentralization and Diversity

Introduction

This chapter is the first of three dealing with the public police in Britain. The following two chapters consider, respectively, national and transnational developments while the present one examines the local dimension. This is a particularly important issue given the general tendency for police organizations throughout Britain, Europe and North America to devolve responsibility for routine policing matters to local commanders (Bayley, 1994). Yet, despite this tendency, other elements of police policy are subjected to greater and greater degrees of centralization. In order to consider the relationship between these two seemingly incompatible trajectories of police governance, the present chapter is divided into three sections. The first outlines some major themes and events of the last thirty years in order to indicate how the discourse of local police governance has been remoulded. The second focuses on the relationship between centralization and decentralization and considers, among other things, whether recent legislative changes, and the community orientated model of policing associated with them, offer genuine prospects for the enhancement of locally accountable policing. The third section outlines some of the key issues at stake in the debate about local police accountability and suggests that a pluralistic model is appropriate for the future.

Accountability and governance: from tripartism to 'governance without politics'

The formal structure of police governance in England and Wales is laid out in the Police Act 1964 and the Police and Magistrates' Courts Act 1994 (PMCA) which were consolidated in the Police Act 1996. The 1964

Act defined a 'tripartite' system of police accountability for the 41 provincial police forces, the chief constable having responsibility for the 'direction and control' of the force, the local police authority (composed of two-thirds elected councillors and one-third non-elected magistrates) being required to maintain an 'adequate and efficient' force and the Home Secretary having the duty to 'promote the efficiency of the police'. The Home Secretary was designated as the police authority for the Metropolitan Police. Under the 1964 Act the only statutory responsibility of the chief constable to the police authority was the submission of an annual report. The authority could also 'require' the provision of a written report on any matter relating to the policing of an area though the chief constable could refuse to provide one where disclosure of information would not be in the public interest or would not be needed for the authority to discharge its functions. For these reasons Marshall (1978) defined the form of accountability enshrined in the Act as 'explanatory and co-operative' rather than as 'subordinate and obedient'.

The legislation left a number of issues unresolved. Despite the fact that the term 'operational' did not appear in the Act, chief constables claimed that their powers of 'direction and control' gave them full 'operational autonomy', not only over decisions in individual cases, but also over general policing policy. This view had been reinforced by the 1962 Royal Commission on the Police. Here, it was claimed that while elected committees had the right to determine policy throughout the rest of the public services, chief officers merely advising and implementing decisions '[i]n the case of the police these positions will be reversed. The role of the police authority will be to advise the Chief Constable on general matters ... decisions will be the responsibility of the Chief Constable alone' (HMSO, 1962: para 166). In fact, the legal basis for restricting police authority involvement in matters of general policy was never a convincing one (Lustgarten, 1986). Indeed, even Marshall, a strong supporter of the principle of operational autonomy, had once argued that police authorities should be able to influence general policy, only later changing his view on practical, rather than legal, grounds (Marshall, 1965; 1978).

The Home Secretary was granted considerable authority under the Act, virtually all of the powers of police authorities being open to Home Office revocation. Thus, as Newburn and Jones (1996) point out, despite repeated concern about the relative impotence of police authorities relative to their chief constables, the most influential pillar of tripartism was, arguably, the Home Secretary. In addition, the duty imposed on the Home Secretary merely to 'promote' (rather than to achieve) police efficiency led to much parliamentary 'buck passing', successive Home Secretaries refusing to address failings in parliament on the grounds that they were 'operational' matters coming under the domain of chief constables.

As for police authorities, they rarely tested the extent of their powers, preferring to accede to the professional expertise of chief constables. This 'cosy consensus' (Reiner, 1997: 1029) broke down during the highly politicized period of the late 1970s and early 1980s when Labour-controlled metropolitan police authorities clashed with chief constables and with the Conservative Government. These clashes exposed the real limits of police authority powers under tripartism and revealed what was, effectively, a bipartite system of police governance dominated by chief constables and the Home Office. That situation was affirmed when the Local Government Act 1985 abolished the metropolitan authorities and replaced their police committees with joint boards composed of councillors and magistrates nominated from the metropolitan districts. Following the recommendations of the Scarman Report 1981, s 106 of the Police and Criminal Evidence Act 1984 (PACE) made statutory provision for police–community consultation. Empirical studies of these groups (Morgan and Maggs, 1985; Morgan, 1987; Savage and Wilson, 1987) reported pessimistically on their effective influence over policing matters, noting regular poor attendance, the domination of agendas by police concerns and committee memberships composed of 'the local great and the good' (Morgan, 1987: 25). However, the Home Office encouraged the development of police consultative committees 'to maintain the myth of local accountability' (Reiner, 1997: 1030) and to further depoliticize matters of police governance.

Home Office influence continued to grow during the 1980s, Home Office Circulars, though officially advisory, becoming more and more policy specific (Jones and Newburn, 1997). A particularly important example was Circular 114/83 ('Manpower, Effectiveness and Efficiency in the Police Service') which signified the government's intent to subject police forces to the same 'value for money' ethos which was being applied to other public services. One effect was that chief constables were required to set clear force objectives which could be measured, monitored and reviewed systematically. A later Circular 105/88 ('Civilian Staff in the Police Service') linked the civilianization of police posts to future establishment levels. These initiatives led some to conclude that a 'privatization mentality' was beginning to dominate official thinking about the police (JCC: Avon & Somerset Constabulary, 1990). That conclusion was, to a large extent, borne out with police forces being encouraged by government to initiate private sector styles of management and to engage in 'load-shedding', contracting-out and charging for some services (Johnston, 1992a; Leishman, Cope and Starie, 1996).

These developments were further consolidated in the late 1980s and 1990s. During this period the Audit Commission, a body whose remit is to evaluate local government management in terms of economy, efficiency and effectiveness, began to play an increasingly significant role in policing. Initially, the Commission had addressed relatively peripheral questions such as vehicle fleet management. However, within a relatively short time it shifted its attention to core issues such as crime detection and financial management. The Commission proved to be a vigorous critic of police practice, its managerial (and implicitly apolitical) focus claiming a degree of impartiality which was difficult to challenge. In due course, what emerged was a template of 'best practice' for police organizations (Savage and Charman, 1996): the devolution of decision-making and budgeting to the lowest appropriate levels; the use of output-based quantitative performance indicators to facilitate cross-force comparison; devolved delivery of police services and local determination of priorities; the establishment, where possible, of client–contractor relations in the delivery of services; the more effective management of crime investigation and patrol (Audit Commission, 1990; 1993; 1994; 1996).

Increasingly rigorous scrutiny has also been exercised by Her Majesty's Inspectorate of Constabulary (HMIC). Far from being, as in the past, a sinecure for retired chief constables, HMIC began to recruit both younger chief constables and civilians to its ranks. The implementation of a more rigorous programme of inspections, the increasingly directive nature of Home Office Circulars and the publication and circulation of inspection reports have, in the view of many, been a significant factor in the further centralization of policing policy. Another influence in policy formulation has been ACPO, no longer a loose confederation of chief officers but a body with a corporate character and a capacity to articulate the collective views of its membership (Savage and Charman, 1996). However, ACPO's corporate character, combined with its lack of any statutory basis, continued to pose questions of accountability, not least when the 'directive' advice laid down in Home Office Circulars was drafted with ACPO involvement.

One theme linking many of these developments has been NPM, a philosophy composed of several elements: the application of commercial business methods to public sector management and accounting; the creation of an accountable professional managerial stratum capable of 'doing more with less'; the setting of measurable performance targets; the costing of all possible activities; the encouragement of competition – both within the public sector and between it and commercial service providers; the publication of league tables to demonstrate comparative performance; the shedding of peripheral tasks; the overhauling of work cultures and practices to produce the flexibility demanded by markets or quasi-markets; and the recasting of public sector clients as the 'customers' and 'consumers' of revitalized services (cf. Leishman *et al.*, 1996; McLaughlin and Murji, 1997). These principles – either singly or in combination – have informed a number of initiatives in recent years. In 1990, ACPO produced its *Strategic Policy Document* (ACPO, 1990), a statement dedicated to the designation of policing as a 'service' and to the adoption of a strategic approach to management which would ensure the provision of high quality performance to a wide range of 'customers'. In order to facilitate that process, mechanisms were to be established to evaluate and monitor police performance and to assess public satisfaction with service delivery. One main element of this initiative was the commitment to 'quality of service' reforms (Waters, 1996).

The ethos of NPM also lay behind two enquiries undertaken during the early 1990s. The first of these, the *Inquiry into Police Responsibilities and Rewards* (HMSO, 1993) was chaired by Sir Patrick Sheehy and recommended, among other things, flattening the rank structure of police forces by eliminating the ranks of deputy chief constable, chief superintendent and chief inspector; introducing a severance programme to facilitate termination of the contracts of up to 5,000 middle ranking and senior officers; reducing the initial salaries of, and instituting fixed-term contracts for, police recruits; and putting into place a system of fixed-term contracts and performance-related pay for senior officers. Predictably, these proposals met massive resistance from the police associations and all but two of Sheehy's main recommendations – the elimination of the rank of deputy chief constable and the introduction of fixed term contracts for ACPO ranks – were shelved. A similar fate met the *Review of Police Core and Ancillary Tasks*, (Home Office, 1995) whose implicit aim was to consider whether certain police functions could be undertaken more cheaply by commercial providers. Such was the resistance of police associations to the threat of widespread privatization that the report, far from imposing radical surgery on the police, limited itself to peripheral matters such as proposing that the escorting of wide loads on motorways might be a suitable candidate for contracting out.

The principles of NPM also impacted on the legislative programme. In March 1993 the then Home Secretary, Kenneth Clarke, announced his proposals on police reform to the Commons. Clarke spoke of making a 'fundamental shift' in the relationship between the Home Office and local police forces; of police authorities and their forces having greater freedom to decide how best to spend their money; of the formation of a police authority for the metropolis; of responsibility being devolved, more and more, to local police managers; of the establishment of 'more businesslike' police authorities with fewer members; of the development of national objectives to complement local ones; of measuring performance against such objectives; and of simplifying the statutory procedures for the future amalgamation of forces. Many of the recommendation made in the White Paper were also contained in the Police and Magistrates' Courts Bill published in December 1993. The major dispute surrounding the Bill related to the composition of police authorities. Clarke's trenchant criticism of the existing authorities – strikingly similar to that made by radical criminologists – had been that they were ritual organizations, exerting little control over the police and taking few genuine decisions. The proposals contained in the Bill – put forward by Clarke's successor Michael Howard – were, however, controversial. This was particularly true of the clause allowing the Home Secretary to nominate the chair and five members of the revised authorities. Following severe attacks in the Lords, over twenty amendments were made to the Bill, PMCA eventually receiving Royal Assent in July 1994.

The Act enables the Home Secretary to set national objectives for the police; imposes a statutory obligation on police authorities to publish an annual local policing plan; requires authorities to set performance targets for measuring the achievement of objectives; and reforms the structure of police authorities. The new, smaller and more businesslike, police authorities are normally limited to seventeen members, uniformity of size, regardless of area or population, signifying 'a departure from the conception of police authorities as primarily *representative* local bodies' (Reiner, 1997: 1031). The democratically elected component of the authority is reduced from two-thirds to just over half (nine out of seventeen members). Three members are magistrates; the remaining five are appointed under a system of Byzantine complexity, the outcome of revisions made after the House of Lords' rebellion against Howard's original proposals to secure powers of appointment for the Home Secretary. The rationale for this system is captured in Reiner's observation that it 'seems to allow the Home Secretary as many bites at the cherry as possible, without simply letting him or her choose' (Reiner, 1997: 1031). The terms by which the 1964 Act defined the role of the police authority are also amended under the (consolidated) 1996 legislation, the authority's role now being defined as the maintenance of an 'efficient and effective' (rather than an 'adequate and efficient') force.

These events suggest that during the last two decades an attempt has been made to shift the discourse of police governance from the domain of politics to the domain of administration ('governance without politics'). Two issues arise in respect of NPM and the legislative changes associated with it. First, there is the question of whether, as in the past, organizational inertia and police resistance will be effective in blocking structural change. McLaughlin and Murji (1997) note that while some aspects of NPM have been implemented others, such as the rationalization of police work, the review of core and ancillary tasks, the maintenance of hierarchies based on rank rather than competence and the implementation of new appraisal systems remain contested issues. Similarly, Leishman *et al.* (1996) point to the role of police policy networks in resisting elements of NPM though, on balance, feel that further consolidation of managerialist practices is likely. Second, there is the question of how far these organizational and legislative changes represent a centralization of governmental power. Reiner suggests that '[t]he intention is to make police authorities more "businesslike",' but that 'the business they will be doing is that of central government rather than the local electorate' (Reiner, 1997: 1031). Jones and Newburn (1997) are more equivocal, claiming that the reforms might give scope for local police authorities to exert more effective influence than hitherto. Both of these examples raise the question of the balance between the centralizing and decentralizing elements of the reforms and it is to a consideration of that issue that the following section is directed.

'Steering', 'rowing' or 'rocking the boat'?

One of the paradoxes of the recent police reforms is that while the majority of academic opinion emphasizes their centralizing thrust, central government insists that they constitute a form of devolution. This latter claim rests upon a number of propositions (Reiner, 1997): that under the legislation chief constables are now free of the budgetary controls which used to determine how they spent their resources; that, in consequence, their spending will be responsive to the demands of the local policing plan, rather than to the demands of central government; and that in meeting those demands they will follow the advice of HMIC and the Audit Commission to devolve more and more responsibilities to Basic Command Units thereby empowering local police commanders. Yet, as Reiner (1997) suggests, the aborted Sheehy reform package (short-term contracts, performance-related pay) and the original plans for the Home Secretary to control key police authority appointments would together have produced 'a formidably centralized system of control over policing' (Reiner, 1997: 1032).

In the event, police and parliamentary opposition resisted some of these developments. Yet, there is much to be said for the view that, on balance, the reforms represent an increase in centralized control. Consider the case of funding. Central government previously provided about three-quarters of police finance (51 per cent from the Home Office and the remainder from the Department of Environment's Rate Support Grant). Under the 1994 Act, police authorities receive a cash limited grant from the Home Office and continue to receive local authority funding through the Revenue Support Grant, non-domestic rates and council tax, the Act defining police authorities as precepting bodies for the purposes of local government finance. These arrangements give police authorities and chief constables much greater budgetary freedom so that the Home Secretary will no longer determine the allocation of funding between staffing, buildings and equipment. Yet, despite this, the Home Secretary will continue to have 'greater control over their *total spending*' (Newburn and Jones, 1996: 126). Interestingly, Butler, himself a chief constable, expresses concern that these general financial controls, coupled with the drive to local 'costed policing plans', will impact on the operational autonomy of chief constables: 'The real danger lies in the government seeking to take de facto operational control by stealth, having been denied it by Parliament' (Butler, 1996: 225). Butler's concern is twofold. First, he believes that, in future, the Home Office will be able to exert greater control over contracted chief constables and will use crudely defined league tables as a means of assessing force performance. Second, he fears that local costed policing plans will not only invite greater Home Office scrutiny, but will also enable police authorities to justify interfering in operational matters by invoking the legitimate role they play in determining how plans are to be met. Butler's argument then identifies two possible developments. On the one hand, devolved powers in respect of the delivery of local police services may simply mask greater central determination over local policing policy. This view is captured in the claim that '[s]teering the police is increasingly centralized, whereas rowing the police is increasingly decentralized' (Leishman *et al.*, 1996: 21). On the other hand, local police authorities may be able to exploit the legislation in order to gain meaningful influence over policing policy.

Recent commentary on the effects of the legislation is uncertain about these two possible futures. This uncertainty reflects an understandable caution about the likely effects of reforms which have only recently been implemented. Reiner and Spencer (1993) had feared that the new 'calculative and contractual' accountability which was implicit in the White Paper would have a deleterious effect on police discretion. Indeed, they had thought it ironic that discretion might be destroyed by a Conservative government in the name of managerial efficiency when generations of radicals had previously failed to achieve it in the name of democracy. More recently, however, Reiner (1997) speculates that the watering-down of the original proposals might give rise to unintended consequences whose effect will rebound on the aims of those who drafted the original legislation. Loveday (1996a), though placing emphasis on the centralizing thrust of the legislation, also notes its ambiguous potential by referring to two examples. The first concerns the composition and function of local police authorities. In 1994 the process of member selection was relatively balanced since, typically, Labour and Liberal Democrat nominations were subjected to short-listing by a Conservative Home Secretary. Yet this balance might alter in the future if those selecting local independent nominees were also members of the same party which controlled central government. Clearly, that situation might undermine local diversity and increase central government control. Yet the opposite is also possible. Central government's attempt to improve policing standards by a combination of short-term contracts, performance-related pay and performance-linked league tables might, ironically, generate alliances between chief constables and their police authorities keen to resist further central government interference in matters of operational policing. Indeed, the situation may be more complicated since, as Butler's (1996) previous comments suggest, the opposite – increased scope for conflict between chief constables and local police authorities over policy matters – is also possible.

This confused state of affairs is, in large part, due to the nature of the managerialist discourse upon which PMCA is founded. This discourse is based upon two sets of assumptions. First, managerialism conceives policy as a technical activity rather than as a political one. For that reason, its objective is to remove policing from the domain of politics and transfer it to the domain of administration ('governance without politics'). Second, as Loader (1996) suggests, managerialism has a dualistic view of 'the public', perceiving it on the one hand as a homogeneous communal mass and, on the other hand, as an aggregate of heterogeneous individual customers. In combination these assumptions produce unpredictable effects. Managerialism is unable to expunge politics from policing – by claiming the latter to be an administrative activity carried out on behalf of a homogeneous community – precisely because the consumerist element of managerialist discourse opens up new contested arenas of debate. For example, newly empowered consumers articulate concerns – about choice, service and quality – and, by so doing, expose political issues which have to be addressed by those responsible for police governance: which service demands should be met? should some demands be given priority over others? should some consumers be given priority over others? In other words, the intended managerialist closure may open up a space for political conflict and resistance, especially when, as in the case of PMCA, initial legislative objectives were diluted by the demands of political expediency.

One obvious question which arises is whether the new police authorities – in alliance with, or in opposition to, their chief constables – can exert meaningful local influence in the face of creeping centralization. Morgan and Newburn (1997) take an optimistic line on this matter, arguing against those who see PMCA as the final nail in the coffin of local accountability and predicting, instead, that the legislation will 'serve to stimulate greater commitment on the part of police authorities to the process of formulating local policing policies than their predecessors ever demonstrated' (Morgan and Newburn, 1997: 148). Here, the critical issue concerns whether the formulation of local policing plans (LPP) might shift the balance of tripartism back towards the local police authority. Although Jones and Newburn (1997) see LPPs as having a significant role to play in that process, they are also mindful of the various limitations imposed by the Act. For one thing, although LPPs are 'owned' by police authorities, they are drafted by chief constables and the authorities must consult with them if they wish to introduce changes. For another, while chief constables must 'have regard' to LPPs in undertaking their responsibilities, they are not bound by them if operational judgement suggests otherwise. Moreover, the demand for national key objectives to be included in LPPs might suggest a significant degree of central determination in the drafting of local policing policy. In view of that, Jones and Newburn's (1997) analysis of all forty-one published LPPs for 1996–7 makes a number of interesting observations. First, the objectives specified in LPPs tend to be strongly influenced by chief constables so that matters of organizational and managerial efficiency, rather than of policing style, tend to dominate. The accountability contained in LPPs is, in other words, typical of that found in business plans, a form characterized by 'administrative' rather than 'political' logic. Second, however, they find no evidence of LPPs being driven by national concerns. Some plans prioritize national key objectives; some incorporate them into local objectives; and some subsume them under local objectives. Third, there is little evidence in

LPPs to suggest that governmental concern with performance objectives has led to an undue emphasis on crime control and enforcement, a concern expressed by some chief constables and academic critics. Fourth, despite the government's intention to introduce costed policing plans, there is little evidence that police authorities and police forces have the capacity, or indeed the desire, to produce them, a fact which places severe limits on the wholesale implementation of managerialist programmes. Overall, then, Jones and Newburn (1997) conclude that while a drift towards 'calculative and contractual accountability' is evident, the decision-making of chief constables is not constrained by national objectives and performance targets to the extent that some commentators had anticipated. National objectives are uncontentious – partly because ACPO was instrumental in their formulation – and the police continue to dominate the drafting of LPPs. Indeed, even those police authorities which had the greatest involvement in their drafting were still, primarily, 'junior partners' in that process. That situation is likely to remain unchanged, of course, as long as police authorities lack the means to challenge police professional domination of policy agendas. For that to happen they would need to be provided with the dedicated research and administrative support necessary for them to fulfil their role to the full.

This analysis suggests two things: that police authorities, as a result of the legislation, have the potential to be more effective than hitherto; and that the shift towards centralization through managerialism is both real and limited. However, each of these conclusions requires qualification. As to the first, Jones and Newburn (1997) are probably right to suggest that the authorities will be more effective than their predecessors – bodies which were, in any case, notorious for their ineffectiveness – precisely because they have a new and specific role to play in the modified pattern of police governance. But this raises several issues. Given their hybrid status – as part-elected quangos dominated by middle aged, middle class, males – will they be adequate to the task of identifying and promoting the complex demands of those (diverse customers) who constitute the local community? If they are able to do that – and not forgetting that such identification and promotion requires dedicated administrative support – will they be able to have such demands incorporated into LPPs which are, currently, drafted by chief constables? And should they succeed in gaining greater control over the formulation of LPPs, would that give rise to unanticipated results? In particular, would it reignite political tensions about the operational autonomy of chief constables, the fear expressed by Butler (1996). In other words, if police authorities were to achieve maximum effectiveness under the 'era of managerialism' would it produce conflicts similar to those which arose during the 'era of politics'? Should that occur central government, despite its devolution of policing policy to the locality, would not be immune from the political fall-out. Ironically, of course, failure by police authorities to articulate local concerns might well reduce the risk of political conflict, but should that happen customers might 'vote with their feet' and look towards the private policing sector for satisfaction (see, Chapter 8).

As to the second point, Jones and Newburn (1997) question whether the power of the centre has been increased to any radical degree at all. After all, they argue, it is the chief constable's position, rather than that of central government or the local police authority, which has become more secure as a result of the reforms. This observation conflicts with the 'steering and rowing' analogy of police reform described earlier. According to that model the legislative programme and the managerial ideology underpinning it, have enabled the central state to monopolize the 'steering' of policing, while devolving its 'rowing' functions to local police forces and their police authorities. In fact, neither interpretation – central state domination or local police autonomy – is particularly convincing. While the 'steering and rowing' analogy is an overly crude (because overly functional) model of late modern governance, the empowerment of chief constables is by no means incompatible with the greater centralization of policing. For one thing, as Leishman *et al.* (1996) suggest, in the long term government may be able to wear down police resistance to the NPM reforms, something which has occurred in other areas of public policy. For another, it should be remembered that PMCA made further rationalization of police forces (through amalgamation) much easier to achieve, thereby leaving room for more overt forms of centralization.

It is easy to regard the reform package as a mere device for centralizing police policy while paying lip service to its devolution. Yet, this fails to take into account the prospect that implementation of the reforms could produce unintended effects, some of which could enhance the prospects of real devolution. There are direct parallels here with a related devolutionary discourse, community policing. As was suggested in the previous chapter, community policing is predicated upon a spurious conception of community which serves to legitimize police domination over the provision of security while purporting to empower community members. Klockars, (1991) certainly sees community policing in that light: '[it is] the latest in a fairly long line of circumlocutions whose purpose is to conceal, mystify, and legitimate police distribution of nonnegotiably coercive force' (Klockars, 1991: 531). Critics of community policing have drawn attention to the paradoxical effects of its devolutionary promise. These include its potential to weaken, rather than to strengthen, community ties; to undermine the community's capacity for self-regulation; to increase, rather than reduce, the power of the police; to limit the prospects of even-handed law enforcement; to reduce, rather than increase, police accountability; to generate impossible expectations among the public; and to appeal to majorities, thereby leaving minorities unprotected (Manning, 1988; Bayley, 1988; McElroy *et al.*, 1993). Weatheritt (1988) gets to the heart of the problem when she suggests that community policing's failings lie in its inability to recognize that policing affects different publics in different ways: 'There are different interests to be reconciled and the appeal to an ideal of a consensual community . . . does not provide a method or a means for doing this' (Weatheritt, 1988: 173).

Yet, the frustrated promise of empowerment contained in community policing (and, for that matter, in the reform package) might, when implemented under conditions of social and governmental diversity, have the potential to generate a demand for real devolution. Were that to happen community policing would have to address its shortcomings head-on. For, as Crawford (1995) suggests, the problem with community policing is not merely that it ignores issues of conflict, diversity and difference, but that it also ignores issues of representation, participation, democracy and social justice. This suggests the need to develop modes of police governance which 'both foster social solidarities yet preserve a cosmopolitan acceptance of cultural difference' (Crawford, 1995: 122). In short, what is required is a pluralistic approach to police governance.

Pluralism and police governance

Pluralism has been significantly absent from the analysis of police governance in the past. This may be illustrated by reference to the debate on police accountability and control which arose during the 1980s, a debate dominated by three approaches (Johnston, 1988). The managerial approach, commonly associated with the Home Office and with senior police managers, adopted a 'top-down' perspective on police organizations. A classic expression of this perspective was the strategy of 'Policing By Objectives' (PBO) (Lubans and Edgar, 1979; Butler, 1984). The aim of PBO was to meet two criticisms: that the police were unaccountable to the public (the charge from the left); and that they were inefficient (the charge from the right). The solution contained in PBO involved the imposition of rational principles on a management which had, hitherto, been 'makeshift', thus enabling the pursuit of 'specific desired results' and the systematic planning, execution and review of decisions (Butler, 1984). Though command structures were rationalized and force goals established at the top of the organization, the action plans by which they were to be achieved were devolved, with each division being responsible for consultation with the community. In effect, PBO aimed to kill two birds with one stone. First, by consulting with the public (through opinion surveys) the police could declare themselves accountable without having to accede to more robust demands for external political control (Lubans and Edgar, 1979). Secondly, by devolving decisions about the implementation of force goals to the ranks, it was hoped that front-line officers would fulfil managerial objectives more willingly, the elimination of traditional rank and file resistance facilitating greater organizational efficiency. However, PBO had two shortcomings. On the one hand, its conception of 'the public' – let alone, of public consultation and accountability – was a remarkably narrow one. On the other hand, its veneer of decentralization often obscured a profound centralism which rank and file officers continued to resist.

Whereas the managerial model assumed that the reform of organizational structures would facilitate internal and external accountability, the interactionist model merely saw accountability and control as problematic. Interactionist writers are particularly interested in how police culture and constabulary discretion may, in combination, undermine attempts to increase accountability through the imposition of internal and external rules. Manning (1979), for example, argues that while it is common in police organizations to have highly specific rules about mundane matters such as uniform, rules for the regulation of operational policing are virtually impossible to create. It is for that reason that police officers repeatedly tell academic researchers who observe them in the field that 'you can't police by the book'. On occasions, such a view is translated into policy. An extreme example occurred when Sir David McNee, the former Commissioner of the Metropolitan Police, presented evidence to the Royal Commission on Criminal Procedure. The Commission's task was to deliberate on the desired balance between police powers and safeguards for suspects, its report eventually providing the basis for the reforms contained in PACE. McNee's argument was that police powers should be extended to legitimate and legalize existing malpractices – specifically the fact that investigating officers habitually ignored the Judge's Rules. Though the argument that laws directed at the control of police conduct should conform with police misconduct was, to say the least, an unusual one, the interactionist position has been used to justify similar – if less extreme – conclusions. Wilson (1968), for example, argued that society's definition of the police function should be based, not on public or judicial preference, but upon the 'street cop's' definition of situation. Though many interactionist writers would reject these particular views, the majority remain sceptical of the impact of rules on police conduct. In so far as the pursuit of accountability is possible within this perspective, it is usually maintained that, in order for rules to be effective, they have to take account of the practices and values of police work. For some, this suggests the need for police organizations to inculcate liberal-professional values within the work force – and particularly among its managers – thereby winning a degree of consent for reform.

While the managerial model aimed to facilitate accountability by means of internal organizational controls, the radical perspective emphasized the deployment of external democratic controls. In practice, this involved the demand for locally elected police authorities to be set up with the power to determine either 'general policing policies' (the view contained in Jack Straw's Private Member's Bill of 1980) or both 'general' and 'operational' policies. A good example of the latter approach – a significantly more radical one than the first – was contained in the Labour Party policy document *Protecting Our People* (Labour Party, 1986). Here, policing was defined as 'unique amongst public services' for its undemocratic character, the document going on to adopt the 1962 Royal Commission's view of the key issue: 'the problem of controlling the police . . . can be restated as the problem of controlling chief constables'. In the light of this formulation, two proposals were put forward: that locally elected police authorities be given statutory responsibility to determine local police priorities, policies and methods; and that they be given the same statutory responsibility for law enforcement as the police. Mindful of the interactionist critique, however, some radical writers went further, recognizing that, in order to effect control, the discretion of all police officers, rather than merely that of the chief constable, needed limitation. Two versions of this argument were put forward. The first accepted that, in practice, even under a system of democratically controlled policing, most police decisions would still be made by the police on the ground. However, in order to restrict police discretion, it was proposed that these decisions be made under 'a delegated authority which could be recalled, limited or extended at any time' (Spencer, 1985: 118). In order to bring this about, it was proposed that police officers give up their 'crown status' (accountability to the crown) for 'employee status' (accountability to the employing authority). In effect, this meant that the recalcitrant police officer could be fired like any other non-compliant public employee. The second was left realism's demand for 'minimal policing' (Kinsey *et al.*, 1986), an attempt to restrict police action to those situations where there had been both an infraction of the criminal law and some public demand for police intervention. Each of these positions raised difficulties. The success of the first depended upon rigorous supervision of police deviance, something which has proved difficult to achieve in the past. As for the second, I have described earlier how left-realism was obliged to make significant concessions to the realities of police work, thereby re-admitting police discretion by the back door.

Far from demonstrating a pluralistic approach to police governance, debate during the 1980s took a unilateral form. Whereas, for managerialism, reform hinged upon internal controls (brought about by changes in the structural planning cycle), for radical critics it demanded external controls (brought about by the actions of democratically elected police authorities). Interactionists, by contrast, merely equated police governance with rank and file autonomy (a form of unilateral 'worker control'). However, interactionism does provide us with one important insight: that since the regulation of police behaviour is problematic, governance of the police is not reducible to the exercise of control over chief constables. On the contrary, effective governance requires a combination of internal and external controls. In the case of the former, the fact that police may resist attempts to control their behaviour should not lead us to conclude that their effective governance is impossible. Though internal controls (rules, procedures, records, supervisory mechanisms, and the like) by no means guarantee compliance, they are by no means ineffective. The relative effectiveness or ineffectiveness of controls varies according to a plurality of conditions: the scope, application and specificity of rules; the rewards and sanctions which accompany compliance and non-compliance; the extent to which controls are compatible with, or contradict, formal organizational goals and informal working practices; the degree of management support they are given; and the adequacy of any supervisory and monitoring mechanisms which accompany them.

It is, however, the issue of external control which is of more significance in the present discussion. It is all very well to demand democratic control of police 'policies, priorities and methods' but that demand raises two problems. First, at the local level, there is, at present, a serious crisis of democratic representation: a general and widespread 'under-participation' in politics; an increasing 'marginalization' of certain sections of the local population who experience exclusion from civil and political institutions; and a failure of the formal political system to represent those diverse interests which are characteristic of late modern communities. Second, there is the problem of majorities. A democratically elected police authority composed of benevolent liberals is one thing. But what if it is dominated by groups which are unwilling to represent minority interests? Such events are not unknown in local politics. During the 1980s the Militant-dominated Liverpool City Council was regularly charged with failing to represent the interests of local black groups. And, even worse, what if a police authority was to be dominated by authoritarian racists? Far from supporting just and sensitive policing, the result might reflect a local bigotry – endowed with democratic legitimacy – which accorded with the worst excesses of police occupational culture. In order to address these issues police governance needs to be driven by a pluralistic approach which encourages social solidarity while, simultaneously, recognizing social diversity.

In an earlier analysis I suggested that policies for the democratic governance of local police should comprise three mutually interdependent elements (Johnston, 1988). First, there should be an effective system of police–public consultation. This should be more than a forum in which the police are left to set agendas because the public are too disengaged from political debate – and too ill-informed about policing – to play any constructive role in its development. Effective consultation has to be more than an exercise in public relations and should enable the public to make critical and constructive comments on key areas of local policing policy. Second, it was suggested that police authorities should take seriously their responsibility for maintaining 'adequate and efficient' (now 'efficient and effective') police forces. This, it was argued, would be a more fruitful tactic than the pursuit of 'operational control', which had dominated much of the debate during the 1980s. 'By fighting for local accountability at this level, rather than at the level of operational policy, it might be possible to construct a programme capable of confronting . . . [police]

resistance . . . [and re-establish] some measure of localism under circumstances of encroaching centralism' (Johnston, 1988: 63). For that reason,
it was suggested that police authorities might expand their activities into
other areas: such as taking over responsibility for crime prevention; and
organizing local public opinion surveys about police policies and their
effectiveness. To a considerable extent, of course, PMCA has established
local police authorities – albeit unelected ones – on just such a basis.
However, the success of those authorities, as bodies responsible for
articulating public demand, is likely to be limited by the nature of their
membership.

These elements, I suggested, should not be seen as 'soft options' but
as components in a plural package, the third aspect of which concerns
democratic policy direction. Undoubtedly, this element is the most problematic one, not least because of the perils of 'majoritarianism' noted
above. There can be no once-and-for-all solution to the problem of democratic policy direction at this level, and suggestions that the duty of law
enforcement might simply be transferred from the police to democratically elected police authorities (GLC, 1983; Spencer, 1985), though neat,
leave many issues unresolved. Some writers have suggested that more
limited forms of legal-democratic control might be exerted in order to
place effective limits on specific aspects of police practice. Jefferson and
Grimshaw (1984), for instance, propose that where the law is unambiguous
and there is an identifiable complainant, individual constables should be
free to exercise discretion since only they can decide, on the basis of the
visible facts, whether an offence has been committed and, if so, to what
category it belongs. By contrast, where the law is ambiguous and there
is no complainant – as is typically the case with breaches of the peace –
they suggest that police practice should be directed by elected public commissioners whose job it would be to produce public policy in the absence
of legal guidance. This approach has some merit. One implication is that
democratic intervention might be applied to those areas of policing policy
where there is least scope for rank and file resistance and most scope for
implementation: as, for example, in public order situations where squad
deployment and paramilitary control minimize officer autonomy.

Jefferson and Grimshaw's (1984) model of a public police commission
– along with Loader's (1996) recent reworking of the idea – provides a
fruitful basis for future discussion within a pluralistic framework. In the
final chapter it is argued that the democratic governance of 'local security networks' requires pluralistic reforms to be implemented within the
context of a rejuvenated civil society. The networks model is one in which
a public authority (a police commission or a local authority) would contract with other agencies in its area for the provision of security according to priorities laid down in the local security plan. Such plans would
aim to maximize public participation and minimize inequity in the delivery
of security. Of course, as I have noted elsewhere (Johnston, 1996a), the
mischievous critic might claim that PMCA ushers in just such a system

through its devolution of finances and its initiation of local policing plans. However, from the perspective adopted here and pursued in later chapters, PMCA – whether confirmed as a radical form of decentralization or as a cynical means of centralization – remains limited in one fundamental respect. It is trapped within a state-centred model of policing which is increasingly incongruent with the diversity of policing forms (commercial and civil) which have begun to emerge at the local level. These forms are examined in detail in Chapters 8 and 9. In the following two chapters, however, attention is directed towards developments in public policing at the national and transnational levels.

Chapter 6

Public Policing: Coordination, Centralization and Order

Introduction

The previous chapter examined one of the most striking paradoxes of contemporary policing: the fact that police services are undergoing a simultaneous process of decentralization and centralization. Whereas, in the previous chapter, that issue was considered from the level of the local community, in the present chapter the emphasis is on developments at the national level. It is here, in particular, that tendencies towards the increased centralization of policing have been most evident. Among these are the reduction in the number of police forces after the 1964 Police Act; the enhanced role of ACPO in police policy-making; the increased influence of the Home Office on senior appointments and on the alloca-tion of grants to police authorities; and the growing impact of 'value for money' principles on policing by the imposition of inspection and audit (Morgan and Newburn, 1997). These developments have been accom-panied by others which, some would argue, are indicative of a 'creeping nationalization' within British policing. Obvious examples include the establishment of the National Criminal Intelligence Service (NCIS), the National Crime Squad (NCS), the National Crime Prevention Centre and the National Crime Faculty; the Home Secretary's right under PMCA to determine national police objectives; and the activation of the National Reporting Centre (NRC) during the miners' strike of 1984–5. Such was the authorities' sensitivity to charges of 'creeping nationalization' in respect of the last of these, that the NRC was renamed the Mutual Aid Coordina-tion Centre. It is for similar reasons of sensitivity that Britain has a Police National Computer (PNC) rather than a National Police Computer.

Wall (1998) suggests that recent police organizational history can be divided into four periods. First, between the middle of the nineteenth century and the First World War, basic aspects of police organization and practice were subjected to *standardization*. Second, between the wars, *centralization* of policing policy gained increased impetus. Third, after the

Police Act 1964 and the Local Government Act 1973, a process of *unification* took place between city and borough forces, local forces being amalgamated into regions or police areas. Fourth, after 1979, a process of police *corporatization* occurred through ACPO's much increased influence over police policy-making. This analysis suggests, rightly, that the consolidation of central influence over policing policy has a long history, much of it being connected to the gradual expansion of Home Office authority during the present century (Spencer, 1985). However, it is also important to recognize the significance of two other processes. First, there is the question of police paramilitarism, an issue which is often linked to allegations about 'creeping nationalization'. Second, there is the question of how far the growth of commercial (Chapter 8) and civil (Chapter 9) policing has led to its increased plurality. Inevitably, the combination of these tendencies begs a question: how far is the model of 'creeping nationalization' compatible with the model of 'creeping pluralization'?

It is to a consideration of that issue that the final pages of this chapter are directed. The chapter is divided into three sections. The first considers the extent to which, and the manner by which, the policing of serious crime has become nationalized, and raises the question of whether nationalization is desirable. The second examines the theme of police militarization and assesses the claim that the growth of paramilitary policing is evidence of an increasingly 'authoritarian state'. This discussion considers recent developments in public order policing in both Britain and Northern Ireland. A short concluding section examines the relationship between the increased coordination of policing (through militarization and nationalization) and its growing diversity.

Nationalization and crime

As Wall's (1998) analysis suggests the centralization and coordination of British policing has a long history. However, in the case of crime control, many of the most significant developments have occurred during the last thirty years. The first Regional Crime Squads (RCSs) were established under the auspices of the Police Act 1964, nine squads being operational throughout England and Wales by 1965. By 1973 some 839 detectives were being seconded from police forces to work in RCSs (Bunyan, 1977). Currently, the figure for secondments stands at around 1200. RCSs, whose number was reduced from nine to six in the 1990s, have three main functions: to identify and arrest those responsible for serious crimes which transcend individual force boundaries; to gather intelligence; and to assist individual forces, when necessary, in the investigation of serious crimes. Yet, as Morgan and Newburn (1997) point out, since the establishment of the RCSs there has been growing pressure to create specialist national units to deal with criminal matters which, it is claimed, cannot be dealt with by existing means. In 1985 the Home Office appointed a National Coordinator for Drugs Intelligence to oversee the transition of the Metropolitan Police's Central Drugs Intelligence Unit into a National Drugs Intelligence Unit (NDIU) which would be staffed by seconded police and Customs officers (Dorn *et al.*, 1992). In 1989 the government, having taken a leading role in the drafting of guidelines for effective police cooperation at European football matches, established the National Football Intelligence Unit (NFIU) to facilitate domestic and international operations. Further impetus was given to the process of centralization when the then Commissioner of the Metropolitan Police, Sir Peter Imbert, predicted that by the year 2000 plans for the creation of a national police force would be under serious consideration (*The Times*, 18 July 1990). In 1989 Imbert had proposed that a British FBI might be established in order to compensate for the alleged inadequacies of the RCSs and in the same year the Home Affairs Select Committee heard evidence from ACPO that greater coordination of specialist units was urgently required. Consequently, by 1990, plans were well under way to establish a national criminal intelligence facility which would incorporate the NDIU, the NFIU, the RCSs, and their associated databases (covering serious crime, football hooligans, animal rights activists, ecological protesters and the like). These objectives were realized in 1992 when the National Criminal Intelligence Service (NCIS) was established. Within three years the government had announced its intention to create a National Crime Squad (NCS) to deal with serious and organized crime, at the same time giving the public an assurance that the NCS would not become a 'British FBI'. The result of these deliberations was the Police Act 1997 under whose terms both NCIS and NCS were placed on a statutory footing.

Prior to the Act, NCIS operated only on the basis of collaboration between forces. The Act established a statutory body, the NCIS Service Authority, with a responsibility for the overall maintenance of the service. Section 2 specified the functions of NCIS as:

(a) to gather, store and analyse information in order to provide criminal intelligence
(b) to provide criminal intelligence to police forces in Great Britain, the Royal Ulster Constabulary, the National Crime Squad and other law enforcement agencies and
(c) to act in support of such police forces, the Royal Ulster Constabulary, the National Crime Squad and other law enforcement agencies carrying out their criminal intelligence activities.

In practice, NCIS supports other police forces as well as being an operational body in its own right. It is headed by a Director General who must hold the rank of chief constable. In addition to bearing responsibility for NCIS, the Director General also coordinates the activities of the Security Services when, under the terms of the Security Services Act 1996, they act in support of the police.

NCIS comprises Headquarters and International divisions plus six regional offices and an Irish Liaison Unit which is based in London. The HQ Division consists of three units: an Operational Support Unit which receives requests from forces for warrants relating to the commission of serious crimes under the Interception of Communications Act 1985 and under s 3 of the Police Act 1997 (which deals with intrusive surveillance); an Intelligence Coordination Unit which aims to improve the quality of the intelligence transmitted to operational units; and a Strategic and Specialist Intelligence Branch which, itself, has responsibility for units concerned with organized crime, economic crime and football hooliganism, as well as specialist crimes such as kidnap, extortion, counterfeiting, organized vehicle crime and paedophilia. The International Division manages a network of European Drugs Liaison Officers, targets UK criminals based in continental Europe and houses the UK Bureau of Interpol.

Section 22 of the Act empowers the Director General of NCIS to enter into collaborative agreements with other UK police forces where shared premises, equipment or facilities are considered appropriate. The fact that the Director General is a senior officer in ACPO – an organization for which, increasingly, 'liaison and cooperation with other forces is the raison d'être' (Uglow with Telford, 1997: 22) – confirms the importance of such collaboration. Under s 22(7) the Home Secretary also has a residual power to direct parties to enter into an agreement where it appears that one or other is refusing to cooperate. Section 23 deals with the provision of mutual aid between NCIS and other forces, the Secretary of State having the powers to require such aid to be given when it is considered expedient for reasons of public safety or in order to enable a force to meet special demands. More generally, under s 26 of the Act the Home Secretary is required to set annual objectives for NCIS after consultation with various parties, the Service Authority's own objectives having to be consistent with those laid down by the Home Secretary.

Two further points are worthy of comment. First, the principles behind the composition of the Service Authority are similar to those which shaped the formation of local police authorities under PMCA. The Authority has nineteen members – although the Home Secretary may increase this number after consulting appropriate parties – of whom ten ('core members') will also be members of the NCS Authority, the aim being to ensure a shared strategic direction between the two bodies. However, five of these ten members are appointed by the Secretary of State. Overall, seven of the nineteen members are appointed by the Home Secretary, seven are drawn from the ranks of the police authorities and five from the police and Customs services. As was the case in 1994 during the debate about PMCA, concern was expressed prior to the Act being passed about central government domination of the Authority's membership and about the lack of community representation on a body which was to be funded by a levy on local police authorities. However, 'the national and international aspects of the work of NCIS, divorced from immediate local concerns, meant that the opposition was more muted than in 1994' (Uglow with Telford, 1997: 10). Secondly, the functions of NCIS, unlike those of NCS, are not limited to 'serious crime' on the grounds that the organization operates in relation to local forces. Uglow with Telford (1997) suggest that this might raise difficulties for NCIS, in its role as the liaison body for Europe, since the Europol Convention limits the communication of intelligence to matters of serious crime. A related question concerns the connection between this broad definition of the NCIS intelligence function and the view that policing has undergone a 'bifurcation, "serious crime" being addressed by coordinated national and international police organizations, "ordinary crime" being tackled by a diverse mixture of municipal, commercial and civil bodies operating alongside increasingly devolved local police units (Reiner, 1992a). Though more is said about bifurcation in later chapters of this book, it is clear that the existence of a *nationally* coordinated body responsible for the collection, collation, analysis and dissemination of intelligence about *local* crime, has implications for our understanding of bifurcation, and also raises questions about the limits of effective and ethical intelligence handling.

Like NCIS, the Act also establishes NCS as a statutory body to be run by a Director General with the rank of chief constable who is accountable to a Service Authority. This arrangement provides clearer lines of accountability than those which have existed under the system of RCSs. (The latter have no statutory basis, having been established under collaborative arrangements contained in the Police Act 1964 and, although there is a national coordinator for RCSs, the incumbent has no powers of direction and control.) Under Part 2 of the Act NCS will not merely coordinate the work of the RCSs but will absorb them into a national structure under the control of the Director General. Section 48(2) of the Act defines the function of NCS as 'to prevent and detect serious crime which is of relevance to more than one police area in England and Wales'. Under s 48(3) it is stipulated that NCS may also act in support of a police force in England and Wales if requested to do so by its chief officer; act in support of the activities of NCIS if requested to do so by the Director General; institute criminal proceedings; cooperate with other police forces in the UK in the prevention and detection of serious crime; and act in support of other law enforcement agencies, whether statutory or not, (including, among others, 'any government department', any person 'charged with the duty of investigating offences' and any person 'engaged outside the UK' in carrying out activities similar to NCS, NCIS or a police force) for that same purpose. Under the terms of the Act NCS is established as an independent agency, both able to employ its own staff and able to enjoy greater operational freedom (Uglow with Telford, 1997).

Like local police authorities the NCS Service Authority is responsible for ensuring that the organization is 'efficient and effective'. Towards this end it must set service objectives – having regard to any national objectives which may be defined for NCS by the Home Secretary after relevant consultation – issue annual service plans and publish annual reports. The NCS Service Authority has seventeen members though the Home Secretary may increase this number after consultation. The authority can also coopt members. The ten 'core' members of the Authority – who also sit on the NCIS Service Authority – comprise three appointed by the Home Secretary, one of whom is chair; two appointed by ACPO; three from the local members of police authorities; and one representative of the Home Secretary in his or her capacity as police authority for London. The additional seven members consist of one appointed by the police members of the Authority and a further six appointed by the local authority members of police authorities. As Uglow with Telford (1997) point out, the NCS Service Authority, like local police authorities, will have little influence on operational matters and is likely to have a withdrawn role. Conversely, they suggest, the position of Director General will become one of the most powerful offices in the ACPO hierarchy. Finally, at the constitutional level, they argue that there will be little accountability to Parliament for NCS operations since, as in the past, Home Secretaries will refuse to comment on operational matters in the House.

These observations beg the question of whether the development of NCS is further proof of 'creeping nationalization'. Uglow with Telford (1997) are unequivocal on this matter: 'Although the initial functions of the NCS are in support of individual police forces, the development of the squad may well be seen as another step towards the eventual nationalisation of policing in the UK' (Uglow with Telford, 1997: 36). Accordingly, they find governmental assurances that NCS's lack of an exclusive operational jurisdiction prevents it from being 'a British FBI' unconvincing. On the contrary, they suggest, the new arrangements – like those for local police authorities – suit both chief constables and Director Generals (who have operational autonomy) and Home Secretaries (who have indirect control). This argument raises two issues. First, there is the question of whether the new Service Authorities for NCIS and NCS constitute an effective third strand under the tripartite structure of accountability contained in the Act. One would have to be highly sceptical on this matter. It is one thing to accept, as Jones and Newburn (1997) do, that local police authorities might, under certain conditions, be empowered by PMCA. It is another to imagine that independent Service Authority members could – even if inclined to do so – question the technical expertise of senior police officers on matters of intelligence-led policing and transjurisdictional organized crime. Second, there is the question of whether 'creeping nationalization' in respect of the policing of serious crime should be regarded as a negative development – the view implicit in Uglow with Telford's (1997) analysis – or a positive one. Contrary to majority opinion, the arguments for the latter view are powerful. For once it is accepted that local police forces, complemented by RCSs, are unable to respond effectively to organized national and transnational crime, the case for unambiguous nationalization is difficult to resist. The problem is that the

1997 Act aims to breathe life into a tripartite model whose primary effect has been to fudge the issue of political accountability. The result of its implementation may be 'the worst of all worlds': a de facto nationalization contained within a de jure statutory framework which provides little genuine accountability. It is for that reason that Morgan and Newburn (1997) insist politicians should 'grasp the nettle': 'We think that there ought to be what the Government claims the National Crime Squad will not be – namely a national police force' (Morgan and Newburn, 1997: 198). If created, such a body would be accountable to Parliament, where its priorities and methods could be subjected to scrutiny, and where Home Secretaries could, genuinely, be held accountable for issues of national policing policy.

Paramilitary policing and 'the authoritarian state'

The changing face of public order policing

During the 1980s the public face of public order policing changed dramatically. As one group of commentators put it: 'Armed with new powers, possessing new equipment and coordinated on a national basis to combat disorder, [the police] appear unfamiliar and discomfiting: less a part of society, more apart from it' (Brewer *et al.*, 1996: 6). Much of this change was evidenced during the miners' strike of 1984–5 when accusations of police paramilitarism were combined with allegations that a national policing policy – obscured as the mere exchange of mutual aid between autonomous constabularies – was being made by Home Office and ACPO under cover of the NRC. Critics pointed to the 'self-evidently national character' (Kettle, 1985: 31) of mutual aid deployments made during the strike. More seriously an *Observer* journalist claimed to have overheard an NRC officer giving 'operational directions' – rather than mere administrative support – to a Midlands police force, in order to get a coach containing pickets turned back upon its arrival at the Nottinghamshire border. ACPO insisted throughout the dispute that the NRC, first activated during the miners' strike of 1972, was merely an administrative mechanism for the rational deployment of Police Support Units (PSUs). What is clear, however, is that even if the NRC did exercise a measure of operational direction, it was not always obeyed by individual chief constables. P.A.J. Waddington (1993) points out that some refused to provide the numbers of officers requested by NRC, while others refused to accept officers from certain forces on the grounds that they were overly aggressive in appearance. Whatever the truth of these contrary claims, the fact is, as P.A.J. Waddington (1993) points out, that central government played a dominant role in the dispute and local police authorities were, effectively, bypassed by the events.

For some, such central control was evidence of the drift to a 'law and order society' in which the state displayed an increasingly authoritarian character (Ackroyd *et al.*, 1977; Hall, 1979; Manwaring-Wright, 1983; Scraton, 1987; Northam, 1988). Developments in public order policing during the 1970s and 1980s undoubtedly confirmed some of the tendencies noted by these writers. Brearley and King (1996) connect some of these changes to key public order events during the period. First, the Grosvenor Square demonstrations of 1967–8 exposed the limits of traditional methods of crowd control. Next, the police's failure at Saltley Coke Depot during the 1972 miners' strike led to the strengthening of organizational mechanisms: national mutual aid was developed and strengthened; a revamped Civil Contingencies Unit of the Cabinet Office was initiated; public order training was reviewed; PSU's were established for every force; and the NRC was set up. In fact, few of these changes had much immediate impact and it was only after the Notting Hill Carnival of 1976 that the police began, systematically, to utilize defensive equipment. Within a year, allegations had been made that the police's use of reinforced helmets and long shields had escalated disorder at the National Front marches in Lewisham and Ladywood and at the 1977 Notting Hill Carnival. Meanwhile, at the long running Grunwick Dispute 1976–8, the police – including the Metropolitan force's Special Patrol Group (SPG) – combined traditional tactics of 'push and shove' with the deployment of 'snatch squads'. By the time of the 1980–1 riots, further technical developments had been initiated including flame retardant overalls, non-traditional helmets, long truncheons, and short shields which were 'more suitable for close combat than static defence' (Brearley and King, 1996: 109). After the second wave of riots in Handsworth, Brixton and Broadwater Farm during 1985, a major review of public order policing occurred which involved the examination of command and control systems, PSU and shield formation training, and post-event evidence gathering. In the Metropolitan Police more officers were trained in the use of baton rounds.

Nowhere was the allegation of state authoritarianism stronger than in respect of Northern Ireland, Jefferson, among others, seeing Ulster as 'a testing ground for a whole range of paramilitary techniques, equipment and weaponry' (Jefferson, 1990: 3) which were later transferred to Britain. In addition to this, the regular renewal of emergency legislation (the Emergency Provisions Act in Northern Ireland and the Prevention of Terrorism Act throughout the UK) have meant that 'departures from traditional legal procedures have become normal in Northern Ireland and spill over into aspects of crime control in Britain' (Downes and Morgan, 1997: 127). The economic costs of the conflict have also been considerable, one estimate suggesting an expenditure of £23.5 billion since 1969 (cited in Hillyard, 1997). An audit carried out in 1986 calculated the annual direct costs of violence to be £1,194 million per annum (cited in Downes and Morgan, 1997). Official figures (cited in Weitzer, 1995: 73) suggest that police expenditure alone during 1990–1 totalled £468 million with a per capita population cost of £265. (The equivalent figure for England and Wales in that year stood at £84). By 1996–7 RUC gross expenditure for the year stood at £641.2 million (PANI, 1997.) A particularly controversial aspect of public order policing has been the RUC's use of plastic baton rounds. During the early 1990s around 200 rounds per annum were being discharged each year. In 1996, following the disorders arising from the parades issue, no less than 6,949 rounds were fired (PANI, 1997: 70). However, the massive investment in security which followed the sectarian conflict not only gave rise to controversy about public order policing, it also led to 'the militarisation of ordinary crime'. As one commentator puts it: 'the fact that the police in "soft" [low crime] areas routinely carry arms, have stations with the look of gulags, and drive reinforced Land Rovers, has been incorporated into what passes for normal policing . . .' (Brewer, 1996: 149).

The security situation in Northern Ireland, the growing sophistication of public order technologies and the British police's decision to replace the philosophy of 'winning by appearing to lose' with one allegedly having a paramilitary basis, raised a number of issues. First, there was the question of accountability for public order policing. During the miners' strike some 1.4 million officer days of mutual aid were worked at an extra policing cost of £400 million (Jefferson, 1990). Yet, police authorities, which bore certain financial responsibilities, had little or no influence over these matters. Second, there was the question of how far aggressive images of public order policing might undermine overall police legitimacy. Fearful of this situation, one writer argued for a radical solution: in order to sustain policing by consent, government should establish a national riot squad so that the majority of officers would be released from the aggressive paramilitary engagement which undermined their everyday policing role (Morris, 1985). Third, there was the issue of whether these developments confirmed the existence of an authoritarian state. Further consideration of this issue requires a more detailed analysis of police paramilitarism.

The debate on paramilitary policing

Any discussion of paramilitary policing in Britain has to engage with continued debate about the meaning of that term and its relationship to the concepts of civil and military action. In recent years there have been three main contributions to that debate. For P.A.J. Waddington (1993, 1994, 1996a, 1996b) the key element of paramilitary policing is its capacity to coordinate actions by means of superior command and control. Instead of allowing individual officers to take discretionary action, paramilitary policing deploys squads under the direction and control of superiors. Far from equating paramilitary policing with unrestrained police violence, Waddington regards it as a necessary means of control over such violence. The same is true, he argues, of the technologies used in paramilitary policing, traditional methods of riot control (such as the use of police charges or the firing of baton rounds) being more likely to inflict violence than paramilitary ones (such as water cannon or CS gas). For Waddington, paramilitarism is more than a mere 'style' of policing, since it involves the grafting of military command on to a civil police force. This process occurs through briefings, debriefings, strategy meetings and sophisticated forms of contingency planning, with commanding officers being divided into 'gold', 'silver' and 'bronze' tiers to correspond to their distinct areas of responsibility over decision-making.

Jefferson (1987, 1990, 1993), by contrast, defines paramilitary policing as 'the application of (quasi)-military training, equipment, philosophy and organisation to questions of policing (whether under centralised control or not)' (Jefferson, 1993: 374). This, Jefferson says, is a 'profane' definition: one which refers to the situation as it often is, rather than to the idealized one proposed by Waddington. For Jefferson, military discipline cannot simply be transferred to the police without altering the nature of policing. After all, he argues, civil policing – with its notion of independently liable unarmed officers – was introduced precisely to counter the provocative effects of military style policing demonstrated at Peterloo. More than that, he argues, military intervention, by its very nature, is provocative and indicative of a failure of democracy. Reversion to a military style of policing may represent a gain in terms of coordination and discipline but this is always bought at the expense of an increase in provocation. The danger is that a combination of provocative military engagement with uncontrolled police discretion will give rise to the worst of all worlds: provocation minus collective discipline.

Hills (1995) disagrees with both of these positions, claiming that they display 'a fundamental misunderstanding of the term paramilitarism' (Hills, 1995: 450). Drawing upon the definition of the International Institute of Strategic Studies, she defines paramilitary forces as those 'whose training, organization, equipment and control suggest that they may be usable in support, or in lieu, of regular military forces' (Hills, 1995: 452). According to this view it is the relationship of the police to the military which defines paramilitarism, not the police's adoption of military systems of command, their use of equipment or their provocative display of force. For that reason PSUs should not be described as paramilitary since they were not acting in support, or in lieu, of the military when deployed at Brixton, Orgreave and Manchester. Though regarding Waddington's definition as more measured than Jefferson's, Hills insists that paramilitary policing cannot be defined by reference to organizational practices such as briefings and debriefings since these are now common to every emergency service, including the social services. And as for the allegation that ACPO policy during the 1980s constituted evidence of the government using the police in lieu of the military, she remains unconvinced, regarding this as an excessively conspiratorial view of a policy arena in which confusion and ambiguity, rather than rational policy, remain the norm.

These three approaches may be brought to bear on two issues. First, there is the question of whether paramilitary policing reduces or increases the risk of violence and disorder, an issue over which Waddington and Jefferson are divided. For Waddington, contrary to the authoritarian state thesis, the police 'massively under-enforce the law' (P.A.J. Waddington, 1994: 40) in most public order situations. Instead, he suggests, they exert control over demonstrators and protesters through informal negotiation. Since police control the conditions by which demonstrations happen (by closing roads, diverting traffic, etc.) they also have the power to stop them happening, merely by refusing to provide these services. In return for negotiating the provision of these conditions, the police 'seek *minimally* disruptive demonstrations . . . they want *control* not just compliance' (P.A.J. Waddington, 1994: 102). For this reason, Waddington draws a distinction between the policing of public order, most of which is done peacefully, and the policing of public disorder. In the latter case, he maintains, violence and disorder are minimized by paramilitary coordination which reduces ad hoc decisions by commanders, controls individual indiscretions by police officers and provides clear lines of accountability for any actions taken (P.A.J. Waddington, 1996b). This view contrasts with Jefferson's (1990) claim that paramilitary organization amplifies violence and disorder, such amplification occurring in four stages: 'preparation for the worst case' (the presence of large numbers of riot-clad officers having a 'self-fulfilling' element); controlling space (the police's movement of people in the crowd causing resentment and reaction which then confirms the 'worst case'); controlling the crowd (the use of 'snatch squads', together with the image of protected officers confronting defenceless members of the public, provoking feelings of anger and injustice); clearance (the use of aggressive, paramilitary styles of clearance adding to that anger).

The dispute between these two positions is, in part, methodological and, in part, political. P.A.J. Waddington (1993) admits that while the conditions for amplification are normally present, disorder is in fact rare. In addition, he provides evidence which appears to refute Jefferson's model: the anti-Thatcher demonstration at Sheffield in 1983 which involved control of space without violence; the 'Battle of the Beanfield' in 1986 which involved violence without the control of space; the anti-poll tax demonstration of 1991 in which control of the crowd did not precipitate violence and the drugs raid at Broadwater Farm in 1985 which, though highly paramilitary in Jefferson's terms, involved no violence and led to the restoration of normal policing within the hour. Jefferson's (1993) response is two-fold. First, he suggests that some of these refutations are questionable: disorder at the anti-poll tax demonstration would, after all, have been unlikely with 5,000 police officers policing a crowd of 11,500. Secondly, he maintains that his model is probabilistic (concerned with identifying the conditions which increase the probability of disorder) rather than absolutist (concerned with predicting individual occurrences of disorder). Methodological disputes aside, however, the fundamental difference is at the political level. Waddington's evidence certainly demonstrates that the relationship between paramilitary policing and violent disorder is complex and contingent. Yet, as Jefferson (1993) insists, this in itself does not vindicate the paramilitary approach. Thus, while the deployment of paramilitary force may, under certain conditions, reduce violent disorder, 'perceived provocations which cannot be dealt with at the time do not disappear but linger on in collective folk memory' (Jefferson, 1993: 379). If that is true it means that the effects of paramilitary policing should not be dissociated from their political context.

Consideration of that political context requires us to address a second issue, the relationship between civil and military action. One of the allegations made against paramilitary policing is that it blurs the distinction between civil and military engagement, giving rise to a militaristic and authoritarian state police. Northam (1988) claims that ACPO's decision during the early 1980s to draw upon the experiences of colonial policing in Hong Kong for the purpose of developing a national public order manual breached two central traditions of British policing: 'the selection of paramilitary tactics raised doubts about the doctrine of minimum force, and the strict code of secrecy surrounding the decision drove a coach and horses through the concept of policing by public consent' (Northam, 1988: 42). For Northam, paramilitarism contradicts the civil basis of consensual policing and leads to authoritarianism. P.A.J. Waddington (1996) disagrees with this view, arguing that the difference between military and civil police engagement hinges upon a distinction between 'enemies and fellow citizens': military action is directed at (mere) enemies of the state while civil police action is directed at citizens of the state (some of whom may have committed criminal acts). Furthermore, he suggests, while in colonial policing systems the distinction between 'enemies' and 'citizens' might have been obscured, that is not the case in a British context where those policed by paramilitary means retain the status of citizens irrespective of their criminal culpability. For that reason, he insists, paramilitary policing retains a core civil component which prevents it from degenerating into a mere tactic of the authoritarian state.

Though this is a valid argument – notwithstanding Mrs Thatcher's notorious depiction of citizens engaged in lawful protest as 'the enemy within' – it both acknowledges and obscures a critical issue: the extent to which the civil-military distinction is, in fact, a stable one. It will be recalled that Hills (1995) defined paramilitary policing in terms of the relationship between two mutually exclusive modes of engagement: civil and military action. The problem with this definition is that the relationship between the two may not always be clear-cut. Sometimes there may be slippage between the categories. Take the case of the police's use of deadly force. What distinguishes police action from military action, in this context, is the police's obligation to discriminate. As Waddington puts it 'a citizen can only be killed when *necessary*, an enemy when *possible*'

(P.A.J. Waddington, 1996b: 123). Yet, prior to his removal from the official enquiry into the RUC's alleged 'shoot to kill' policy, John Stalker had uncovered evidence of Special Branch ' "inclination" (if not policy) to shoot suspects without attempting to make arrests' (Weitzer, 1995: 179). Alternatively, the relationship between the two categories might be highly contingent. Consider two examples. Vogler (1991) notes that during the early twentieth century magistrates' authority over civil disorder was first appropriated by the military rather than by the police. The reason for military domination, he suggests, was that the army developed a corporate structure much more quickly than the police, though such domination was soon destroyed by the demands placed on the military during a time of disintegrating empire. By the time of the 1926 General Strike, it was the police, not the military, who took the leading role. A second example concerns the concept of civil police primacy: the principle whereby chief constables of Home Office forces enjoy primacy over both the military and the military police on public space. Elsewhere (Johnston, 1992b), I have suggested that this concept is as much a rhetorical device as a real guide to operational practice, particularly when applied to sensitive areas such as the security of civil and military nuclear material in public places. In 1987, for example, there was an accident involving a military convoy on a public road at West Dean in Wiltshire. Although the Wiltshire police arrived within a few minutes of the incident, armed marines from the convoy stopped, detained and interrogated members of the public. Not only were the local police unable to exercise civil primacy in this case, they had no knowledge of the rules under which military personnel were operating.

Confirmation of the contingent nature of this relationship is also demonstrated by events in Northern Ireland. During the early years of the troubles the army took the primary role in security. However, in the mid-1970s the government announced a new policy of 'police primacy', itself part of the wider programme of 'Ulsterization' which was intended to reduce British military involvement. As a consequence, the numbers of army personnel in Northern Ireland fell by 50 per cent between 1972 and 1990. At the same time, the army – now providing military aid to the civil power – was placed in a subordinate position to the police, the latter having a dual role in which counterinsurgency work and routine police duties were combined (Magee, 1988; Weitzer, 1995; Brewer *et al.*, 1996). However, in this case, the implementation of police primacy did not result in an unambiguous distinction developing between civil and military action (cf. Hills, 1995). On the contrary, the RUC became more and more paramilitarized. As Magee puts it, '[i]n the face of continuing political violence, the militarisation of policing [was] the inevitable outcome of a policy of police primacy' (Magee, 1988: 79). That is not to say, of course, that all subsequent RUC action has taken a paramilitaristic form, for as Weitzer (1995) argues, one or other strand of the dual role tends to predominate according to the security profile of the locale being policed. The point is, as the previous examples confirm, that the connections between civil and military action, far from being stable, are contingent upon the effects of particular social conditions.

These examples suggest that a definition of paramilitary policing which is based upon the rigid demarcation of civil and military action, such as Hills's (1995), is difficult to sustain. On the contrary, the essence of para-military policing is its fusion of civil and military elements. Whether paramilitary organization minimizes disorder (P.A.J. Waddington, 1993) or maximizes it (Jefferson, 1993) in particular situations is an empirical matter, though any understanding of its long term effects demands an awareness of the wider political context in which it is deployed. However, the suggestion that paramilitary policing – because of its focus on 'citizens' rather than 'enemies' – describes a domain of consensual (because civil) police action is unconvincing. Undoubtedly, paramilitary policing contains the potential for authoritarian action by state police. Should this lead us to conclude, then, that the blurring of civil and military action also confirms the drive to an authoritarian (strong) state?

Centralization, diversity and the state

The strong state thesis rests upon a number of propositions. First, it is supposed that authoritarianism is linked to certain key developmental processes. Two of these – nationalization and militarization – have already been discussed. The third relates to the authoritarian potential of tech-nology, a factor which has been a cause of concern since the 1970s (Ackroyd *et al.*, 1977) and remains so today. Recently, the Omega Foundation carried out an appraisal of present-day technologies of political control on behalf of the European Parliament's Civil Liberties and Internal Affairs Committee. Among the developments listed in the report were 'dataveillance' systems which can build a life-profile and identify the friend-ship networks of those targeted; new 'less-lethal' weapons and incapacita-tion technologies being developed for operations 'other than war'; and new lethal weapons with advanced target acquisition aids whose use would be banned against foreign soldiers, though not necessarily against a state's own people (Ballantyne, 1998).

Secondly, it is assumed that under conditions of hegemonic crisis (Hall *et al.*, 1978), key elements of the state apparatus (the police, the media, the judiciary, etc.) act collectively to bring about an authoritarian response. Thus, many proponents of the strong state thesis maintain that differen-tial law enforcement during the miners' strike was an expression of the common class interests and actions of senior police officers, the media, the courts and the government. However, this second assumption depends on a number of others which are, themselves, highly problematic: that the constituent agents of the authoritarian state possess common objective interests; that they have a means of recognizing those interests and share a willingness to act according to them; that they possess the necessary capacities to carry out such action, including the knowledge needed to decide that one action is more rational than any other; and that, by undertaking such action, they are able to secure their objectives (Hindess, 1982; Johnston, 1986). In view of these conditions it is not surprising that attempts to provide empirical confirmation of the coordinated actions of a strong state are fraught with difficulty. For that reason, differential, biased or aggressive policing, however undesirable, hardly amounts to adequate confirmation of the authoritarian state thesis.

The strong state thesis also makes certain erroneous assumptions about police nationalization and militarization. As to the first of these, it is assumed that nationalization constitutes a singular, dominant, uniform tendency within British policing. Such a view is understandable – after all, this chapter has drawn attention to the nationalization of police functions in respect of serious crime and public order – and may even appear to be borne out by expert commentary. Following the miners' strike, Waddington made the dramatic judgement that Britain had a national police force 'where and when it mattered' (P.A.J. Waddington, 1989). In a similar vein, Brearley and King claimed that 'this was the strike that the political circumstances of the time had determined would require the deployment of the potential to organize a police response on a nation-wide basis in the overt interests of central government' (Brearley and King, 1996: 110). However, nationalization is neither a singular nor a uniform process and it is significant that these authorities have also pointed to the diversity of practices which coincided with the nationalization of public order policing. Thus, P.A.J. Waddington (1994; 1996) notes that, during the miners' strike, police action was far from cohesive, some chief constables being reluctant to take the hard line imposed by their colleagues from other forces. Brearley and King (1996) draw similar conclusions about the strike, suggesting that the tactics deployed varied from event to event and from area to area. Commenting on more recent events, they also note the marked discrepancies which existed between forces during the policing of demonstrations against animal exports in the 1990s. A similar point is made by D. Waddington (1996) who contrasts the relatively confrontational tactics of Essex Police with Sussex officers' attempts to use discretionary legal powers (specifically, testing lorries for roadworthiness) in order to limit traffic convoys, without provoking an aggressive response.

Similar qualifications have to be made about the process of militarization. Brearley and King (1996) argue that the paramilitary model, though important, gives only a partial account of contemporary public order policing. What is missing from this account is any consideration of the diverse range of preemptive strategies which police, increasingly, deploy in order to minimize the risks of public disorder. These risk-based strategies include enhanced surveillance, the use of detective work as a means of intelligence gathering both before and after the occurrence of public order incidents, the construction of tension indicators to improve forward planning and to facilitate preventive negotiation with relevant parties, and the use of community liaison to head off spontaneous acts of disorder. To some extent these developments reflect P.A.J. Waddington's (1994) observation, noted earlier, that much public order policing involves negotiation between the police and the policed. However, such routine practices are, increasingly, informed by risk-based modes of thinking which, in turn, support anticipatory forms of action.

Two things may be noted about these developments. First, though it is, undoubtedly, true that paramilitary engagement is not the only relevant mode of public order policing, it should not be assumed that, in the future, force-based (paramilitary) techniques will simply be replaced by risk-based (anticipatory) ones. Rather, as was suggested earlier, the police's use of 'techniques of disorganization' in public order policing – as in other policing domains – opens up the potential for new combinations of risk-based and disciplinary-based techniques to be developed. Second, the potential for further diversification of police technique is, itself, con-nected to social and political diversity. As Brearley and King (1996) point out, increased diversification of protest (environmental and lifestyle, animal rights, anti-nuclear, new age travellers, etc.) demands a correspond-ing diversity of response if policing is to remain legitimate. One question which arises, however, concerns the legitimate parameters of diversity. In that regard, D. Waddington (1996) notes the significance of the Newbury bypass protests for the future of public order policing. Here, three factors were especially important. First, the protest involved a public order dis-pute on private space. Second, because of that, removal of protesters was carried out by bailiffs and commercial security personnel rather than by police. This meant that there was little confrontation between police and protesters, though much between private police and protesters. Third, because of the private nature of the conflict, severe restrictions were placed on public access to information. D. Waddington (1996) concludes that the Newbury events involved 'the privatization of public order – even though, or perhaps because, the state was one of the protagonists' (Waddington, 1996: 31). The danger is, he suggests, that if reproduced elsewhere, this pattern would give rise to a new strain in public order policing: one where private security companies would be accountable to their clients first and to the law second, with the police having complicity in the preservation of private orders.

The question of the police's relationship with commercial security and its future role in the preservation of private orders will be a major issue in the future. An equally pressing issue will concern the relation-ship between specialist police agencies and specialist commercial security companies in tackling serious crime at both national and transnational levels, an issue considered further in the next two chapters. By whatever means these matters are resolved, however, one thing is clear. The unstable combination of 'creeping nationalization' and 'creeping pluralization' which, increasingly, defines the policing of serious crime and public disorder – itself a product of the late modern changes described in Chapter 3 – cannot be understood through the concept of the authoritarian state. There are two reasons for saying this. First, at the theoretical level, the concept is incapable of recognizing that governance is no longer the exclusive prerogative of the sovereign state. The lesson of the miners' strike is not that the state is an authoritarian one; merely that governance is sometimes usurped by the premeditated and coordinated actions of authoritarian governments willing to override legal and democratic conventions. The miners' strike is, in short, a case of 'governance by government' rather than 'authoritarian statism'. Second, at the political level, there is no reason to assume that the nationalization of police functions – whether in respect of public order or of serious crime – increases police (and state) authoritarianism. On the contrary, as Morgan and Newburn (1997) (with regard to serious crime), Morris (1985) and Magee (1988) (with regard to riot control and public disorder) suggest, nationalization may produce positive benefits for democracy and legitimacy. Such positive effects are, however, conditional upon political mechanisms being put into place which secure genuinely democratic ends. In that regard, the extent to which recent legislation (the PMCA and the Police Act 1997) genuinely increases the accountability of Home Secretaries or further obscures it remains to be seen.

Chapter 7

Public Policing: The Transnational Dimension

Introduction

The previous two chapters have examined a number of processes including devolution and concentration, decentralization and centralization, the combination of which, though apparently contradictory, is a characteristic feature of late modern organization. The present chapter moves outside the local and national spheres of analysis to return to the earlier theme of globalization, a topic addressed, in this instance, through the issue of transnational policing. Transnational policing initiatives are, of course, hardly new. As Sheptycki (1995a) points out, the idea for an International Criminal Police Commission (Interpol) was mooted as early as 1914, the outbreak of war delaying its eventual formation until 1923. The rapid escalation of transnational initiatives during the last quarter of a century has, however, raised the question of whether today 'transnational policing has reached a certain mass which makes it qualitatively different from what has gone before' (Sheptycki, 1995a: 616). In considering these developments my aim is not merely to argue that late modern policing is globalized – a matter on which there would seem to be little ground for dispute – but, rather, to ask what form that globalization might take. Here, one key issue is whether transnational policing represents the supranationalization of governance (and with it the demise of the nation state), or merely indicates supranational tendencies which leave the state with a significant – albeit altered – role in governance. Although the present chapter will focus almost exclusively on developments in Europe, it is worth remembering that transnational organization is no less a feature of North American policing. Here, for instance, the Drugs Enforcement Administration (DEA), alone, deploys more than 200 operational agents in over 60 offices throughout the world, its combined investment in the domestic and international arenas being estimated at $718m in 1993 (Sheptycki, 1995a: 620: footnote 7).

This chapter consists of three sections. The first considers the phenomenon of 'Eurocrime' and, with it, the expressed need for cooperative
policing initiatives to be developed across European nation states. The
second examines existing forms of European police cooperation, explores
the problems of, and the prospects for, their further development, and
speculates on their future trajectory. The third section explores the concept of transnational policing considering, among other things, its relationship to security, its impact on the conventional distinction between 'high'
and 'low' policing (Brodeur, 1983), its implications for police accountability, and its significance for state sovereignty and governance.

Euro-crime and the perceived need for police cooperation

Heidensohn (1991) suggests that there is an emerging congruence
between European nation states on matters of crime, three discernible
trends having contributed to this development. First, there has been an
internationalization of certain crimes which are no longer confined to
single nation states, terrorism, drugs offences and fraud being obvious
examples. Second, common social influences have caused people throughout Europe to object to everyday crimes and to the inadequacies of their
criminal justice systems. Third, a new crime agenda has been diffused
throughout Europe, particular concern being expressed for the needs
of victims. For these reasons, Heidensohn (1991) contends, 'common
definitions of crime as a problem are far more readily understood than
either recent criminological orthodoxy or common sense would expect'
(Heidensohn, 1991: 8).

The view that capitalist nation states in general, and European nations
states in particular, are experiencing common (transnational) crime problems which require corresponding (transnational) policing solutions has
become commonplace. It is widely held that transnational crime in
Europe – what might be called Euro-crime – is prevalent in a number of
offence types which breach territorial boundaries: terrorism, football hooliganism, drugs trafficking, arms trafficking, fraud, money-laundering,
computer crime, environmental crime, kidnapping and extortion, vice
and prostitution, industrial espionage and the theft of high value articles
such as art and antiques, to name just a few. It is also suggested that the
transnational character of such crimes is underpinned by their level of
organization. In recent years it has been argued that Eastern European
criminals have laundered billions of dollars throughout the world engaging, in particular, in illegal financial practices in the USA and Canada.
Though the lack of a large émigré community has protected Britain
from equivalent levels of infiltration, British police have, nevertheless,
taken preparatory measures. For example, the murder of two Chechen
businessmen in 1993, together with a retaliatory murder in 1994, led to

an investigation into the mafia activities of criminals from the former Soviet Union. Though it was concluded that they posed little threat at that time, a database was set up by NCIS to monitor future activities (Graham, 1996; *Police Review*, 31 May 1996).

Yet, despite the development of initiatives predicated upon the existence of transnational criminal activity in Europe, the concept of Euro-crime is far from unproblematic. There are several reasons for suggesting this. First, there is concern that the concept both overestimates the similarity of crimes within Europe and underestimates the prevalence of global transnational criminal activity outside Europe. Second, it has been noted that the concept of Euro-crime is, strictly, baseless without the existence of a European-wide criminal justice system. On these grounds 'the only appropriate application of the term . . . is to crime committed against the EU itself' (Anderson *et al.*, 1995: 15). Third, contrary to Heidensohn's (1991) prediction about the growing congruence of crime definitions in Europe, significant levels of incongruence have been observed. Anderson *et al.* (1995) suggest that two of the most contentious classifications relate to terrorism and organized crime, though drug trafficking also lacks consistency of definition across national boundaries. Fourth, and most significantly, a number of writers have pointed to the absence of reliable empirical data on the extent of transnational criminal activity in Europe. Sheptycki's (1997) view that there is, as yet, no reliable and valid method for evaluating the scope of transnational crime is shared by Hebenton and Thomas (1995) who argue that there is little hard data about numbers of cross-border crimes in Europe and little information about the economic costs of such activity. Lack of such reliable data has, however, neither deterred police and criminal justice professionals from speculating about the growth of car crime, drugs trafficking, or art and antiques theft, nor from constructing control policies informed by such speculation. Yet, as Anderson *et al.* (1995) suggest, police officers do not have privileged access to information about the scale and scope of international crime: '[t]heir professional expertise cannot overcome the limitations of the objective knowledge base' (Anderson *et al.*, 1995: 19).

Despite these qualifications about the scope and coherence of Euro-crime the problems assumed to be associated with its growth have provided a rationale for increased police cooperation. This rationale has been underpinned by a focus on two particular issues, cross-border crime and immigration (Benyon, 1996). Clearly, one of the main arguments for increased police cooperation since 1992 has been that the removal of frontier controls in the European Union (EU) would exacerbate the problem of cross-border crime. As Benyon (1996) suggests, much of this concern is linked to governmental anxiety about national security and social stability, the 'high policing' issues identified in Brodeur's (1983) analysis. Consequently, terrorism and drug-trafficking have been identified as cross-border issues of particular significance. One question which arises here is whether preoccupation with these 'high policing' issues might distort the character of policing in general. Sheptycki (1996), for example, fears that policing practices informed by 'the war on drugs' might condition other forms of transnational policing in undesirable directions. Linked to this has been a growing concern with the need to create a 'ring of steel' around the EU in order to repel a threatened 'flood' of immigrants from the less developed regions of Southern and Eastern Europe. Immigration has now displaced terrorism and drug trafficking in the EU as the main 'internal security threat' (Benyon, 1996) though, paradoxically, official concern about that threat is often expressed in terms of the alleged linkages between illegal immigrants and serious crime.

A significant part of the rationale for enhanced cooperation is, of course, derived from police concerns about the criminological effects of the loss of control over territorial borders. Yet, these effects are, by no means, straightforward. In the case of terrorism, for instance, Benyon (1994) suggests that 'the removal of internal borders is likely to have little impact on the overall levels of these types of serious crime as frontier controls have not prevented terrorist activity in the past' (Benyon, 1994: 499). The same point applies to drug-trafficking. Hebenton and Thomas (1995), having reviewed a number of European studies on drugs control mechanisms, conclude that while the issue of border controls has been an important one in terms of the rhetoric of police cooperation, professional traffickers 'have never been so impressed by border controls as to be frightened out of business' (Hebenton and Thomas, 1995: 165). Indeed, with a given level of demand, strict border controls have usually driven up street prices and, thereby, increased profits. Leaving aside matters of their utility, the question of borders raises two further issues. The first concerns their rhetorical and symbolic function in the construction of discourses on European police cooperation, an issue to which I return in the final section. The second concerns their definition as locations occupying an essential physical space, a definition whose shortcomings are, increasingly, exposed. Though, understandably, debate on European police cooperation has been preoccupied with the control of terrestrial crime, criminal activity, in the form of electronic and cybercrime, is now breaching terrestrial boundaries. Grabosky (1996) notes that while transnational crime has proven a difficult challenge for law enforcement in the past, telecommunications-related crimes – such as the theft of intellectual property rights, the electronic dissemination of offensive material, electronic money laundering, and electronic vandalism – will pose even greater challenges in the future. As Wall (1997) suggests, cyberspace poses fresh problems for policing since, by cutting across geographic, social, political and gendered boundaries, it calls into question conventional notions of space, place and time. It also transforms our conception of property, physical property being displaced by intellectual properties 'in the form of images, and likenesses, copyrightable, trademarkable and patentable materials . . . [which] have value and are therefore vulnerable to being appropriated' (Wall, 1997: 211). Such developments impact on the nature and significance of borders. They also raise implications for national sovereignty and governance far beyond those posed by European cooperation.

European police cooperation

Anderson (1994) suggests that, until recently, police cooperation in Europe was largely a story of 'pragmatic responses to particular pressures' (Anderson, 1994: 11). Though, since its inception, Interpol's workload has been dominated by European police communications, it is only during the last twenty-five years that attempts have been made to develop formal cooperative structures in Europe. The classificatory scheme outlined by Benyon and his colleagues (Benyon *et al.*, 1993; Benyon, 1996) provides a useful means of describing these structures. In that classification a distinction is drawn between three interrelated levels of police cooperation. The macro level entails constitutional and international legal agreements and the harmonization of national laws and regulations. The meso level focuses on the operational structures, practices and procedures of police and law enforcement agencies. The micro level consists of the investigation of specific offences and the control and prevention of particular forms of crime. It is worth noting that some criticism has been made of this classification. Sheptycki (1995a: 619), for instance, claims that, for all its utility, the classification fails to portray the European 'system as a system'; while Hebenton and Thomas (1995: 49) suggest that all attempts to impose settled meaning on European policing arrangements are undermined by the dynamics of 'process'. Those criticisms notwithstanding, Benyon's classification is useful for the purpose of describing recent developments and debates. Critical analysis of these developments and debates is reserved for the following section.

At the macro level government ministers take decisions on matters relating to rights of entry to and exit from sovereign states (extradition procedures, asylum policies and visa harmonization) and on legal issues about operational powers across borders in respect of arrest, detention, investigation and surveillance. The main instrument of cooperation has been – and at the operational level remains – Interpol (Anderson, 1994). However, that organization was never established through an international treaty, its constitution being written by a group of police officers who never submitted their draft for governmental approval (Sheptycki, 1995a). Interpol currently has a membership of 176 countries, the 46 European member states accounting for eighty per cent of its communications traffic (Benyon, 1996). The organization's aims are twofold: to ensure and promote mutual assistance between criminal police authorities within the legal limits laid down in different countries and in the spirit of the Universal Declaration of Human Rights; and to establish and develop institutions likely to contribute to the prevention and suppression of ordinary law crimes (cited in Benyon *et al.*, 1993: 122). Contrary to its popular public image Interpol is not an executive agency with specialist international detectives but an international communications system between different police forces, advising officers when they visit foreign jurisdictions and carrying out research and analysis of international crime patterns. Each Interpol member is required to nominate an office for communication with the Lyon headquarters, these National Central Bureaux (NCBs) being the mechanism through which Interpol enquiries are channelled. Police information is circulated between NCBs on 'international notices' which contain photographs, fingerprints and physical descriptions of persons and are colour coded according to the nature of the enquiry.

Clearly, Interpol's role as a communications network restricts it to the exchange of information on a case by case basis and, partly because of this, its capacity to promote greater police cooperation in Europe is limited (Benyon, 1996). It is also restricted in other ways. Article 3 of its 1956 Convention, mindful of the sensitivities surrounding national sovereignty, defined the organization's mission as the 'efficient repression of common law crimes and offences to the strict exclusion of all matters having a political, religious or racial character' (cited in Sheptycki, 1995a: 619). It was largely because of this exclusion of political crime from Interpol's operational brief that, following terrorist acts of the late 1960s and early 1970s, the European Council of Ministers instigated the Trevi initiative.

The Trevi Group was set up in 1976 having been preceded by a number of intergovernmental meetings on terrorism in 1971 and 1972. Trevi is a high level ministerial group which includes senior police officers, its meetings being attended by the twelve members of the EU plus seven 'friends of Trevi' who attend meetings as observers: Austria, Canada, Morocco, Norway, Sweden, Switzerland and the USA (Sheptycki, 1995a). Trevi operates at three levels. At the macro level the Ministerial Group meets every six months, being serviced at the meso level by the Senior Official's Group which prepares agendas and reports and monitors the progress of the micro level Working Groups (Benyon, 1996). Subsequent to the 1976 Luxembourg meeting five Trevi Working Groups were established with specified areas of responsibility. Trevi 1 focused on measures to combat terrorism. Trevi 2 was concerned with scientific and technical knowledge and with police training, its work later being expanded to embrace public order and football hooliganism. Trevi 3 was originally set up to deal with security procedures for civilian air travel, a role later passed on to Trevi 1. However, at the 1985 Rome meeting of Trevi Ministers its role was redefined to address the problems of organized crime and drug trafficking, thus preparing the way for the eventual creation of the European Drugs Unit. Trevi Groups 4 and 5, responsible respectively for nuclear security and for disaster management, were never convened (Bunyan, 1993). Four other ad hoc groups were set up to promote cooperation in related fields. The first of these was established in 1991 to develop the idea of a European Criminal Police Office (Europol). The other three, though not formally part of the Trevi structure, followed the same cycle of meetings and reported to the same ministers. The Group on International Organized Crime was established in 1992 following the murders of two Italian anti-Mafia judges. The Group on Immigration was founded in 1986, its work being directed to issues of admission, expulsion, visas, asylum and refugees among others. The Group on Judicial Cooperation on Criminal Matters had the remit to prepare conventions and agreements to facilitate mutual legal assistance in matters of extradition, fraud against the EU budget and combating terrorist funding (Benyon *et al.*, 1993; Benyon, 1996).

There seems to be widespread agreement that Trevi's role in stimulating European police cooperation 'cannot be underestimated'. Benyon (1996) confirms that from the late 1980s onwards the activities of Trevi were characterized by political commitment at the macro level of ministerial meetings and at the meso level of liaison and information exchange. However, it should also be noted that such macro and meso level success has been achieved through intergovernmental means which have excluded the Group from accountability to, or scrutiny by, the European Commission and the European Parliament. (This factor, above all others, has made the UK a strong supporter of the Trevi process, given governmental desire to secure national sovereignty against the alleged federal tendencies of the EU.) It is also worth noting that some police criticism has been made of the effectiveness of Trevi at the micro level of operational policing though, as Benyon (1996) suggests, it could equally be argued that one of the aims of Trevi was to develop meso level procedures which would, in due course, facilitate future police cooperation at the micro level.

The Schengen Convention provides the most complete model for European cooperation. The original agreement was signed in 1985 by Belgium, France, Germany, Luxembourg and the Netherlands, Italy joining in 1990, Spain and Portugal in 1991 and Greece in 1992. The 1985 agreement acknowledged the need to remove all internal frontiers between the parties in order to facilitate the free movement of goods and people, ensuring at the same time that external borders were strengthened in order to control the entry of external aliens. According to the Convention, non-EU citizens will need a visa – normally of three months duration – to ensure entry to Schengen countries while asylum applications will be made to one member state, any decision reached being binding on all others. Denmark, Ireland and the UK have not joined Schengen because of their desire to maintain control over their borders.

The agreement provides a number of measures to compensate for the establishment of a frontier free area. These include increased border surveillance, right of 'hot pursuit' of criminals across borders, and the coordination and sharing of information between the police forces of member states. The last of these is underpinned by the establishment of a computerized data exchange, the Schengen Information System (SIS). SIS is intended to be a common database shared by members with a capacity of eight million personal records and seven million records on objects. SIS is regarded by the Schengen membership as a critical compensatory measure for the removal of frontier checks, enabling police agencies in the different countries to have identical information on wanted persons, 'undesirable aliens', asylum seekers and those extradited or under surveillance (Benyon *et al.*, 1993; Hebenton and Thomas, 1995; Benyon, 1996; Morgan and Newburn, 1997).

Like Trevi, Schengen also works at three levels, macro level agreements deciding policies such as 'hot pursuit'; meso level structures, such as SIS, being put into place to facilitate micro level policing. Like Trevi, Schengen is also immune from overall judicial and parliamentary accountability to EU institutions, an issue which has particular implications for human rights, data protection and police powers. In addition to that, there is the issue of sovereignty. It has been noted that Schengen members are prepared to lose some degree of sovereignty in return for 'an enhanced capability to combat crime, limit clandestine immigration and enable internal border controls to be removed' (Benyon, 1996: 361). However, the success of this endeavour depends upon members adopting a common policy on matters such as immigration. In January 1998, Italy's decision to grant political asylum to Kurds fleeing persecution, led to demands for the 'stamping out' of such immigration from French and German ministers, fearful of their entry into Northern Europe. Indeed, such was the level of concern in Germany that the Social Democratic Interior Minister for Lower Saxony called for the entire suspension of the Schengen accords (Traynor and Smith, 1998).

The fourth element of European police cooperation is Europol, this initiative being contained within new structures which would replace Trevi. The original intention put forward by German Chancellor Helmut Kohl in 1991 was to develop a fully operational European Police Agency similar to the Federal Bureau of Investigation in the USA. However, as Sheptycki (1995a) points out, such an event is still a long way off and subsequent developments have been more measured. In December 1991 Art K1 of the Maastricht Treaty referred to 'the organization of a union-wide system of exchanging information within a European Police Office (Europol)' (cited in Benyon, 1996: 366). As a first step in this initiative a Europol Drugs Unit (EDU) was established, becoming operational in February 1994, its task being the collection and analysis of information on drug trafficking, money laundering and related criminal organizations, together with the facilitation of intelligence exchange between law enforcement agencies in the member states. Subsequently, its brief has been extended to cover illicit traffic in vehicles, nuclear and radioactive substances and the smuggling of illegal immigrants. Though member states pressed ahead with the establishment of the EDU, the creation of a European Police Office (Europol) required agreement on a convention. The Europol

Convention was signed in July 1995 and must, eventually, be ratified by all EU member states. Within two years of such ratification it is accepted that the organization will have additional powers to tackle terrorism (Gibbons, 1997a).

What, then, are the prospects for, and the obstacles to, future European police cooperation? Benyon, (1996) suggests that the emergence of meso level policy networks, consisting of senior officials and police professionals, gives rise to common agendas which may lead to 'a gradual evolution of some specialist forms of European police units with limited cross-border operational capabilities' (Benyon, 1996: 342). On a related theme, Anderson (1994) suggests that closer collaboration will give rise to further pressures for cooperation in a number of areas: the harmonization of criminal justice procedures; the identification of serious crimes as 'Euro-crimes' subject to similar penalties; the necessity for agreed general rules on data protection; the centralization of intelligence; common training and professional standards; and common systems of accountability.

Undoubtedly, some of these ends will be difficult to achieve not least because, as Benyon (1996) suggests, arguments about national sovereignty may impede future cooperation. In addition to that there are other obstacles that need to be recognized. First, the diverse working experience of police in different jurisdictions, combined with the existence of different legal systems and organizational structures, places cultural and procedural obstacles on cooperation. Second, there is the problem of rivalry between different policing agencies both within and between states. In Britain, for example, there is increasing disagreement between the police, Customs and MI5 over the right to police organized crime and drugs trafficking (Hyder, 1996). Third, there is the problem of public sensitivity. As Anderson (1994) suggests, increased public acceptance of transnational policing will, inevitably, go hand in hand with greater sensitivity about the ways in which nationals of 'one's own' country are treated by police from another. That problem is, in turn, part of a wider one concerning public perceptions regarding the relationship between national citizenship and European citizenship.

It is also worth noting the limitations imposed by what Anderson *et al.* (1995) term the 'micro-political dynamics' of European policing. Here, they note a number of dichotomies which appear in the discourse of officials and senior police officers when discussing cooperation. First, despite significant progress towards formal cooperation, police insist on the continued need for informal contacts. Second, there is the tension between the demands of 'high politics' and the exigencies of 'practical policing'. Third, police invariably point to the numerous differences between their system and other 'foreign' systems, and to the consequent obstacles such differences pose for cooperation. Fourth, tension exists between officials in those states pledged to federalism (notably Germany and the Netherlands) and those, like the UK and France who favour inter-governmentalism. Fifth, there remains the issue of whether Europol should, eventually, possess operational powers or merely serve as an information exchange.

Finally, within what parameters might European police cooperation develop in the future? Van Reenen (1989) makes a useful distinction between four types of supranational engagement. 'Cooperation' occurs between independent police forces and requires no change to the nature and powers of national police systems. An example would be informal collaboration for the exchange of information. 'Horizontal integration' arises when officers obtain authority to operate in another country as, for example, with 'hot pursuit' across borders. 'Vertical integration' exists when a police organization is created with European-wide operational powers. This is a distant prospect for mainstream policing, though as both Van Reenen (1989) and Anderson *et al.* (1995) suggest, such developments are more likely in the field of 'administrative policing' (that concerned with the enforcement of EU regulations on health and safety, the environment or the nuclear industry). 'Competition' occurs as European policing becomes, more and more, a market in which different police systems trade their products and services. There are three ways in which that process develops. First, commercial security companies compete for a slice of the market in police services and facilities. Second, defence companies, on the look-out for new markets after the collapse of communism, turn their attention towards matters of internal security. Third, the military, faced with a shrinking role in conventional defence, seeks new opportunities in the field of policing and internal security (Johnston, 1992a). This last issue is discussed in the following section, the role of transnational commercial security companies being considered in Chapter 8.

Transnational policing

In discussing transnational policing, a distinction should be drawn between mere international developments and those which are genuinely transnational. It is clear, for example, that some of the cooperative endeavours discussed in the previous section (e.g. in respect of Trevi) have been international (intergovernmental), rather than fully transnational. Indeed, ideological differences about the relative advantages and disadvantages of these alternative cooperative routes continue to preoccupy European debate. For that reason, transnational activity should be distinguished from the mere interaction of sovereign states. So defined, transnational policing is hardly new, Interpol being an early example of a non-governmental organization established without recourse to international agreements between sovereign nation states. Since the inception of Interpol, however, transnational policing has developed in a variety of different ways: through formal organizations such as the International Association of Chiefs of Police and the Police Executive Research Forum, as well as through a myriad of informal, invisible and subterranean channels (Sheptycki, 1995b). Such transnational arrangements have an increasingly significant impact on matters of law, politics and justice.

Consider the issue of law enforcement, an area where three developments may be identified. First, it would seem that transnationalization has already 'outdistanced our ability to adequately theorize its implications' (Sheptycki, 1995b: 306). Sheptycki (1995b) supports this claim by citing two legal cases where, despite the circumstances being similar, judgment was entirely contradictory. In the first (*United States v. Alvarez-Machain*, 1992), the defendant was forcibly kidnapped from his place of work in Mexico, flown to Texas and arrested for alleged involvement in the murder of a DEA agent. Conviction was upheld by the US Supreme Court despite a criminal act having been committed in the process of arrest. By contrast, the conviction was set aside in a South African case (*S v. Ebrahim*, 1991) involving the forcible abduction of a member of the African National Congress from Swaziland by South African agents on the grounds that it would involve the state in 'sanctify[ing] international delinquency' (cited in Sheptycki, 1995b: 303).

Second, there is the relationship between law, police discretion and justice. Though this issue is an 'old chestnut' in domestic policing circles, transnational developments give it a new lease of life. Sheptycki (1996), once again, illustrates this point when quoting the words of a Dutch police officer, deliberating on the relative merits of arresting a drug dealer in the Netherlands (maximum penalty six months in prison) or in Germany (maximum penalty six years in prison): 'We arrest them in Germany. It is better I think' (cited in Sheptycki, 1996: 61). In other words, transnational practices provide new sets of conditions which will affect the exercise of low-level police discretion and, with it, the administration of justice.

Sheptycki (1996) also draws attention to a third issue, the fact that, increasingly, transnational legal practice is shaped by transnational police practice. A clear example of this tendency arises in respect of drugs enforcement where techniques of 'controlled delivery' (by which officials allow shipments of illicit drugs to proceed, under surveillance, in order to secure evidence against the organizers of drugs traffic), though not legally condoned are, nonetheless, widely used by agents. Pressure from enforcement bodies has now succeeded in persuading prosecutors to sanction, and judges to legalize, such techniques. The problem here is that, increasingly, transnational law is dictated by the working practices of middle level operatives and officials who are unaccountable and invisible. In effect, transnational law enforcement is dominated by unaccountable bureaucratic and professional police interests.

Though, as I have suggested in Chapter 2, transnationalization is linked to the wider structural trajectory of globalization, police and bureaucratic interests have played a major role in developing the rationale for transnational police cooperation in Europe. Fundamental to this process was the construction of a discourse concerned with the problem of the security deficit: the view that late twentieth century Europe faced new security challenges which demanded unprecedented solutions. Critical analyses of the concept of the security deficit fall into three types. The first, illustrated in Den Boer's (1994) discussion, subjects the concept to discourse analysis, the basic proposition being that '[t]he quest for international policing is a public exchange of rhetorical statements which reveal minimal empirical or analytical scrutiny' (Den Boer, 1994: 193). Den Boer (1994) argues that the evolution of police cooperation is subject to various conceptual transformations which are inspired by changing evaluations of the efficacy and accountability of existing mechanisms. To that extent, police cooperation constitutes a form of 'evolutionary politics' (Den Boer, 1994: 176) constructed around various rhetorical justifications: in this instance, the threat allegedly posed by international crime, loss of border controls and immigration.

Where Den Boer (1994) examines the dynamics of discourse, a second approach focuses on discursive constructions at the transnational level of what, in the domestic sphere, have been termed 'moral panics' (Hall *et al.*, 1978). This approach shares much with the previous one in terms of its account of the dynamics of cooperation, the main difference being that it aims to locate transnational discourse within the social interests of the participants who construct it. In order to do that Benyon *et al.* (1993) draw attention to the use of exaggerated terminology and crude moral sentiments by police, public officials and politicians when predicting future crime levels in a Europe without borders. Though such predictions are based upon no valid empirical data, their effect is to produce real and rapid changes in two areas of policy. First, 'constructing a "moral panic" around serious crime is likely to prove effective in the promotion of international police cooperation' (Benyon *et al.*, 1993: 58). Second, the explosion of interest in fighting crime may generate repressive social policies which may be disproportionate to the size, and inappropriate to the character, of the social problems which they are meant to address. Hebenton and Thomas (1995) share this view, arguing that during the early 1990s the British police constructed a 'shopping list' of demands on the back of the moral panic which they had, themselves, helped to instigate. Among the items on this list were demands for the extension of the powers of s 14 of the Prevention of Terrorism Act, for the strengthening of the Aviation and Maritime Security Act 1990 and for the introduction of identity cards. At the same time, in the wider European arena, police, politicians and bureaucrats engaged in a 'linking and glossing' process 'whereby separate activities of drug trafficking, terrorism, money-laundering, illegal immigration, extreme right movements and football hooliganism were assembled into a causal "field of intervention"' (Hebenton and Thomas, 1995: 135). One particular feature of this process was the conjoining of criminality with immigration so that any distinction between immigrants, asylum seekers, drug-traffickers and terrorists became confused in the public mind.

These two approaches are subject to obvious – and contrasting – limitations: the first because the analysis of the dynamics of discourse is divorced from its political and organizational context; the second because discourse is seen as a reflection of the social and political interests of those who construct it. A third approach, emphasizing the conflicts which arise during the process of discourse construction, avoids some of these difficulties. Bigo (1994) suggests that while the concept of a 'European security field' has, undoubtedly, been constructed by participating agents – and while that construction certainly involved the conjoining of hitherto unrelated elements such as terrorism and immigration – the process was 'not a sinister plot of ministerial power-seekers to attack civil liberties' (Bigo, 1994: 164). On the contrary, the concept of the internal security field, arose out of a 'battleground of bureaucracies' (Bigo, 1994: 163). The critical moment in this process of bureaucratic conflict arose when the elaboration of a common immigration policy was handed over to officials from different ministries (Justice, Interior, Transport, etc.). As a result, officials, acting on their own experience, broke down the boundaries between issues, unaware that they were, simultaneously, engaged in philosophical and political reconstruction of the security agenda. Terrorism, drugs, crime and asylum came to be treated together in an attempt to gain an overall view of their connections, not because of the ideological predispositions of those engaged in construction. For that reason, Bigo (1994) insists, the security deficit cannot be explained as a product of the interests and ideologies of the agents who construct it; nor, for that matter, can it be seen as the exclusive preserve of the right. Only by recognizing the conflict within the construction of security discourse, Bigo (1994) insists, is it possible to explain the fact that differences continue to arise within and between states as to the character and extent of future transnational initiatives.

The processes described in these three accounts have given rise to a new security politics in Europe. Significantly, this politics is shaped by the same interplay between risk and security described in Chapters 2 and 4. Two aspects of this interplay are particularly significant. First, there is the impact of global political and military factors (normally considered as part of the field of 'international relations') on the internal security of the EU and the domestic security of its constituent member states (normally considered as part of the field of policing and criminal justice). Carr (1996) suggests that the character of security politics in Europe has changed since the collapse of communism, Cold War conceptions of threat being replaced by those which include political and economic, as well as military, elements. In particular, he suggests, the 'Cold War perception of military threat has ended and given way to the notion of risks' (Carr, 1996: 395). Thus, for instance, the New Transatlantic Agenda and Joint Action Plan agreed between the USA and the EU in 1995, though still seeing NATO as the centrepiece of transatlantic security, also pledges to cooperate on risks from 'international crime, terrorism and drug trafficking, mass migration, the degradation of the environment and nuclear safety and disease' (cited in Carr, 1996: 395). The net effect of these changes is twofold. On the one hand, a widening spectrum of ever more broadly defined security issues emerges. On the other hand, an overlapping plurality of agencies competes for participation in and influence over the expanding security arena.

Second, there is the growing importance of new techniques for the collection, collation, storage and retrieval of information for the purpose of minimizing risk and maximizing security. Hebenton and Thomas (1995) suggest that this process of 'informatization' enables the police to move from the mere tactical use of intelligence (deploying it in the course of particular investigations) to its strategic use (deploying it for the achievement of more general objectives). Though, as I have suggested in Chapter 4, these tendencies are already apparent in domestic policing, they are especially pertinent to the transnational arena where the security deficit is defined in terms of its complex, organized, global and systemic nature. It is precisely for this reason that transnational policing focuses less and less on arrest, detention and prosecution and more and more on surveillance, targeting, disruption, inhibition, disorganization and subversion – techniques usually associated with those engaged in military intelligence and state security.

Anderson *et al.* (1995) suggest that these developments are indicative of a merging of external and internal security, the result of which is that conventional divisions between the police, state security and the military are eroded. One implication of this development is that Brodeur's (1983) influential distinction between 'high' policing (that concerned with the protection of the state) and 'low' policing (that concerned with routine matters of crime prevention and order maintenance in civil society) becomes less and less tenable. Inevitably, that raises dangers. For if the (undercover and invisible) techniques of 'high' policing are transferred to the civil sphere, there are likely to be serious implications for accountability and justice. As Anderson *et al.* (1995) put it, the issue will be 'whether the balance of the common European policing effort will tip towards repression and authoritarianism or to an affirmation of democratic values' (Anderson *et al.*, 1995: 289).

The problem is that the discourse of the 'security deficit' which sanctions the expansion of transnational policing in Europe has not, simultaneously, generated corresponding forms of transnational accountability. On the contrary, as Anderson *et al.* (1995) argue, the European arena is the site of an 'accountability deficit'. This deficit arises for a number of reasons. Many security initiatives involve ad hoc and informal cooperation on the grounds that formal ones (and the formal accountability which might accompany them) would undermine the sovereignty of member states. It is also the case that the new security politics has been dominated by bureaucratic and professional interests to the extent that issues of police accountability have been marginalized. In part, this has been possible because the public have had little, if any, direct involvement in the development of European police cooperation, such lack of involvement meaning that there is little popular demand for enhanced accountability. Finally, there remains limited judicial control over matters of operational policing at the transnational level. The Amsterdam Treaty signed in 1997, amending the Treaty of European Communities and the Maastricht Treaty, stipulates that the Court of Justice has 'no jurisdiction to review the validity or proportionality of operations carried out by the police . . . of a member state . . . with regard to the maintenance of law and order and the safeguarding of internal security' (cited in *Statewatch*, Vol. 7, 3, May–June: 13).

Under these circumstances it is not surprising that concern is repeatedly expressed about the secretive nature of transnational developments. In 1994, for example, the EU and the FBI agreed to collaborate in the creation of a global system for the surveillance of telecommunications (phone calls, faxes and emails). This decision was taken by officials in the EU's K4 Committee, the body responsible under the Maastricht Treaty for cooperation on law and order, immigration and asylum, without being discussed by ministers. In contrast to its handling in the EU, the initiative was the subject of widespread debate in the USA, that debate eventually giving rise to legislation. These arrangements have developed under the auspices of a group of twenty countries (EU members plus the USA, Canada, Australia, New Zealand and Norway) though there is no accountability to the Council of Justice, to the European Parliament or to national parliaments (Norton-Taylor, 1997; *Statewatch*, Vol. 7, 4 and 5, July–October 1997).

Some critics have suggested that the secretive implementation of transnational policies without adequate accountability indicates the emergence of an 'authoritarian European state' (Bunyan, 1991). In Bunyan's view this state has two features. First, its practices are informal, secretive and unaccountable. Typically, its core groups operate multifunctionally, shifting from drugs to immigration to organized crime with much 'shuffling of chairs' between the key members of different committees. Second, this state is preoccupied with the functions of internal and external control. In Bunyan's view this security agenda cannot be divorced from its racist roots: 'The new European state is set to exclude Third World peoples from its shores and to create a system of internal controls which will criminalize black settlers and illegal immigrants alike' (Bunyan, 1991: 26). Such an institution, it is claimed, 'has all the hallmarks of an authoritarian state' (Bunyan, 1993: 33), its power residing in the hands of officials immune from legal or democratic accountability.

Though undoubtedly reflecting serious concerns about justice and accountability, claims of this sort should be treated with caution. The suggestion that transnational police cooperation constitutes proof of the existence of a fully operational European (authoritarian) state can be questioned on a number of grounds. Robertson (1994), for example, has pointed out that there are practical obstacles to the development of European wide intelligence systems which make predictions about the dominance of the 'surveillance state' at least premature, and at most unconvincing. It also has to be said that transnationalization of policing in no way implies its homogenization. It is certainly true that the practices of police, military, state and commercial security have merged in crucial respects, but this does not imply their fusion into a unified institutional bloc. On the contrary, as van Reenen's (1989) analysis suggests, competition between diffuse security agencies is likely to be a feature of any transnational future.

Predictions about the emergence of a European state are, then, unconvincing. Despite the existence of supranational policing initiatives, most police cooperation has occurred through intergovernmental (bilateral and multilateral) arrangements between nation states. The long term impact of such transnational activity on the sovereignty of nation states is both unpredictable and paradoxical. As Hebenton and Thomas (1995) point out, the more there is a perceived need for transnational cooperation against crime, and the more this is instigated by bilateral and multilateral state action, the greater is the likelihood for the resulting institutional arrangements to place limits on the autonomy of states. The likely outcome, they suggest, is a 'patchwork . . . of contexts, coalitions and interactions within and between national societies that escape the effective control of the central policy organs of government' (Hebenton and Thomas, 1995: 3). Interestingly, in talking about the impact of informatization on transnational policing, Sheptycki, (1995a) uses the same analogy, describing a 'vast and ungovernable patchwork of informated spaces, existing in the transnational interstices of state power [which] might . . . be a significant diminution of the nation state's near monopoly of policing' (Sheptycki, 1995a: 629).

Of course, recognition of this diminution of one near monopoly (at the level of the nation state) should not lead us to invoke its replacement by another near monopoly (at the level of the European state): even less to conjure up a European authoritarian state with an unlimited monopoly of coercive powers. It may be that in the future the EU will take on some 'state-like characteristics' (Anderson et al., 1995: 107). But, if it does so, it will be in a context where the state is 'a less cohesive political entity' than hitherto (Anderson et al., 1995: 107) and where governance, itself, is remoulded. As far as policing goes, one factor in that remoulding will be the capacity of the commercial security industry to produce pockets of 'governance without government' at both domestic and transnational levels. It is to a consideration of commercial security that the following chapter is directed.

Chapter 8

Commercial Policing

Introduction

The previous three chapters have examined contemporary developments in public policing at various jurisdictional levels. Many of these developments have, of course, taken place during a period when governmental restructuring has altered the balance between the public and private sectors. In the case of policing that restructuring has coincided with a 'rebirth' of private modes of provision (Johnston, 1992a) and it is to a consideration of one of these modes – commercial security – that the present chapter is directed. The chapter is divided into three sections. The first gives a brief account of the size and structure of commercial security, looking both at particular countries (Britain, the USA and Japan) and at European and transnational developments. The second examines the range of functions undertaken by commercial security organizations, an issue which has to be considered in the light of those functional changes in police work identified in Chapters 3 and 4. The third section considers some major explanations for the expansion of commercial security during the post-war period and examines the impact of its growing interaction with and penetration of the public security sector. This interaction raises a number questions about the governance, accountability and justice of diverse policing systems which are considered in the final chapter.

The structure of commercial security

The present chapter is concerned, primarily, with contract security since it is that sector of the industry which has provoked most controversy due to its operation in and around 'public space'. The contract security sector may be divided into three categories (cf. Jordan & Sons,

1989; Jones and Newburn, 1998): physical/mechanical security (locks, safes, strong rooms, shutters, vehicle security, cash bags, boarding up services etc.); electronic security (alarm manufacture and installation, control panels, CCTV, access control, security cameras, etc.); and staffed services (guarding, cash transportation, key holding, alarm monitoring, investigation, bailiffing and debt collection). It should not be forgotten, however, that commercial security also comprises a large proprietary or 'in-house' sector whose task is to protect the assets of factories, banks, hotels, universities and government departments. The significance of in-house security should not be underestimated. Writing in the mid-1970s, O'Toole (1978) noted that General Motors' force of 4,200 plant guards gave it an organization larger than the municipal police forces of all but five American cities. In Britain, during the same period, estimates suggested that the in-house sector employed around 60,000 people (Shearing and Stenning, 1981). More recent work suggests that by the early 1990s around 91,000 personnel were employed in the proprietary sector (Jones and Newburn, 1995).

Calculation of the numbers employed in the contract and in-house sectors is notoriously difficult due to an absence of official data, ambiguity about which occupational roles in the in-house sector may be deemed 'security' and the diverse range of security and non-security activities undertaken by the major contract corporations (South, 1988). There is broad agreement, however, that the industry has undergone significant expansion during the post-war period in all western economies. Early predictions in the USA (Kakalik and Wildhorn, 1972) suggested that despite the expansion of contract guarding, public police forces would continue to grow more rapidly than their commercial counterparts. By the early 1980s, however, the first 'Hallcrest Report' (Cunningham and Taylor, 1985) indicated that the number of uniformed guards, alone, exceeded the 580,000 police officers then in post and concluded that private police outnumbered public police by a ratio of 2:1. The second Hallcrest study (Cunningham, Strauchs and Van Meter, 1990) confirmed that by 1990 a total of 965,300 personnel were employed in commercial security, 54 per cent of them in the contract guard sector. The same report predicted that by the year 2000 total employment would grow to almost one-and-half million with a private-public policing ratio in the USA of almost 3:1.

Elsewhere, estimates of the size of the industry are less reliable. In Europe a small number of companies operated between the wars in Britain, France, the Netherlands, Sweden and Finland (South, 1988; de Waard and van der Hoek, 1991; Johnston, 1992a) though the most significant expansion did not occur until the 1960s and 1970s. That same pattern of development occurred elsewhere. In Japan the first company was established in 1962, the industry being given a boost by the security demands of the 1964 Tokyo Olympic Games (Miyazawa, 1991). Since then, growth has been dramatic. Between 1989 and 1993, the number of Japanese security businesses expanded from 5,248 to 7,062 and the number of guards from 232,617 to 321,721. By comparison, the combined authorized police strength for the Japanese National and Prefectural Police stood at 259,000 in 1993 (National Police Agency, 1994). Estimates of the size of the British security industry have been notoriously inaccurate. However, recent research, based on data drawn from the Yellow Pages Business Classification and the Labour Force Survey (Jones and Newburn, 1998), is more reliable. Here it is suggested that total employment could be as high as one-third of a million, with 100,000 working in the electronic security sector and more than 180,000 employed in security services and equipment. Indeed, the total employed in this second category alone is equivalent to the combined police and civilian staff of the 43 constabularies in England and Wales.

Attempts to carry out comparative analyses of the size and structure of the industry are fraught with difficulty. A study undertaken by the Dutch Ministry of Justice (de Waard and van der Hoek, 1991; see also, de Waard, 1993) examined numbers of police personnel, numbers of private security personnel, total security personnel (public plus private) and the ratio of public to private security in each of ten European countries. The authors suggest that while Southern European countries such as Portugal, Spain and France exhibit higher numbers of public police per 100,000 inhabitants than Northern European countries, the position with commercial security is less geographically polarised. In fact, their analysis shows that Germany (307 private security personnel per 100,000 inhabitants) has the highest number, followed by Sweden (182) and Spain (165). By combining the two categories, it is suggested that Portugal (636 security personnel per 100,000 inhabitants), Germany (634) and Spain (587) 'are well in the lead in Europe as regards security services' (de Waard and van der Hoek, 1991: 27).

This research suggests that despite the rapid expansion of the last twenty years the private security industry in Europe – unlike that in North America – remains the secondary, rather than the primary, protective resource. According to these estimates, the highest ratio of private to public police in Europe (Germany at 0.94:1) still falls well short of the 2:1 or 3:1 ratios claimed for the USA. However, one has to be cautious about some of the figures used in the Dutch research. In the case of Britain, the estimate of private security employees used in the study (70,000) appears to include only those working for member companies of the British Security Industry Association (BSIA). On that basis, Britain ranks sixth in terms of private security employees (123 per 100,000 inhabitants) and has a private-public police ratio of 0.39:1. However, if Jones and Newburn's (1998) figures are applied, these estimates are transformed dramatically. This transformation occurs whether one bases the calculation on guard numbers alone or on total security employees. Restricting oneself to the 182,596 employed in security services and equipment (the Yellow Pages category under which guarding companies usually provide services) would give an employment figure of 321 per 100,000 inhabitants and a private-public ratio of 1:1. Including those employed in the provision of mechanical and electronic security, investigation, bailiffing and debt collection – Jones and Newburn's basis for calculating total employment in the industry – would give a figure of 588 per 100,000 inhabitants, producing a private to public police ratio of 1.85:1, roughly similar to the totals recorded in the USA during the early 1980s. Two conclusions may be drawn from this discussion of the Dutch research. First, as the authors suggest, 'international comparisons entail many problems' (de Waard and van der Hoek, 1991: 3). The Dutch study certainly underestimates the size of the industry in Britain, though whether their estimates for the remaining European countries are similarly wanting is open to question. Second, at least as far as employment in Britain is concerned, Jones and Newburn's figures refute the claim that commercial security remains the secondary protective measure relative to public policing.

As for market size, turnover in Britain grew from £5m per annum in 1950 to £55m in 1970 (Randall and Hamilton, 1972), that figure rising to more than £120m by the mid-1970s (Home Office, 1979). The industry enjoyed continued expansion during the 1980s, annual growth rates reaching as high as 22 per cent in mid-decade (Jordan & Sons, 1991). Today, there is broad agreement that turnover exceeds £2 billion per annum (House of Commons, 1995) and similar rates of expansion may be found elsewhere. Cunningham *et al.* (1990) suggested that by the year 2000, gross revenue from sales and services in the US security sector would reach $103 billion per annum. Though the European market is smaller than the American one, it is also expanding rapidly. Research carried out by McAlpine Thorpe and Warrier (Narayan, 1994) indicated that the total market for security products and services in Germany, France, Italy, Spain and the UK stood at £11.2 billion in 1992, Germany representing the largest market (£3.7 billion) followed by the UK (£2.4 billion) and France (£2.2 billion). MTW predicted that the market would grow at an average rate of six per cent per annum, reaching a total of £14 billion by 1996. Though security services – mainly guarding and cash-in-transit – still retain the largest market share (£4.3 billion), electronic systems account for £3.9 billion and it is here that the highest annual growth rates are found (CCTV 11.4 per cent, access control 7.7 per cent and integrated systems 11.8 per cent).

In market terms it is also important to recognise the difference between large corporations and small businesses. In Jones and Newburn's (1998) British study, 51 per cent of the companies sampled employed five or fewer people and 88 per cent employed fewer than fifty people. However, these figures must be treated with caution. For one thing, as Jones and Newburn point out, size of company is related to function, businesses in the investigative and physical security sectors generally being smaller than those offering guard or bailiff services. For another, it is clear that a small number of companies dominate the market. Between 1985 and 1987, for example, the combined market share of three British-based companies (Racal-Chubb, Securicor Group, Group 4 Total Security) rose from 48 per cent to 60 per cent (Jordan & Sons, 1987; 1989). Currently, four major security corporations (Williams Holdings, £372 million; Securicor £310 million; Group 4 £158 million; and Rentokil Initial £110 million) account for almost £1 billion of UK market turnover (Garrett, 1997). The domination of large corporations over domestic markets is mirrored by their increasing penetration of overseas ones. Between 1985 and 1989 British, Swiss, Australian and Japanese corporations invested over $4 billion in US security companies (Cunningham *et al.*, 1990). This pattern of activity is commonplace, with major corporations engaging in acquisitions and joint ventures overseas. To that extent, commercial security is far more 'transnationalized' than the public police organizations discussed in the previous chapter.

To confirm this one has only to consider the size and operational scope of some of the major protagonists. The Pinkerton organization employs 45,000 personnel in 250 offices throughout the USA, Canada, Mexico, Asia and Europe. Its main American rival, The Wackenhut Corporation, employs 39,000 staff, Wackenhut's international sales growing by 26 per cent in 1995. Significantly, most of that growth occurred through the company's involvement in South America, Africa and Europe (Wackenhut Corporation, 1995). In the UK the Securicor Group employs 41,000 staff in a multifunctional organization whose subsidiaries engage in a variety of security and non-security activities: cash transportation, mobile and static guarding, telephone billing, vehicle fleet servicing, electronic surveillance and alarms, the construction and design of prisons, office cleaning, personnel recruitment and hotel and leisure services. In recent years Securicor has undertaken joint ventures in South Africa, South East Asia and the Americas. Racal-Chubb spans both the commercial security sector and the defence industry. Chubb Security, one of its UK-based holding companies, employs over 18,000 people in the manufacture and sale of locks, safes, banking and prison equipment, alarms and CCTV. Chubb International Holdings employs over 11,000 people and represents groups supplying similar services to South East Asia, Australasia, Canada, the USA, Africa, the Middle East and Europe. Racal Electronics Plc also employs over 11,000 people and specializes in data communications, radio communications, defence, radar and avionics (UK Equities Direct, 1996).

These multinational security corporations operate from metropolitan centres and have branch plants situated throughout the world. Such corporations operate nationally or subnationally (within national jurisdictional boundaries) and transnationally (across national jurisdictional boundaries). Two things are worthy of note about their activities. First, security corporations, like all commercial organizations, keep an eye open for new opportunities. These may lie in particular operational areas.

In recent years security commentators have identified airline security, counter-terrorism and the policing of migrants and asylum seekers as potential new areas of service activity (Johnston, forthcoming). Alternatively, opportunities may arise in particular geographical locations. The opening up of Eastern Europe during the 1990s spawned a number of security companies specializing in the anticipation, assessment and minimization of the personal and corporate risks arising from the penetration of new foreign markets (Rainey, 1996). Likewise, rising crime rates in post-apartheid South Africa have attracted the attention of leading British corporations. Britain is now a major supplier of high technology products such as surveillance cameras, alarms and infra-red detectors though, in recent years, it has also become more involved in heavy duty armed defence systems. Chubb now supplies its South African customers with 'armed reaction teams', fully equipped with automatic weapons and capable of providing an instant response to incidents of crime (Woolf, 1996). Second, there is the question of how transnational commercial security relates to other dimensions of international security. Clearly, one issue concerns the relationship between commercial and public police in a transnational context: the recurring question of the public-private sectoral divide. However, the involvement of corporations such as Racal-Chubb in both commercial and military security opens up another sectoral issue: that of the relationship between civil and military security. In particular, this has led some writers to suggest that a new 'military-industrial complex' is emerging to dominate the field of security (Lilley and Knepper, 1992).

Commercial security functions

As was suggested earlier, commercial security companies undertake a vast, and growing, range of activities. In Britain, for example, one of the most significant areas of expansion has been in the management of defendants and of those in receipt of custodial or community sanctions. To date, commercial companies have been contracted to manage immigration detention facilities (Green, 1989), to escort prisoners and to secure courts (Caddle, 1995), to build and manage custodial institutions (James et al., 1997) and to participate in trials on the effectiveness of curfew orders with electronic monitoring (Mair and Mortimer, 1996). Though these 'custodial and control' functions raise important questions about the propriety of commercial involvement in punishment (Taylor and Pease, 1989; Logan, 1990; Sparks, 1995) and indicate a fundamental reorientation of the criminal justice policy-making arena (Johnston, 1992a), the present discussion will focus on those functions undertaken by commercial security which constitute policing in the strict sense defined here. Broadly speaking, those activities can be considered under four headings.

Guarding and asset protection

This category includes, among other things, the protection of industrial, commercial, retail and residential property by foot and mobile patrol, bodyguard services, the transportation of cash and other valuables, the protection of public buildings and other state facilities, alarm response services, the security provided to clubs, pubs and leisure facilities by door managers (bouncers) and the collection of debts, in cash or in kind, by companies offering specialist bailiff or debt collection services. Some of these activities have provoked controversy. Some years ago, concern about the excessive zeal shown by bouncers in night clubs led to the establishment of a Home Office Working Party. Many police forces and local councils have now established registration and training schemes for door managers, both in order to control standards of job entry and to eradicate undesirable practices. However, the financial rewards available to unscrupulous bouncers through controlling drug distribution on club premises may undermine such initiatives.

Commercial companies can combine with public bodies in the provision of guarding and asset protection in a number of different ways. In North America, as well as in Holland and New Zealand, concern about the excessive waste of police time arising from false burglar alarm calls has led to the contracting out of initial alarm response to commercial companies (Johnston, 1992a; West, 1993). To date, that solution has been avoided in Britain, though the high cost of false call-outs may lead to its consideration in the future. For now, contracting out of services has been limited to areas such as the clamping and storage of illegally parked vehicles and the enforcement of on-street parking. Some areas of cooperation are, however, more controversial. In Britain military bases are secured by a complex combination of agencies, including local (civil) police constabularies, the (civil) Ministry of Defence Police, military police, military personnel, contract security guards, civilian guard forces and company guard forces. A similar complex of agencies may also be involved in the transport of civil and military nuclear material both within and between national boundaries, something which raises serious questions about rational coordination, operational jurisdiction and public accountability (Johnston, 1992b; 1994). Such complexity is also increasingly evident in the policing of demonstrations. The conflicts arising from the construction of the Newbury bypass (Vidal, 1996) were handled by a cocktail of security agencies consisting of officers from the local constabulary, contract security, local authority personnel, officers from the Health and Safety Executive, sheriffs and bailiffs. A similar situation has developed in the continuing conflicts between hunt saboteurs and the British Field Sports Society. In this case, the cocktail is a more complicated one, bodies such as The Hunt Saboteurs Association alleging that the security companies employed by local hunts recruit military personnel for 'cash in hand' (House of Commons, 1995). These allegations are almost certainly justified. In the rural areas adjoining one large military base in the North of England reports of military personnel 'moonlighting' for commercial security companies are by no means uncommon, despite the fact that such activity is proscribed by the military authorities.

Prevention

One of the defining characteristics of the commercial security industry is its proactive and preventive role. Indeed, one writer (Morn, 1982) has argued that, historically, there has been a reversal in the roles of public and private police; the former moving from a preventive orientation to one based on detection; the latter moving from a focus on detection to one emphasizing prevention and the protection of property. Though there is much to be said for this historical generalization, it should not be adopted too rigidly. Nowadays, commercial security agencies engage, more and more, in specialized investigative activity, while much of the rhetoric of public policing is community-orientated and preventive.

It is also important to differentiate between two aspects of prevention, the commercial security industry being, primarily, concerned with the prevention of individual (private) client loss and the police with the prevention of (public) crime. Although this distinction is an important one, however, it does have its limitations. Take the case of preventive patrols undertaken by commercial security organizations. Boothroyd's (1989) survey indicated that in Britain there were at least 504 non-police patrols funded by local authorities, businesses and, in a few cases, residents. All of these are, undoubtedly, engaged in the prevention of individual client loss, though whether their activities can always be so restricted is less clear. Consider a situation where a public authority contracts with a commercial security organization for preventive policing within a given jurisdiction, granting the officers of that company full police powers. Such a situation has not yet occurred in Britain – though some of the cases of municipal policing discussed in the following chapter raise interesting parallels. However, such developments have taken place in the USA, the best known one being at Starrett City, an apartment complex of 20,000 residents located in East New York (Donovan and Walsh, 1986; Walsh and Donovan, 1989; Shearing, 1996). Here, the owner of the properties, the Starrett City Realty Corporation, employs a Security Department having unrestricted access to all areas and full police powers. Evaluations of this experiment declare it to be a community orientated style of policing in which 'private interests and community needs are combined in a positive crime prevention strategy' (Shearing, 1996). Here, then, the rigid distinction between (individual/private) loss prevention and (social/public) crime prevention is undermined. The potential inherent in such arrangements is considered further in Chapters 9 and 10.

Surveillance and intelligence

Though these two functions are considered together, the former is a generic term, and the latter a specific one. As to the first, Shearing and Stenning (1981) suggest that the single feature uniting the diverse preventive activities of commercial security is surveillance. Indeed, as they point out, the slogan originally adopted by the Pinkerton Detective Agency – 'the eye that never sleeps' – confirms the centrality of surveillance to the security function. Nevertheless, despite the sinister connotations of the term, much surveillance is both mundane and routine. This is certainly the case with the general preventive activities undertaken by officers engaged in security patrols; checking locks, doors, alarms, windows and generally keeping an eye out for potential security breaches. As both South (1988) and Shearing and Stenning (1981) argue, however, surveillance is more than mere watching. In particular, it is concerned with eradicating opportunities for security breaches rather than with reacting to the breaches themselves. That, after all, is the rationale of risk management, the effect of which is to expand the category of 'offender' to include those who might be guilty of violating security procedures as well as those who have been guilty of committing offences.

The other issue concerns the extent to which surveillance, so defined, may be integrated with the specific intelligence gathering functions of the commercial sector and the state. This is a particularly critical question when the technical sophistication of intelligence gathering is growing. For some writers the combination of risk-based surveillance practices and sophisticated computer technology poses the threat of a 'maximum security society' (Marx, 1988). Whether or not such a view is justified, an issue reconsidered in the final chapter, the intelligence gathering potential of contemporary technologies raises two issues. First, there is the danger that the machinery may be directed against particular social groups: radicals, minorities, protesters and the like. It would be foolish to ignore the long historical connections between commercial security and employers' interests, just as it would be naïve to ignore the links between some security personnel and right wing political organizations (Johnston, 1992a). Second, there is the danger that public police might use the intelligence gathering capacities of commercial security to circumvent lawful constraints placed upon them by the state. In the USA the Law Enforcement Intelligence Unit is a private body whose members – some of them police forces – can gain access to confidential information not available through regular police channels. The ethical difficulties raised by these practices have neither prevented the LEIU from receiving state grants, nor from having the authority to share data with the US Justice Department (Marx, 1987).

Investigation and detection

Despite the broad accuracy of Morn's (1982) observation, investigation and detection remain significant features of commercial security work.

Private investigators may be involved in a range of investigative activities including tracing missing persons, obtaining proof of evidence, insurance claim investigation, employee vetting, obtaining witness statements, matrimonial and adoption enquiries, accident investigation and fraud investigation. In the past, there has been concern about the extent to which private investigators threaten individual privacy by engaging in illegitimate activities such as bugging and burgling. As Jones and Newburn (1998) suggest, the fact that the two main trade associations in Britain strongly support regulation – something which is lacking throughout the industry – indicates that malpractice is still considered to be a problem. Yet, malpractice may also reside in the commercial relationship between client and service provider, the law giving only limited protection from abuse. Recently, some security companies have expressed concern that stalkers are using their services in order to keep track of their victims. However, legislation proposed to make stalking a criminal offence is unlikely to prevent 'stalking by proxy' since private investigators, police and security services will have immunity from its restrictions (Todd and Elsworth, 1997).

One of the main growth areas for private detection is fraud investigation and there are now a large number of companies advertising themselves as specialists in the prevention and detection of commercial and computer fraud. In Holland, for example, police detectives have been recruited by banks, insurance companies and industrial corporations to investigate insurance and cheque frauds and during the last decade the private sector has developed extensive computerised data banks on commercial fraud far superior to anything held by the public police (Judge, 1988; Hoogenboom, 1989). Privatization of fraud investigation, of course, may be undertaken for two reasons. First, commercial companies might be regarded as more effective than public police due to their ability to respond rapidly to changing technologies. Second, privatization might be considered preferable because it is private. After all, corporate victims of fraud rarely like to have their dirty linen washed in public. A bank which has been the subject of major fraud – particularly where that fraud has been engineered from the inside – will, more often than not, invoke private rather than public justice when dealing with perpetrators. This 'calculated exercise of discretion against invoking the formal criminal justice process' (Stenning and Shearing, 1980: 222) is perfectly consistent with the principles of loss prevention. Indeed Clarke (1989), in describing the activities of insurance loss adjusters, suggests that there is 'a fundamental incompatibility between the profit-oriented objective of the insurance industry . . . and vigorous fraud control' (Clarke, 1989: 17 and 18).

It is not merely that a policy of fraud control grounded in the public justice system is incompatible with the ethic of profit, however. The pace of technological change exposes new tensions. One of the most interesting issues arising in respect of computer crime – particularly where it relates to the Internet – is whether the traditional means of public justice (law and police) are adequate to the task demanded of them. Wall (forth-coming) has observed that public police culture and organization are singularly unsuited to policing a 'virtual' environment in which legal, spatial and experiential parameters are fundamentally different from those pertaining to 'terrestrial' forms of communication. Already, the task of policing the Internet is dispersed across a variety of agencies: govern-mental bodies; public police; service providers; and groups of Internet users, themselves. The second Hallcrest Report (Cunningham *et al.*, 1990) identified 'computer security and electronic intrusion' as a key area of criminal activity which the industry should address in future years. The potential for 'cybercrime', coupled with the problem of applying public standards of law and justice to a jurisdiction which transcends conven-tional notions of time and space, suggests that commercial security will have a major role to play in the future diversified realm of policing.

Summary: the functional division of labour

Consideration of these four areas, coupled with our earlier discussion of the industry's structure, would suggest that commercial security does everything that the public police do and rather more besides (Johnston, 1992a). Recently, this claim has been subjected to empirical scrutiny in Jones and Newburn's (1998) analysis of the policing division of labour in Wandsworth. Here, it is observed, policing was dispersed among a number agencies including the Metropolitan Police, the Wandsworth Parks Police, the British Transport Police, the Environmental Health Department, the Health and Safety Executive, the Post Office Investigation Department, the local authority Housing Patrol, and a range of commercial security companies. During the course of the research the authors identified certain key policing functions, derived from those which they believed to be undertaken by all Home Office Constabularies. These included, responding to calls from the public, investigating crime, arresting offenders, maintaining public order, providing visible patrol, controlling traffic, enforcing parking regulations, investigating accidents, undertaking crime pattern analysis, carrying out security surveys, responding to alarms, deal-ing with noise and harassment, escorting prisoners and monitoring CCTV systems. One striking conclusion from the study was that while the three uniformed policing bodies (the Metropolitan Police, the British Transport Police and the Wandsworth Parks Police) all engaged in the majority of these tasks, only the Metropolitan Police and the commercial security industry fulfilled all of them. Though this evidence would appear to bear out my earlier claim, however, the authors insist that this 'superficial functional similarity camouflages a number of rather important dis-similarities' (Jones and Newburn, 1998: 240). The most important of these dissimilarities is that while commercial security is specialized and narrow in its remit, the mandate of the public police is so wide as to be virtually unlimited. According to that view a less superficial analysis of Wandsworth would suggest a clear functional demarcation between specialized private policing agencies and the generalist Metropolitan Police.

While the Wandsworth study confirms that commercial security does everything that public police do and rather more besides, it reminds us that a distinction needs to be drawn between the 'generalist' remit of single local police forces (such as the Metropolitan Police) and the wide totality of functions undertaken by multiple security companies whose particular functions are often quite specific. However, while this qualification is, undoubtedly, correct for Wandsworth – and will probably be true for other localities as well – one has to be cautious about its wider application. Two considerations are particularly relevant. First, there is the question of the level of analysis at which empirical confirmation of functional similarity or dissimilarity is being sought. From what I have suggested earlier, examination of the functions undertaken by major corporations in the global security market would indicate the existence of organizations whose activities encompass a wide range of functional activities. This would suggest that the degree of functional generality or specificity is likely to vary according to the level at which the analysis is undertaken. In the case of transnational policing, for example, it would seem that public police organizations are engaged more and more in specialized crime control activities (against drugs, terrorism, organized crime and the like) while commercial security companies pursue a diverse range of functions. Second, while it remains the case that local police forces maintain generalist services in their localities, this does not preclude them from adopting some of the functional priorities and practices of the commercial sector. As I have suggested previously, police forces engage in anticipatory practices, target particular groups of high risk offenders, adopt 'disorganizing' (as well as enforcement-based) strategies against known criminals and look for ways of spreading risks to other service providers in ways similar to those employed by the commercial security sector. For that reason, functional dissimilarity in certain operational areas may be entirely compatible with functional similarity in others.

Explanations for and implications of the growth of commercial security

There have been two dominant explanations for the growth of commercial security. The first is based upon the view that the state experienced a fiscal crisis (O'Connor, 1973) from the early 1970s, the period during which commercial security experienced particularly rapid expansion. One version of this thesis maintains that public expenditure restrictions have led to a security 'vacuum', the private sector 'filling the void' and becoming the 'junior partner' of public police (Kakalik and Wildhorn, 1972). A more radical version explains both the initial growth of public policing, and its later supplementation by commercial 'policing for profit', through an examination of the historical connections between capital and the state (Spitzer and Scull, 1977). Each of these arguments provides a useful structural framework for understanding the growth of commercial policing, though they also have weaknesses. For example, there is no direct connection between fiscal prudence and the timing of the relative contraction of public policing. In Britain during the 1980s the commercial security industry certainly enjoyed the expansion predicted for it by fiscal crisis theory. Yet, despite fiscal rectitude during the Thatcher years, expenditure on the public police grew considerably, rising by almost 50 per cent in the decade after the 1979 election. Significantly, in the USA, Scull's (1977) prediction that 'private' punishment in the community would grow at the expense of public prisons required drastic revision after continued public sector growth. Thus, the predicted contraction of public policing never occurred in Britain or the USA, though fiscal policies contributed towards redefining the relative balance between public and commercial providers in security markets undergoing absolute expansion.

The other dominant explanation for commercial security growth relates to those processes of commodification and mass consumption which are characteristic of 'risk society'. Commodification increases demand for security products and services but, as Spitzer (1987) claims, may fail to engender greater feelings of security among consumers. Mass consumption is associated not only with a change in the culture of consumption, but also involves a fundamental reshaping of capitalist property relations. Shearing and Stenning (1981) maintain that a key feature of twentieth century society is the emergence of 'mass private property' – tracts of ambiguous space which combine apparently contradictory social relations. The archetypal example of mass private property is the shopping mall, which combines private property ownership with relatively unlimited public access. The function of commercial security is to resolve the contradiction inherent in that relationship: to maximize public access (and, with it, mass consumption) while restricting entry to those who might undermine the commercial imperative (vagrants, drunks, beggars and the like).

This thesis has been an influential one since it encapsulates many of the paradoxes of commercial policing. It has been pointed out, however, that it may be more appropriate to North American conditions than to those found elsewhere. Jones and Newburn (1998) argue that the thesis is only partly relevant to Britain where the physical forms characteristic of mass private property – such as malls, residential complexes and university campuses – are as likely to be publicly owned as privately owned. Thus, while both the retail and leisure industries have developed physical forms (shopping complexes, leisure parks) which confirm the thesis, there is little evidence of mass private property in housing and education, fields which have been dominated by public sector intervention. All in all, Jones and Newburn (1998) suggest that Britain has experienced a 'gradual transition' to mass private property, rather than the 'quiet revolution' (Stenning and Shearing, 1980) witnessed in North America.

This conclusion is a valid one and suggests that the mass private property thesis might need to be adjusted if it is to take account of the conditions pertaining in particular societies. It is also interesting to speculate on how the particularities of property relations within given societies might impact on the future division of policing labour. Earlier in the chapter reference was made to the policing experiment at Starrett City which Shearing (1996) regards as a model of how to produce community policing from the marriage of private interests and community needs. The feasibility of such experiments may, in part, be conditioned by past configurations of property relations and by the nature of their governance. For example, the particular conditions which Jones and Newburn (1998) identify in Britain – the fact that mass private property sits side by side with what one might call 'mass public property' – may be favourable to developing the initiatives Shearing (1996) describes. For the deployment of commercial security within publicly accountable security networks (the marriage of private interests and community needs which Shearing advocates) might be more feasible where there is a long established – albeit dormant – history of municipal government such as that found in Britain.

The prospect of incorporating commercial security into policing networks raises immediate questions about accountability, justice and governance. The problems associated with the most publicly visible sector of commercial security in Britain – the contract guard industry – are well-documented: inadequate vetting, poor training, limited supervision, rapid staff turnover, poor wages and lack of regulation, to name but a few (Button, 1998). One consequence of this state of affairs has been the presence of too many 'cowboy' companies at the local level, something which has been a matter of police concern for many years (ACPO, 1988). During the last two decades a number of Private Member's Bills, seeking regulation of the industry, have failed to win parliamentary support, though a recent Home Affairs Select Committee Report (House of Commons, 1995) recommended that statutory measures would be necessary both to regulate standards and training and to license individuals in the contract guard sector. Prior to the last election, the incoming Labour government expressed its commitment to the principle of statutory regulation though, as yet, no firm proposals have been put forward for consideration either in respect of the guard sector or in respect of the wider security industry (George and Button, 1998).

Whether or not regulation is introduced in the near future, however, the police face a dilemma. Given the demand for security services and their own stretched resources, how should they respond to commercial expansion, especially in areas hitherto considered a public police monopoly? One proposal has been to adopt the 'Profitshire Constabulary model' of policing (Johnston, 1992a) whereby local police forces would compete directly with commercial security businesses in their areas, setting up companies to sell 'extra' police services, such as preventive patrols, to those able and willing to pay for them. At least two British police forces have argued along these lines in the last few years: South Wales Police proposing the setting up of a security company for hire to local housing estates; West Yorkshire Police evaluating plans to set up a business to install burglar alarms and carry out street patrols. The advantages of this approach, it is said, are twofold. First, the police can control the vetting, recruitment and training of the personnel employed in security companies. Second, such personnel can be employed to undertake precisely those tasks – crime prevention and preventive patrol – for which public demand is highest. One proponent of this view (Blair, 1994) notes that its successful implementation would require the Home Office to initiate various policy changes. First, the police would have to be given the authority to deploy police auxiliaries and commercial security personnel on street patrols. Second, police authorities would have to be given the right to generate income from services, such as crime prevention, which are now offered free to the public. Rather than providing free call-out to burglar alarms, Blair (1994) suggests, the police should market and fit alarms themselves. By establishing partnerships with private companies for the sale of security equipment, personal security or drugs awareness, the police could both guarantee high service standards and generate the income to fund additional street patrols. Significantly, Blair (1994) sees this reform package as a means by which the public police could retain a monopoly over the control of private patrols, thus ensuring an acceptable level of public accountability.

The 'Profitshire' model raises a number of obvious issues. In order to meet the conditions of the Police Act 1964 commercial services would have to be defined as 'extra' services available only to those wishing to consume them. In other words, there would need to be an assurance that such services would not lead to a reduction in 'normal' police cover. However, it would be naïve to think that police-run commercial patrols – or the municipal patrols discussed in the following chapter – would have no impact on 'normal' policing. Consider a situation in which 'Profitshire Constabulary Security Services' is contracted to undertake residential street patrols by local tenants worried about the problem of burglaries on a private housing estate. Are we to believe that such provision would have no impact on normal police cover? Or is it more likely that the hard-pressed local commander, aware of the extra (private) resources being channelled into the locality in question, would take those extra personnel into account when allocating officers to their duties? Where public resources are stretched it might be difficult for the police to ignore the availability of private provision. In addition to that, there is the possibility that such commercial patrols might displace offenders and offences into areas lacking such provision, thereby giving rise to 'two-tier policing'. In short, the operation of commercial patrols, whether run by the police or by private companies, raises problems of equity. While resolution of these problems is by no means impossible, it demands careful consideration of how to govern diverse policing systems. That issue is addressed more fully in the final chapter.

Chapter 9

Regenerating Locality: Municipal and Civil Policing

Introduction

People's relationship to policing is undergoing fundamental change, those who hitherto regarded themselves as the mere recipients of a public service now being prepared to consider alternative forms of provision. In 1993 a MORI poll found that 55 per cent of respondents supported residents setting up, or paying for, local security patrols. When asked, 27 per cent said that they would be prepared to take part in such patrols, the same proportion being willing to pay extra council tax in order for them to be run on municipal lines. A further 23 per cent of respondents said that they would be willing to pay for patrols run by private security companies (*Police Review*, 6 August 1993). Such views have to be put in the context of two developments. First, there is the question of the rights and responsibilities accruing to citizenship, something which has increasing pertinence in the field of policing and crime prevention. Second, there is the apparently insatiable rise in public demand for security, something which is connected, at least in part, to its commodification. The product of the public's demand for 'more policing' has initiated both market and state-led responses. On the one hand, commercial companies have taken a greater role in the provision of routine security (see, Chapter 8). On the other hand, the police have developed various initiatives – such as problem orientated policing and zero tolerance policing – to render police patrol more responsive and effective (see, Chapters 3 and 4). Reaction to escalating demand has not, however, been restricted to the state and the market. More recently, there has been growing interest in the role of the locality in initiating new forms of policing provision. Here, two developments are of particular interest: the re-emergence of municipal policing in Britain after more than a century of decline; and the growing significance of citizen-based forms of self-policing. These municipal and civil initiatives are the subject of the present chapter.

The chapter consists of three sections. The first examines recent developments in municipal policing in Britain and Europe. The second considers the role of the 'active citizen' in the provision of security, paying particular attention to the apparent growth of so-called vigilante activity. In the third section I explore the concept of vigilantism in more detail and suggest that the analysis of it is crucial to an understanding of late modern policing. In particular, I argue that a distinction needs to be drawn between two dimensions of vigilantism: 'judicial vigilantism' (which is, invariably, illegal, violent and retributive) and 'civil policing' (which, in principle, may involve none of these).

Municipal policing

Although the centralizing tendencies of the British state have reduced local authority influence over the police, the legislative basis for some form of municipal police provision remains intact. Two pieces of legislation, the Public Health (Amendment) Act of 1907 and the Ministry of Housing and Local Government Provisional Order Confirmation (Greater London Parks and Open Spaces) Act of 1967, empower local authorities to swear in employees as constables for the purpose of securing local bye-laws. Under the Local Government (Miscellaneous Provisions) Act of 1982, s 40 it is also possible for municipal personnel to be sworn in by magistrates as constables with powers of arrest in designated parks and open spaces. Some local authorities have also used specific local acts to establish constabularies for policing parks and open spaces (CIPFA 1989) and a significant amount of local legislation still exists. For example, the 'Paving Act' of 1824 permits 'Paving Commissioners' to appoint 'Watchmen and Patroles' to police Regent's Park in London at night. Such persons, once appointed, will be sworn in as constables, will enjoy full police powers within their jurisdiction and will be provided with proper 'Arms, Ammunition, Weapons and Clothing' (Johnston, 1993a).

Experiments in municipal policing are by no means peculiar to Britain. In 1983 the French government passed legislation allowing for the formation of municipal forces to supplement the services provided by the Police Nationale and the Gendarmerie Nationale (Kania, 1989). Municipal initiatives undertaken in the Netherlands arose as part of the government's comprehensive plan for social crime prevention developed in the mid-1980s (Ministerie van Justitie, 1985). This plan was based upon a mixed model of social control in which formal and informal, public and private, and local and national agencies were encouraged to combine in an integrated preventative network. In practice, this has involved several components: design policies which facilitate surveillance (of young people in particular) and which make the commission of offences more difficult; the involvement of occupational groups such as janitors, shop assistants, sport coaches and youth workers in the surveillance of potential law breakers; and 'the strengthening of non-police surveillance of possible law breakers' in private, public and semi-public areas of life. This last measure was to be achieved by 'involving the citizen more and more in the maintenance of law and order' as well as by 'strengthening the supervisory function of the intermediary structures' of family, work and recreation (Van Dijk and Junger-Tas, 1988: 264–5).

Two of the Dutch initiatives justify brief comment. In 1988 the government subsidized the appointment of 150 social caretakers in 130 public housing estates throughout the country. As well as undertaking cleaning and repair work, research suggests that almost one-quarter of the caretaker's time is spent in handling residents' social problems while over one-fifth of their time is spent on patrolling the estates in order to deter vandalism and other petty crime. Though social caretakers possess no special powers and have no effect on more serious forms of crime, evaluation indicates that the percentage of residents satisfied with the safety of estates increased after the first year of their deployment (Hesseling, 1995). There have also been new initiatives in street patrol. The police surveillant is a new rank of police officer, the incumbent holding full police powers, though not being permitted to carry a firearm. In practice, police surveillants only perform certain police tasks and are deployed in such a way as to minimize the chance that they will be called upon to exercise their powers of arrest (Hesseling, 1995; Police Foundation/Policy Studies Institute, 1996). Public demand for a uniformed presence on the streets also led to the introduction of City Guards by a number of municipal authorities. The first of these was introduced in 1989 and by the end of 1993 around 650 guards were engaged in patrols in 28 Dutch cities. Possessing only citizen powers, their basic functions are to provide a visible daytime patrol, to respond to public enquiries, to assist in the prevention of crime and nuisance and to provide public reassurance. Though the municipality has responsibility for all City Guard projects, some are completely autonomous from the police, while others are integrated with the police to varying degrees. Evaluation of the City Guards scheme suggests that they contribute towards an increase in citizens' feelings of safety and that some municipalities have experienced a drop in petty crime (Hauber *et al.*, 1996). It is also noted that City Guards appear to enjoy good relations with the public (Hesseling, 1995), a particularly important factor given the philosophy which underpins the Dutch programme of social crime prevention and functional surveillance. Here, the objective is to use agents without police powers to remind citizens of their social responsibilities and obligations without recourse to formal law enforcement. This has led the authorities to deliberate on whether the granting of minimal legal powers to City Guards might enhance their effectiveness or merely undermine their relations with the public and, by so doing, compromise the principles of informal social control (Hauber *et al.*, 1996).

The previous Conservative government in Britain was far less willing to embrace the principles of social crime prevention than its Dutch counterpart. However, there have been significant developments in municipal policing. Broadly, these are of two types: those involving bodies of constables holding police powers within a jurisdiction; and those consisting of unsworn personnel. The history of the former is a long one, many local authorities having established parks police forces earlier in the century. Though many of these organizations went into abeyance, in recent years they have enjoyed a revival. This trend has been particularly evident in a number of London boroughs over the last two decades. At Brent, staff from the Borough Security Department have been sworn in as constables since 1979, the organization adopting the official title of 'Brent Parks Constabulary' in the early 1990s. Similar organizations exist in Greenwich, at Barking and Dagenham and at Holland Park where patrols began in 1991. In the last case the decision to establish a force was taken following public concern about anti-social behaviour, crime and vandalism in parks. There was also evidence of increased bye-law violations, including illegal parking, cycling, skateboarding, loose dogs and the occurrence of 'unseemly behaviour' after dark (Royal Borough of Kensington and Chelsea, 1992). The force has an establishment of twelve, all three senior staff being former regular police officers. Four weeks training is provided by a special course run by the Metropolitan Police.

The best known of the London municipal forces is the Wandsworth Parks Constabulary which was established when personnel from the 'Mobile Parks Security Group' were attested as constables in 1985. By 1995 the Constabulary employed 35 full-time staff and a further 25 part-time staff having the status of Special Constables. Officers carry out both foot patrols and mobile patrols in marked police vehicles, covering parks, cemeteries and other open spaces over an area of about 850 acres in total. Training is received in fingerprints, taped interviewing and crime reporting from the Metropolitan Police. The Constabulary also sells training to other organizations and provides an advisory service to other councils interested in setting up similar bodies of their own. In 1991, £135,000 was generated from selling services (Johnston, 1993a). One of the main roles of the Constabulary is to maintain public compliance with bye-laws on municipal open spaces. To that extent it acts as a deterrent rather than as an enforcement body, dealing with problems of dog control, traffic violations, low level violence, drunkenness and indecency. Constables are also responsible for monitoring CCTV cameras situated in the parks and provide security patrols for libraries, leisure centres, youth and recreation facilities and cemeteries. In addition, officers provide a full alarm call service for Leisure and Amenity Service buildings; provide security services to the Borough Council, maintaining a visible presence at Housing Advice Offices to deter unruly clients and at Council Chambers when public demonstrations are anticipated; act as key holders to a large number of local authority buildings; and provide a cash in transit service between council offices and banks (Johnston, 1993a; Police Foundation/Policy Studies Institute, 1996; Jones and Newburn, 1998).

Though the principal remit of municipal constabularies is to police bye-law offences, it is clear that they undertake a wide range of duties. Jones and Newburn (1998) note that the Wandsworth Parks Constabulary Report for 1995 listed 21 duties routinely undertaken by officers. In addition to that, there are occasions when officers travelling between parks and open spaces within the Borough – and thus outside their territorial jurisdiction – are stopped by the public and asked to assist in incidents. Occasionally, this may involve officers using citizen's powers to make arrests of those engaged in the commission of crimes. These two issues – the range of functions undertaken and the extent of officers' legal powers – have been the source of some dispute with the Metropolitan Police. Essentially, this dispute is about accountability, municipal constabularies regarding themselves as a valid local authority response to local concerns about crime and disorder, the police calling into question their status as publicly accountable organizations.

Legal opinion on these matters has been inconsistent. When, in 1989, one non-London council sought Home Office advice about the powers of parks constables, the view expressed was that they enjoyed all of the powers of Home Office constables within the jurisdictional confines of the park, a view that was later reversed (Johnston, 1993a). Subsequently, counsel's advice to the Metropolitan Police attempted to draw a distinction between police officers and 'bodies of constables which are not police forces' (Wiggs, 1990). Here, an implicit distinction was drawn between 'real' (Home Office) police and others whose legal powers would be limited strictly to the enforcement of bye-law legislation. However, the basis for this opinion is unconvincing (Johnston, 1993a) and it is hardly surprising that the matter remains unresolved, Wandsworth Parks Constabulary continuing to assert that its officers possess full police powers within the perimeters of council parks, commons and open spaces (Wandsworth Parks Constabulary, n.d.).

This dispute has broader ramifications. It is not merely that Parks Constables in Wandsworth enforce the Theft Act and other elements of the criminal law. Bye-laws, themselves, endow officers with considerable powers. The Holland Park bye-laws stipulate that 'it shall be lawful for any officer of the Council to exclude or remove from any open space any person committing any breach of the . . . bye-laws, and all gypsies, hawkers . . . beggars . . . rogues and vagabonds' (Royal Borough of Kensington and Chelsea, n.d). Moreover, as Jones and Newburn (1998) point out, when dealing with an offence Parks Constables may invoke bye-laws in preference to the criminal law on the grounds that the burden of proof is less in the former than in the latter. The fact that constables have discretion over the deployment of these different legal resources makes them an effective and flexible policing resource and helps to explain why in 1994 the local authority sought to extend their routine patrols to the 'open spaces' of council housing estates. Metropolitan Police resistance has, for the moment, put this proposal on hold, regular police seeing further municipal expansion as a threat to their primacy over the policing of public space. Significantly, police spokespersons have argued forcefully that any future implementation of City Guard-type programmes – with or without accompanying constabulary powers – should be under the strict control of the police rather than of the local authority (Davies, 1989).

Many local authorities also deploy security forces consisting of uniformed personnel without police powers. As in Holland, many of these initiatives have recruited unemployed people, using funds from state employment initiatives. One of the earliest schemes emerged on Merseyside where the boroughs of Sefton, St Helens, Wirral and Knowsley developed anti-vandalism patrols in the late 1970s. At the height of their recruitment, these organizations employed large numbers of staff, the St Helens and Knowsley operations each having around 200 officers in post by the mid-1980s. When financial support from the Manpower Services Commission and the Community Programme eventually dried up in the late 1980s, the forces were reduced in size. Nevertheless, in the early 1990s, each of the boroughs ran operations comparable in size to Wandsworth, with Knowsley having 23 officers, Sefton 28, St Helens 39 and Wirral 88. As in Wandsworth, operational responsibilities included the protection of schools, libraries, recreational facilities, void properties and indoor markets, as well as the provision of keyholding, cash in transit and alarm response services. Wirral's Metro Security Service, the largest of these organizations, also provided a property marking facility to the Education Department and a risk management service to all council departments. Here, the Chief Security Officer claimed that regular patrols of Wirral Education Department premises had reduced break-ins from over 700 per annum, prior to the organization's establishment in 1988, to around 250 per annum by the early 1990s. Interestingly, he also suggested that the Association of Chief Police Officers Alarms Policy – whereby repeated false alarms might lead to a withdrawal of police response – would, inevitably, lead to the expansion of dedicated municipal security forces. (All information obtained from interviews undertaken on Merseyside during 1991.)

The other Merseyside organization – the Liverpool City Security Force – was established in 1972, following the abolition of the Parks and Airport forces. By the early 1980s the Force consisted of some 200 officers organized into three territorial divisions. However, during the late 1980s allegations were made that the Force had become a 'private army' for the Deputy Council Leader and prominent Militant supporter Derek Hatton. In 1991 redundancy notices were issued to a large number of security staff, the result being a significant reduction in the size of the Force. These particular events raise obvious questions about the quality of staff recruited to municipal security organizations. In a recent move aimed at obviating this problem, the 70 officers of North Tyneside Council's newly established security force are vetted by Northumbria Police and trained by the local Training Enterprise Council (Gibbons, 1996b).

Undoubtedly, the best known recent initiative in municipal security has been the establishment of the Sedgefield Community Force in County Durham. The Force became fully operational in January 1994 and was the first municipally-run body to be given the task of patrolling the streets in a local authority area. To that extent, the Community Force bears some similarity to the various City Guard schemes in the Netherlands though, unlike the Dutch example, it provides services over a full 24 hour period. The main objectives of the Force are to increase public safety and reassurance by the provision of foot and mobile patrols, to consult with local residents and the police on local problems of crime and anti-social behaviour, to provide advice and information to local residents on crime prevention, and to adopt a non-confrontational policy of observing and reporting incidents to the local police when they occur. In this last respect the Community Force insists that its role is not to compete with the officers of Durham Constabulary but to serve as the 'eyes and ears' of the police. The Force is headed by an ex-Chief Inspector from a local constabulary and its officers receive four weeks' training in theoretical and practical subjects, assisted by Durham Constabulary who provide instruction in evidence gathering, scene of crime reporting and procedure for bomb threats (I'Anson and Wiles, 1995).

The Sedgefield experiment raises a number of issues. First, research undertaken by I'Anson and Wiles (1995) suggests that more than four-fifths of respondents sampled in a telephone survey aged 26 and over (including 100 per cent of those aged under 25) found the Community Force acceptable. Interestingly, this research also found support both for private security patrols and for citizen patrols, levels of support ranging from one-third among older age groups to between one-half and two-thirds among the under 25s. Support was also significantly higher among women than among men. Second, 72 per cent of those sampled believed that the Force would provide a deterrent to criminals, though whether this indicates public faith in the effectiveness of patrol or merely a demand for more police (Loader, 1997) is open to question. Third, there is the question of the Force's relationship to Durham Constabulary. In principle, the Force restricts itself to being the 'eyes and ears' of the police. However, it has been reported that the local police control room, faced with excessive demand, has passed on work to the Community Force (Northern Eye, 1995). Finally, there is the question of the Force's operational role. Here, a comment from the council's Customer Relations Officer is especially pertinent: 'The Police have to focus on priorities that move away from minor criminal activity and nuisance. We believe that we are filling that gap' (cited in I'Anson and Wiles, 1995: 4). This is a particularly interesting comment since it seems to suggest that the Community Force will focus on those very 'incivilities' which regular police forces are now claiming to address as part of a sustained zero tolerance strategy.

Citizenship and security

Autonomous and responsible citizenship

A second series of developments may be identified at the level of local civil society. In order to put these developments into context it is necessary to say something about the debate on citizenship which has been at the forefront of British politics during the last decade. Both Conservative and Labour governments have been keen to extol the virtues of the active citizen and it is clear that much of the discourse of citizenship is concerned with balancing rights (enshrined in various Citizen's Charters) with personal responsibilities (which, for example, limit state responsibility for welfare and encourage individuals to subscribe to personal health schemes). To that extent, Conservative commitment to citizenship was linked to the wider project of re-designing the balance between the public and the private sectors of government. However, both the left, in general, and the Labour Party, in particular, have also embraced citizenship, emphasizing – contrary to the views of neo-liberals within the Conservative Party – that rights and responsibilities have a social, as well as a personal, dimension attached to them. In that regard, left discourse has used the concept of citizenship both as a means of criticizing the flawed institutions of contemporary democratic politics and as a basis for extending social and political rights. Hirst (1994) has pointed to the limitations of this 'new republican' view of citizenship: '[It] is ill-adapted to current circumstances . . . [since it] re-emphasizes the idea of a single effectively self-governing political community at the very moment when the nation state is being undermined and a complex multi-focal politics is developing' (Hirst, 1994: 13). In fact, Hirst's critique is no less applicable to the Conservative philosophy of citizenship than it is to the new republican one. Both are predicated on an idealized view in which citizenship provides the mechanism for securing 'unity in diversity': citizenship being seen as the cement which will bind together the disparate elements of a fragmented order.

Far from being a stabilizing factor, however, citizenship is a brittle entity. This may be illustrated if we consider its application in the field of policing and personal security. In the past, debates on citizenship have focused on matters of social and economic security rather than issues of personal security. Yet, Marshall (1963) insisted that citizenship was a relative, rather than a fixed, notion: 'the right to . . . live the life of a civilised being according to the standards prevailing in the society' (Marshall, 1963: 74). Nowadays, there are good grounds for arguing that people regard personal security as a right: a measure of civilized life. The problem is, however, that all social rights have fiscal costs and it is for this reason that governments since 1979 have 'denied social protection on the ground that [a person] was equipped with the means to protect himself' (Marshall cited in Barbalet, 1988: 21). In short, individuals have been encouraged to engage in acts of 'responsible citizenship' (Johnston, 1992a) in order to maximize their own security. Such acts might include enrolling in the Special Constabulary, joining a Neighbourhood Watch group or passing on information to the police via a telephone crime line.

Responsible citizenship consists of those acts which are sanctioned by the state. The problem is that governmental control over citizenship is fragile. It is easy to find examples which confirm this fragility. Recently, it has been stated that of the four groups of people giving information to the Crimestoppers phone line, the smallest consists of 'ordinary good citizens'. Perversely, the largest group of those giving information consists of drug dealers using the facility to inform on rival dealers so that they can steal their business (Campbell, 1996). Alternatively, consider the case of victims of domestic burglary who invoke their rights of self-defence when victimized. In 1996 the Home Secretary gave instructions to the police that they should exercise greater discretion when charging crime victims who tried to defend themselves. Yet, the implications of this proposal are unclear. Were the state to uphold victims' rights to shoot dead those committing aggravated burglary on their properties, might this constitute a case of state collusion in an act of violent vigilantism? A similar problem arises in respect of the previous Home Secretary's decision to reverse past policy and sanction the mobilization of Neighbourhood Watch street patrols. In the past, government had refused to legitimize such action on the grounds that members might quickly degenerate from responsible citizens into irresponsible vigilantes, taking the law into their own hands.

Elsewhere, I have suggested that the unstable character of citizenship can be expressed in the distinction between its 'responsible' and 'autonomous' forms (Johnston, 1992a). Responsible citizenship is directed, sponsored, supported and legitimized by the state, while autonomous citizenship is independent of the state. The fragmentation of statehood to which Hirst (1994) alludes, renders state control of responsible citizens increasingly problematic. The difficulty for politicians, having mobilized active citizens, is how to contain them within the bounds of central state authority when that very authority is undermined by governmental diversity. Under late modern conditions there is the probability that acts of autonomous citizenship will increase and the possibility that acts of responsible citizenship will mutate into autonomous forms. Contrary to the dominant view (encapsulated in the 'community policing' and 'partnership' models), the challenge is not only how to mobilize and manage responsible citizens – a task which, in any case, becomes more and more difficult under late modern conditions – but, also, how to incorporate autonomous citizens so that their actions do not degenerate into arbitrary violence and injustice. It is to a consideration of the character and potential of autonomous citizenship that the remainder of this chapter is devoted. In order to address this issue it is necessary to consider the question of vigilantism.

Vigilantism

For some years there has been growing speculation that the United Kingdom is experiencing a wave of vigilante activity. Reaction to this has been mixed. For some commentators, 'taking the law into one's own hands' can never be justified since it undermines the police and replaces public standards of justice with private ones. Yet, for others, it is the apparent breakdown of the public system – its failure to provide effective and equitable policing for all sections of the community and its inability to deliver just judgments through the courts – which has, itself, precipitated the growth of vigilantism. Proponents of this latter view tend to regard vigilantism as indicative of some fundamental social malaise. An editorial in *The Daily Telegraph* during December 1993 suggested that 'a vigilante . . . is a symptom, often also a victim himself, of an underlying collapse of order which is not his fault'. A later editorial in *The Sunday Telegraph* during March 1994 ('We Need Vigilantes') goes further, suggesting that the government should legitimize the growing vigilante movement by encouraging 'normal solid citizens who see guarding their areas as an extension of their duty to their family, their community and their country' to undertake street patrol.

Most publicized incidents of vigilantism have been crime related, something which undoubtedly reflects the preoccupation of the mass media with crime stories. However, examination of reported vigilante incidents (for further details see, Johnston, 1993b; 1996b) would suggest three broad – though by no means mutually exclusive – forms of engagement.

(a) Retributive justice

Here engagement takes the form of violent reaction by an individual or group to the perpetrator(s), or alleged perpetrator(s), of an offence (or alleged offence). In some circumstances this reaction precedes the arrest, trial and conviction of the putative offender: the three Exeter men sentenced to periods of community service after beating a fourth with a baseball bat, having heard from an 'impeccable source' that he had burgled a house belonging to the father of one of the offenders; the Leicester farmer given an eighteen months suspended sentence for shooting, and partially blinding, a burglar who had been apprehended following an armed patrol on a caravan site located on the farmer's land; the mob which attacked the homes of two teenage girls charged with the murder of an elderly spinster in Penywaun, Aberdare; or the two Norfolk men, initially gaoled for five years following their conviction for kidnapping and threatening a youth suspected of involvement in a spate of local burglaries, whose sentences were reduced to six months by the Court of Appeal after a major campaign to release them. In other circumstances, the reaction arises at the 'post trial' stage: the father acquitted by a jury after admitting shooting the lorry driver – a man with no driving licence and a string of convictions for motoring and violence offences – who had been sentenced to eighteen months in prison after knocking down and killing his son.

(b) Crime prevention and order maintenance

Here individuals, though more often groups, engage proactively in behaviour aimed at the prevention of crime and the maintenance of order. Such activities may be peaceful or they may involve force or the threat of force: the various Guardian Angel street patrols and vigilance committees which sprang up in London, Bristol, Birmingham and the North East of England during the early 1990s; the anti-racism patrols set up to protect Asians and others from attack; the various anti-drug patrols reported on Merseyside and in other major cities; various mobilizations by farmers and others against New Age Travellers in the West Country.

(c) The maintenance of communal, ethnic or sectarian order

This form of engagement is usually collective and organized, rather than individualistic and spontaneous. Usually, it is proactive rather than reactive. Its purpose is to protect or, if necessary, to reconstitute, the order and values of a particular community. These values may have an ethnic or sectarian component to them. As with the previous categories, however, this one may overlap with the others. Factor and Stenson (1987; 1989) give an account of what is, effectively, communal vigilantism in a London Jewish community. Here, adult members ('Bozos') are deployed to protect affluent Jewish youths from street crime (drug pushers, muggers and skinheads) while, simultaneously, reaffirming the values of a Jewish identity, itself undermined by the young people's exposure to street culture. The most extreme form of communal vigilantism is found in Ulster where Loyalist and Republican paramilitaries have engaged in punishment shootings and beatings for many years. Some of this activity is directed at criminal deviance (particularly burglary and joyriding) while some merely seeks to ensure that paramilitiaries stay in line with the rules and values of the organization. Communal vigilantism is particularly important because it confirms that vigilante activity is by no means exclusively directed towards crime control. Indeed a key component of the 'American vigilante tradition' (Brown, 1975) has been its long historical concern with the regulation of travellers, vagrants and social misfits.

In the USA the re-emergence of vigilantism during the last twenty years has generated a small amount of research. Though some of this work has examined the general preconditions of vigilantism – one suggestion being its tendency to arise in communities which are socially or ethnically homogeneous (Shotland and Goodstein, 1984) – most research has focused on the activities of citizen patrol groups such as the Guardian Angels. Here, a paradox has been found. On the one hand, groups receive the highest levels of support from areas experiencing the greatest risk of victimization (Perry, 1989). On the other hand, willingness to participate in street patrols – rather than merely to support them – has been found to correlate with a lower than average fear of crime (Troyer and Wright, 1985).

Public attitudes towards citizen patrol groups, such as the Guardian Angels, are generally positive. People, fearful of crime and disorder – yet aware of the limited prospects of more police officers appearing on the beat – accept citizen patrol as an alternative, albeit a less desirable one. On the whole, public reaction to patrols is favourable. In a study undertaken in San Diego (Pennell *et al.*, 1985) over 60 per cent of respondents said that they felt safer as a result of Angels' patrols, women and older people being especially positive. However, the same study found that patrols had no impact on violent crimes – despite these being the primary target offences for patrols – and only a limited, short-term, effect on property crimes. The general conclusion – that patrols are good at reducing fear of crime but poor at reducing recorded levels of crime – is, of course, to be expected, given that much the same has been said about the effectiveness of police patrol.

There is also the question of whether the willingness of some to join patrol groups encourages others to follow them, thereby regenerating informal social control in communities. The probable answer to this question is that it depends on the location under consideration. American studies of subway patrols have found little evidence of increased citizen mobilization (Kenny, 1986), though this is hardly surprising given the anonymous terrain of the subway. Whether patrols might flourish in residential streets where some conception of 'ownership' of space may be prevalent is a different matter. Here, however, communal self-policing of public space can degenerate into the consolidation of private fiefdoms under certain conditions. In Britain, right wing commentators from the Adam Smith Institute have demanded the right of residents to 'close their streets' to outsiders in accordance with policies adopted in parts of Los Angeles and St Louis (Elliott, 1989). This proposal that residents in 'stable and well-maintained areas' should exclude entry to 'footloose populations' is, in fact, the latest in a long line of attempts to exercise containment over the so-called 'dangerous classes'. However, 'dangerousness' is perceived here as a moral, rather than a criminal, failing. Tucker's (1985) demand for a 'vigilantism of the majority' involves 'rediscovering a certain unwillingness to tolerate bizarre, dangerous or irresponsible behaviour and redeveloping a taste for public order' (Tucker, 1985: 224). Significantly, there is no mention of crime control here. Nor, for this proponent of 'morally sanctimonious vigilance' (Burrows, 1976: xv), is there any recognition that the toleration of bizarre behaviour might be a measure of social integration rather than an indicator of social pathology.

We are left, then, with a question. Are there conditions under which vigilantism might contribute positively to the regeneration of informal control within communities without giving rise to a morally censorious and socially divisive backlash? In order to address that question it is necessary to define vigilantism more precisely.

Judicial vigilantism and civil policing

Vigilantism may be regarded as the practice of autonomous citizenship when applied to policing and security. The term vigilantism will not be used here in its normal pejorative sense to describe illegal acts of violence and retribution – 'taking the law into one's own hands', 'lynch-law', and the like. Rather, I shall outline five defining features of generic vigilantism (see, Johnston, 1996b for a full discussion), after which a distinction is drawn between two types: 'judicial vigilantism' is the vigilantism of popular imagery – violent, illegal, arbitrary and retributive; 'civil policing' is a mode of autonomous policing which may, in principle, involve none of these pathological features.

First, an act of vigilantism presupposes at least minimal planning by the initiator of the action. Typically, this might involve the surveillance of an intended victim or the observation of a particular location. Mere acts of reactive violence, such as defending oneself against an assailant, do not constitute vigilantism, though the mass media sometimes describe them as such. Vigilantism involves preparation, though that preparation may vary in intensity and character: anything from having a gun in one's house as a defence against potential burglars to participating as a member of an organized vigilante group engaged in anti-crime patrols.

Second, vigilantism is undertaken by private citizens. Though several writers define violent acts committed by the police, as vigilantism (Rosenbaum and Sedeberg, 1976; Bowden, 1978) the concept of 'state vigilantism' is unhelpful. That is not to deny that state representatives engage in violent and illegal acts – witness the involvement of Colombian and Brazilian police in 'death squads' – it is merely to insist that subsuming these acts under the concept of vigilantism makes it impossible to differentiate between public and private abuses of power. To insist that vigilantism is the exclusive preserve of private citizens also means that violent acts undertaken by private commercial bodies are, similarly, excluded. Vigilantism is a voluntary activity not a commercial one carried out under contract. Commercial activities, no less than the activities of public representatives such as the police, are authorized by the state through commercial and other laws. As such, they cannot be defined as autonomous of the state's authority.

Third, vigilantism uses or threatens the use of force – or, at the very least, retains the potential to exercise force. Groups engaged in actions without this feature – such as Neighbourhood Watch members undertaking street patrols under conditions laid down by the local police (Routledge,

1993) – do not constitute vigilantes. By contrast, similar acts undertaken by the Guardian Angels constitute vigilantism because that organization maintains the right to use or threaten the use of force – albeit for defensive purposes – training its members in martial arts and in the use of non-lethal restraining techniques (Pennell *et al.*, 1985). In reality, of course, there might be slippage between the two if responsible members of Neighbourhood Watch groups were to engage in autonomous acts of violence and retribution.

Fourth, vigilantism is an attempt to impose or re-impose normative control over situations of instability and disorder. Such disorder may not be exclusively criminal in origin. Brown's (1975) analysis of North American vigilantism distinguishes between 'classic' vigilantism (directed against horse thieves, outlaws and the rural lower classes before 1900) and 'neo-vigilantism' (directed at urban Catholics, Jews, Negroes and labour leaders from the late nineteenth century onwards). A similar distinction is made by Rosenbaum and Sedeberg (1976) who differentiate between 'crime control' and 'social control' vigilantism, though there may, of course, be overlap between the two forms. Loyalist and Republican paramilitary groups in Ulster have carried out punishment shootings and beatings both against those accused of criminal deviance (e.g. joyriding and burglary) and against those accused of social deviance (e.g. contravention of the rules and mores of paramilitary organization) (Munck, 1988; McCorry and Morrisey, 1989; Conway, 1993). It is not enough, however, to define vigilantism in terms of crime control and social control. The latter, in particular, is a nebulous concept which, if combined with our definition so far ('planned voluntary actions undertaken by private citizens without the state's authority and using or threatening force for purposes of social control') could encompass anything from slapping a disobedient child in jurisdictions where such punishment is forbidden, to assassinating a radical politician in order to stabilize a given regime. Part of the solution to this problem lies in the normative aspect of vigilantism. Vigilantism occurs when some established order is perceived to be under threat from the transgression, potential transgression, or imputed transgression of institutionalized norms. Vigilantism is, in other words, a reaction to real, perceived or anticipated deviance. Thus, the actions of paramilitary squads in Ulster constitute vigilantism because they are directed at infractions of institutionalized norms (such as joyriding) or anticipated infractions (such as contemplating 'resignation' from paramilitary membership). By contrast, when paramilitaries assassinate civilians from the 'other side', shoot soldiers or bomb buildings they engage in political acts which have no function in the internal regulation of deviance and, thereby, do not constitute vigilantism.

Vigilantism is not, however, merely about the re-imposition of normative controls. It is also about security. For that reason security is a fifth element in our definition. As I suggested in Chapter 1, security involves the preservation of some established order against internal or external threat (Shearing, 1992). Like Spitzer (1987), Shearing emphasizes that the essence of security lies in an 'absence': an aspiration on the part of subjects that nothing should occur to alter the status quo. Yet, 'peace is seldom something that simply happens: it requires an *assurance* of security' (Shearing, 1992: 401). Security, thus, consists of strategies which are deployed for the purpose of offering subjects assurances (or 'guarantees') that an established order will prevail. Vigilantism is one such strategy: a popularly initiated one whose locus lies in civil society. Vigilantism is a mode of policing – a strategy for offering guarantees of security – located neither in the state apparatus (public policing) nor in the market place (commercial security) but in the sphere of civil society. Because of its civil origins, historical and anthropological commentators have defined it as a popular social movement. Brown (1975) locates American vigilantism within the specific context of the 'American frontier tradition', while specific examples of African vigilantism are traced to the socio-cultural complexes of particular tribal societies (Heald, 1986; Abrahams, 1987). Contemporary vigilantism is, no less, a popular civil movement whose origins lie in specific social conditions: in this case, the social diversity and governmental fragmentation which is a characteristic feature of late modern societies.

To sum up. Vigilantism is a civil movement giving rise to premeditated acts of force or threatened force – or where there is a potential for force to be exercised or threatened – by autonomous citizens. It arises as a reaction to the transgression of institutionalized norms by individuals or groups – or to their potential or imputed transgression. Such acts are focused on crime control and/or social control and aim to offer assurances (or 'guarantees') of security both to participants and to others.

The definition of vigilantism presented here, unlike previous ones, neither assumes it to be illegal nor orientated, exclusively, to punishment and retribution. In fact, vigilantism is a paradox. On the one hand, it may consist of the most pathological forms of behaviour: vicious acts of retribution against those who have committed deviant acts; acts of violence and threatened violence against those who, it is anticipated, might commit deviant acts in the future – or against those who 'deviate' merely by virtue of their particular lifestyle, politics, ethnicity or colour. On the other hand, some forms of vigilante action may be relatively benign: preventive anti-crime patrols; or patrols mobilized to protect those who are susceptible to sexual or racial attacks. Taylor (1976) captures this paradox well. Vigilantism may be uncontrolled, arbitrary in its effects, illegal and open to political manipulation; yet it may also be the best means available to those – especially the poor and the weak – who are confronted not just by crime and disorder, but by an insensitive and bureaucratic criminal justice system.

Taylor's (1976) analysis suggests that a full understanding of vigilantism demands consideration of both its authoritarian and liberating potential. For this reason, a conceptual distinction needs to be drawn between *judicial vigilantism* and *civil policing*. The former – as in traditional pejorative imagery – is usually illegal, violent, retributive, arbitrary and judgmental. The latter, by contrast, is primarily preventive, protective and orientated towards security. That is not to deny that the latter has the potential to degenerate into the former. Benign citizen street patrols may, sometimes, mutate into violent punishment squads. Yet, the potential for slippage is by no means peculiar to citizen-based forms of civil policing. Klockars argues that public police work is dominated by the 'Dirty Harry' problem – those routine moral dilemmas which are inherent in policing and which may predispose officers to use 'bad means' for what are, arguably, 'good ends' (Klockars, 1980). In other words, policing in all of its forms, raises moral conflicts whose resolution demands ethical, organizational and political debate. In the case of civil policing, one issue is immediately posed. If, as we have suggested, the character of policing is one of growing diversity and plurality, does civil policing have a legitimate role to play within the diverse local security networks of the future? And, if so, what role?

Both civil policing and the municipal experiments described earlier are symptomatic of the drive towards governmental distanciation and diversity. Their growth raises a number of issues. Are they likely to satisfy the public's apparently insatiable demand for 'more policing'? Should we accept that demand as a legitimate one which governments have an obligation and a capacity to meet? If so, how can municipal and civil policing initiatives be integrated into local security networks so as to ensure their operational effectiveness, their responsiveness to public demands and their delivery of just policing? These and other issues are addressed in the final chapter.

Part Four:

Conclusion

Chapter 10

The Future of Policing

Introduction: the governance of risk

In previous chapters I have demonstrated that the concept of risk is fundamental to the understanding of late modern change and to the analysis of contemporary policing. However, I have also maintained that risk should not be seen as a singular force with a homogenizing effect on society. Thus, in Chapter 4 it was argued that while risk-based forms of policing are increasingly adopted by public police, these are combined – under determinate political conditions – with disciplinary based forms of policing, thus giving rise to new combinations of police philosophy and practice.

It is because risk is mediated by social and political conditions that the concept of risk society (Beck, 1992) is particularly inappropriate to the analysis of policing. For Beck, risk society is a stage of development in which social and technical innovation generates global risks – nuclear war, chemical pollution – which are beyond effective control. Risk society is a society of fate in which all members share the same uniform level of insecurity. Not only are victims equal in their fate, those offenders who instigate global disasters and conflicts will share the same experiences as those whom they victimize. This equivalence in the status of victim and offender – coupled with a uniform level of insecurity for all – is combined with an entirely negative conception of security. Those living in risk society are unconcerned with the attainment of 'good' normative ends such as justice and equality, being preoccupied merely with 'preventing the worst'. Risk society is obsessed with security in its most negative sense.

Beck's (1992) argument is certainly suited to the analysis of some global risks. Yet, the sociological determinism contained in this argument makes it particularly invalid to the analysis of policing and security. For, while risk is undoubtedly a driving force in the transition to late modern policing, its effects are far from uniform. On the contrary, one of the most striking features of late modern societies is that individuals and groups experience unequal and inequitable degrees of security. Indeed, under conditions of social diversity and plural policing, the likelihood is that, left to their own devices, those who provide security will distribute it in an increasingly uneven fashion.

The aim of this chapter is to speculate about the future of policing while, simultaneously, discussing some of the normative issues which have to be addressed if that future is to be a just and democratic one. Despite rejecting the concept of risk society, an understanding of risk is critical to this analysis. The transition to late modern policing is based upon the interaction between risk and security described in Chapter 2, that interaction giving rise to two parallel developments. On the one hand, social diversity is accompanied by the growing fragmentation of policing. On the other hand, the impact of risk-based thinking corresponds with its proliferation. The former fragmentation, if left unchecked, will give rise to a patchwork system of policing which combines ineffectiveness (due to lack of coordination) with injustice (due to inequity of distribution). The latter proliferation, if left unchecked, threatens us with a 'maximum security society' (Marx, 1988). This combines the quantitative excess of policing (due to providers merely acceding to the public's insatiable demand for 'more security') with its qualitative distortion (due to the proactive deployment of increasingly invasive technologies). The contention of this chapter is that diversity and proliferation demand good governance. As was suggested at the end of Chapter 4, the paradox of risk is that it poses new problems for policing while, simultaneously, making new questions – and, in the longer term, new solutions – thinkable.

The chapter consists of three sections. The first engages with some contemporary debates about the problem of governing fragmented and distanciated systems of rule. Drawing upon that discussion, the second discusses the problem of the governance of complex and diverse security networks. The final section examines the issue of security from the point of view of its quantitative and qualitative expansion. One question posed here is whether policing should continue to expand or whether, on the contrary, such expansion should be restricted. It is suggested that, in the long term, what is required is neither the maximization nor the minimization of policing but its optimization. In order for that to happen, however, it is necessary to embrace diversity.

State rule at a distance: 'pulling the strings that unravel . . .'

Previous chapters have emphasized the growing diversity of policing. Bayley and Shearing's (1996) account of the position in North America is also applicable to Britain: 'Policing has become a responsibility explicitly shared between government and its citizens, sometimes mediated through commercial markets, sometimes arising spontaneously. Policing has become pluralized' (Bayley and Shearing, 1996: 588). In North America, as in Britain, diversity has not only been the result of a growing commercialization. Equally significant has been the influence of 'community crime prevention' and 'community safety' discourses on the mobilization of active citizens: 'citizen automobile and foot patrols, neighbourhood watches . . . protective escort services for at-risk populations . . . While once [volunteer policing] was thought of as vigilantism, it is now popular with the public and actively encouraged by the police' (Bayley and Shearing, 1996: 587). Though commercial and voluntary developments are more advanced in North America than elsewhere, they are having an increasing impact on domestic policing and security throughout Europe. In addition, the growing transnationalization of commercial policing, coupled with the blurring of distinctions between civil and military security, suggests that these developments will far exceed the boundaries of individual nation states.

Of course, this process of diversification is by no means restricted to policing. In Chapter 2 it was suggested that government itself has been subjected to a similar process. In this case, four components – all implicated in the wider process of global restructuring – were deemed to have significant impact: privatization; internationalization; new public management; and the interdependent discourses of 'community' and 'multi-agency partnership'. The impact of these processes, it will be recalled, is a complex one, globalization being compatible with a bewildering mixture of ends: the centralization and decentralization of government; the pursuit of internationalism and the invocation of national identity; the fragmentation and the consolidation of rule. One result of that complexity has been the development of a conceptual imagery aimed at describing this confusing pattern of government. According to this imagery the state has been described as 'stretched', 'unravelled', 'hollowed out' and 'filled in'; rule has been declared 'distanciated'; and distinctions have been drawn both between the state's capacity for 'steering' and 'rowing' and between its 'core' and 'peripheral' functions.

As was suggested in Chapter 2 these discourses on the 'reinvention of government' (Osborne and Gaebler, 1993) have two related – though conceptually distinct – emphases. On the one hand, there is a focus on the distanciated *processes* of government. Frequently, this distinction is represented by the analogy of the state maintaining a 'steering' role while devolving 'rowing' responsibilities to others. On the other hand, there is an emphasis on *functional* differentiation, the lean state retaining control of 'core' activities and devolving 'peripheral' ones elsewhere. There is, however, a need to explore the view of state power contained in these approaches. Each is intended to cast doubt on the view that the state enjoys undiminished sovereign authority under late modern conditions. Yet, in both cases, the purported diminution of sovereignty is deemed to arise from strategies of distanciation which are undertaken by the state itself. To express this in terms of an analogy, it seems as if the state 'pulls the strings' which lead to its own 'unravelling'.

Garland's (1996) analysis is worthy of consideration since it combines both of the emphases mentioned in the last paragraph, the process of distanciation being said to coincide with a differentiation in criminal justice functions. For Garland (1996) the state engages, increasingly, in strategies of 'responsibilization', non-state bodies being encouraged to bear much of the burden for crime prevention and control. This strategy involves the state taking on a new role for, as Garland suggests, distanciation will pose new problems of coordination and present it with 'many more difficulties than the traditional method of issuing commands to state agencies and their functionaries' (Garland, 1996: 454). The distanciation of responsibility for crime control is combined, however, with an increasingly harsh approach to punishment which, in Garland's (1996) view, constitutes a reassertion of state power. In effect, a distinction may be drawn between 'the *punishment* of crime, which remains the business of the state (and . . . a significant symbol of state power) and the *control* of crime, which is increasingly deemed to be "beyond the state" in significant respect' (Garland, 1996: 459: emphasis in original). Garland contends that the realistic prospects for a sustained strategy of responsibilization are, however, limited. Overall, he suggests, the state is not particularly good at 'acting at a distance', governments tending to combine responsibilization with measures intended to consolidate further central state power.

Undoubtedly, that view has some justification, previous chapters of this book having drawn attention to the complex process whereby policing has been, simultaneously, centralized, decentralized and recentralized. However, for all its apparent plausibility, this view should not lead us to place inherent limits on the process of distanciation. After all, similar predictions have been made with equal conviction in the past. A decade ago Cohen (1983) asserted that while the private sector might supplant the state in some areas '*this would be an impossible outcome in crime control. For the state to give up here would be to undercut its very claim to legitimacy*' (Cohen, 1983: 117: emphasis added). The fact that developments in the last fifteen years have demonstrated the error of Cohen's prediction – and may, in another fifteen demonstrate the error of Garland's (1996) – suggests the need for caution in discussing state power. It is one thing to contend that distanciation occurs along functional lines. It is quite another to contend that those lines are fixed within essential parameters. That view invariably rests upon two dubious assumptions about the state and state power. First, there is the assumption that the state is a rational actor with the capacity to secure its own desired objectives. Crawford castigates proponents of the 'lean state' thesis for this shortcoming and for their tendency to 'conflate intentionality with effectivity' (Crawford, 1997: 221). The fact that the state may not be good at 'acting at a distance' and may, indeed, adopt strategies of recentralization, neither assures their success nor ensures that unintended consequences will not arise from their deployment. A second problem relates to the issue of state power. The view that distanciation leads either to a dispersal of state power to the periphery or to its reconsolidation at the centre hinges upon a zero-sum model. However, as Crawford (1997) suggests, the view that peripheral power can only expand at the expense of central power – or vice versa – obscures a far more complex pattern of displacement and restructuring.

The implication of these criticisms is that power, rather than being defined as a *capacity* – exercised effectively by rational actors and distributed along zero-sum lines – should be conceived in *relational* terms. Such a relational view of power is necessary if distanciation is to be regarded as more than an instrumental strategy for the consolidation of 'core' and 'peripheral' functions. The ends of distanciation are by no means predetermined. That much was demonstrated in the previous chapter where it was seen that the 'responsibilization' of active citizens – and the slippage between 'responsible' and 'autonomous' citizenship associated with it – has the constant potential to compromise the state's authority. In deploying distanciated strategies, then, state power may be undermined or it may be consolidated. But where the latter occurs, there is no reason to assume that it will follow fixed functional lines. Shearing notes that whereas the state still deploys violence and retribution as a basis for security, non-state bodies pursuing security through actuarial means, that division of labour is by no means fixed. Rather, 'a significant movement has developed under the rubric of "restorative justice" which aims to . . . challenge, and it is hoped eventually replace, the conception of justice that lies at the heart of the retributive paradigm' (Shearing, forthcoming). In fact, Shearing's observation mirrors the analysis of ZTP contained in Chapter 4, both examples indicating that, far from being focused exclusively on disciplinary techniques, state agencies deploy shifting combinations of strategies. It is difficult to speculate on what the future configuration of those combinations will look like. What is unlikely, however, is that their functional alignment will be fixed along sectoral lines. More probable is a melding and overlapping of strategies between state and non-state agencies.

That melding and overlapping raises an obvious issue. Elsewhere, I have suggested that it is increasingly difficult to identify what is 'inside' and what is 'outside' the state (Johnston, 1992a). Others have expressed similar views about the plasticity of the state's boundaries: '[t]he very notion of "the state" as a separate and autonomous institutional entity, intimately connected with "politics" and the "public sphere" and clearly separated from the domain of the economy, the societal community and culture, is increasingly problematical' (Crook *et al.*, 1993: 104). What these comments suggest – and what the analysis of late modern policing confirms – is that governmental action emerges from an increasingly amorphous space occupied *inter alia* by formal political institutions, non-governmental organizations, commercial entities, 'private governments', voluntary agencies and civil bodies. It is not merely that the boundaries between state and non-state institutions have developed 'blurred edges', those boundaries have been transformed, sometimes coagulating into specific configurations, sometimes dissolving back into themselves or into one another. This suggests that any understanding of policing under late modernity requires careful analysis, not just of the state, but of the changing morphology of governance.

Such an approach is incompatible with 'capacity' theories of state power. If government is plastic and the state merely one agency within a shifting governmental complex – an agency whose exclusively 'public' status may, moreover, be compromised by 'private' commercial penetration – state sovereignty is problematic. What, then, of the concept of state rule at a distance? Jessop (cited in Edwards 1994: 9) is, undoubtedly, right to insist that contemporary rule no longer consists, in the Weberian sense, of 'centralised imperative coordination'. Yet, the statement begs an obvious question. Does distanciation merely imply '*decentralised* imperative coordination'? Clearly, such a notion is unacceptable since it reduces rule to a self-fulfilling capacity. However, this reduction is by no means inevitable. To return to our earlier analogy, there is a fundamental difference between seeing rule at a distance as mere 'decentralised imperative coordination' and seeing it as a process whereby the state 'pulls the strings which may produce its own unravelling'. The latter notion neither endows the state with governmental primacy nor grants it an essential capacity for self-reproduction. It accepts that the pattern of state power – the extent to which and the manner by which power is consolidated and/or dispersed – together with the configuration of state functions relating to that pattern, will be contingent upon social and political conditions.

Such a relational approach raises a problem. How, under the diverse circumstances of late modernity, and without the traditional assurances of state sovereignty, can good governance be achieved? How, in other words, can plurality be managed so as to ensure effective and efficient administration while also maintaining desired standards of democratic accountability and equity? In the recent past three types of responses have been given to this question. The neo-liberal answer – a minimal state contained within a free market economy – has been particularly influential in Britain. However, it contains logical and substantive flaws which render its proposals for government in general, and for policing in particular, unconvincing. (For a critique of this position see, Johnston, 1992a: ch. 3.) 'New republican' solutions have extolled the virtues of citizenship as a basis for good governance. However, these suggestions have two failings. First, they are based upon the idea of a single political community when evidence points to growing political diversity. Second, the community they envisage, rather than facilitating the expression of difference merely exhorts people to be the same (Hirst, 1994). More recently, communitarianism has been proposed as a foundation for social and political reinvention (Etzioni, 1993) though in Britain the moral agenda associated with it – most notably through its connection to the debate on the 'underclass' (Dennis and Erdos, 1992; Murray, 1996) – has led to deprived communities being seeing less as victims of their circumstances than as blameworthy for their predicament. There is a strong antipathy within communitarian thought to both the market and the state, each being seen as a threat to the cultivation of organic communities (Hughes, 1996). Social cohesion and compliance, it is maintained, are best achieved through the duties and responsibilities of community members rather than through the freedoms and rights of individual citizens. However, these non-state solutions are unconvincing. Governance through the market produces systematic inequity if some consumers enjoy less 'free choice' than others. Governance by citizens assumes that the communities which contain them share a social and moral consensus when, in fact, they are just as likely to generate conflict and dissent.

This would suggest that if the demands of good democratic government are to be met, the state, albeit reshaped and remoulded by the rigours of late modernity, must play some role in governing diversity. That view is held by Hirst and Thompson (1995) who suggest that while the state may no longer function to sustain national culture it 'will probably find a new rationale in managing . . . diversity, acting as the public power that enables . . . communities to coexist and to resolve conflict' (Hirst and Thompson, 1995: 420). However, this raises a critical question to be considered in the following section. Does the remoulded state constitute the exclusive domain of authoritative public power or does such power also reside elsewhere in the governmental complex? The first part of the section considers Hirst's discussion of 'associative democracy' (Hirst, 1989; 1993; 1994; 1996), a concept which raises many of the issues at stake in respect of public power, interests and authority. The second part applies that discussion to the problem of governing diverse local security networks.

Governance, diversity and security

Diverse government

The governmental complex under late modernity consists not merely of the state and the market but also of the institutions of civil society. Cohen and Arato (1992) define civil society as 'a sphere of social interaction between economy and state, composed above all of the intimate sphere (especially the family), the sphere of associations (especially voluntary associations), social movements, and forms of public communication' (Cohen and Arato, 1992: ix). However, liberal political theory in both its traditional and contemporary variants has simplified the character of the governmental complex, reducing it to a dichotomy between 'public' and 'private' spheres. As Hirst (1996) points out 'what all these positions have in common is a conception of the private sphere or civil society as a spontaneous order independent of and separate from the state' (Hirst, 1996: 98). Subsequently, libertarians, neo-liberals and left-wing radicals alike, have been preoccupied with a single problem: how to protect the spontaneous private order from encroachment by the state?

There are two difficulties with this argument. First, as Hirst (1996) suggests, the problem is misconceived. Civil society is far from a spontaneous apolitical realm separate from government and the state. Indeed, 'structural changes over the last century [make] any attempt to equate "state" with "the political" or "civil society" with "the private" seem anachronistic' (Cohen and Arato, 1992: xiii). In particular, the fact that 'both state and civil society are made up of large complex organisations . . . [means that] the boundary between the two is not all that clear' (Hirst, 1996: 99). Secondly, as I have argued elsewhere (Johnston, 1992a), public and private should not be seen as distinct 'places' with inherent characteristics, but as strategic sites of political debate. The changing boundaries of the public and private spheres are constituted in political conflict rather than given in the nature of things. What is important about the public–private divide is not the search for its 'natural' boundary but rather to explore 'the ways in which it has been successfully deployed to support political and economic orderings and to see whether it cannot be fruitfully reframed as an analytically useful concept' (Shearing and Stenning, 1987: 22).

Hirst's (1989; 1993; 1994; 1996) analysis of associative democracy is, at least in part, addressed to the latter task. His contention is that existing ideological positions – socialist collectivism, social democracy and free market liberalism – are unable to provide a solution to the problems of democratic governance and public welfare. He maintains that voluntary associations, organized on territorial and functional bases, can establish the foundations for pluralist democracy. Associative democracy aims, where possible, to decentralize and devolve social affairs to publicly funded, voluntary, self-governing associations. By these means civil society becomes the primary – and the state the secondary – public power. As such, it 'ensures peace between associations, protects the rights of individuals and provides the mechanisms of public finance whereby a substantial part of the activities of associations are funded' (Hirst, 1993: 117).

Associative democracy aims to regenerate civil society, establishing it as a primary locus of governance. This objective arises, in part, from Hirst's view that there is a need to create 'a civil society for the poor' (Hirst, 1993: 115). Here, he argues that centralized state bureaucracies cope badly with the pathologies arising under a 'two-thirds versus one-third society'. The effect of unmitigated social exclusion is to generate an 'uncivil society' (Hirst, 1996: 101), something which requires political solutions rather than the police solutions described in Chapter 4. Indeed, the sources of an 'uncivil society' are as much political as social, Hirst contending that society is dominated by unaccountable 'large-scale quasi-public and private institutions possessed of powers that dwarf those of many pre-modern nation states' (Hirst, 1996: 101). The problem, then, is not the traditional liberal one – the threat of state domination of civil society – but the combined domination of state and civil society by unaccountable modes of top-down administration: 'the main danger to liberty is the piecemeal authoritarianism of unchecked managerial elites' (Hirst, 1996: 102).

Hirst claims that if the problem of authoritarianism is to be resolved the whole of society – not just the state – has to be viewed politically: as a 'complex of institutions that require a substantial measure of public and private control' (Hirst, 1996: 101). The problem is that, at present, individuals define freedom as something to be realized through the private domain of leisure rather than through the public world of politics. Nowadays, it is difficult to pursue freedom in formal organizations, such as the workplace, since managerialism has – as was demonstrated in Chapters 5 and 6 – 'been remarkably successful at redefining [political] accountability [as] accounting' (Hirst, 1996: 105). The implication of Hirst's argument is that politics needs to be reinjected into society in general and, for our purposes, into policing in particular.

Hirst maintains that while there is little wrong, in principle, with some of the democratic political reforms proposed by contemporary critics – referenda, electronic democracy, citizens' juries and the like (see, Crawford, 1997) – they address only the problem of democratic decisions, rather than the authoritarian structures which will inevitably limit them. These limitations 'are structural, a product of the increasingly problematic division between the public and private spheres' (Hirst, 1996: 106). Genuine democratization of public and private governments requires two institutional reforms. First, the constituencies served by organizations need to be given a voice within their government and, where possible, a choice between alternative service providers. Second, the organizations themselves need to be protected from unwarranted interference by managerial elites. For that reason they should be guaranteed a level of autonomy consistent with their members' empowerment.

Hirst's model of associative democracy is particularly relevant to the problem of establishing 'good government' within diverse systems. For that reason, one of his main concerns is to establish a democratic framework for coordinating relations between the state, the market and civil society. In order for this to happen, the market has to be embedded 'in a social network of coordinative and regulatory institutions' (Hirst, 1994: 12). This idea of embedding commercial provision in a coordinated and regulated social network underpinned by state and civil institutions is considered in a policing context in the second part of this section. Interestingly, however, Hirst is somewhat ambiguous about its application to policing. He emphasizes that the state's function is to ensure peace between associations, to protect individual rights and to provide the necessary means of public finance 'whereby those forms of provision that are regarded as necessary and available as of right to all members are administered through voluntary associations that those members elect to join in order to receive such services' (Hirst, 1994: 26). Yet, far from seeing policing as such a 'necessary and available' service, Hirst adds that there are certain facilities common to all members of society 'that cannot be administered in this way'. These include 'the defence of the territory, *certain* police powers, certain environmental and public health provisions, and certain forms of compulsory control of individuals . . .' (Hirst, 1994: 33: emphasis added).

Hirst elaborates no further on *which* police powers might be considered inappropriate for associative governance, though he does offer an explanation for their exclusion. Some elements of public welfare, he suggests, cannot be entrusted to voluntary agencies since 'in the last instance, rights of entitlement, standards of service and principles of equity must be maintained by the public power at the federal level' (Hirst, 1994: 42). Now there are three problems with this statement. First, it could be applied, with equal conviction, to any area of public welfare. Matters of entitlement, equity and service quality are, after all, as relevant to education, housing and health as they are to defence, policing and incarceration. Second, the statement – as one of principle – appears to exclude all areas of policing from associative governance thus making the earlier reference to the exclusion of only 'certain police powers' puzzling. Third, and most importantly, the statement makes several unwarranted assumptions. To say that matters of entitlement, equity and quality must be maintained by a public power neither means that that power has to operate *exclusively* at the federal level, nor that the exercise of such power precludes all service delivery at the level of associative networks. Indeed, Hirst's statement would only be true if public services, such as policing, comprised a single unified whole and public power was reducible to the singular capacities of the federal state. That this assumption should be implicit in an analysis dedicated to establishing a political framework for what might be termed 'the diverse governance of diversity' is, to say the least, puzzling.

To sum up. Associative democracy provides us with an excellent framework for exploring the problems of diverse government. However, the issue of authoritative public power remains unresolved. Hirst begins by defining civil society as the primary locus of power and the state as the secondary locus. Yet, in the last instance, the state is defined as the exclusive domain of authoritative public power. As Hirst puts it 'there must be a common public power [and such] a public power would be, in effect, a liberal constitutional state, but with limited functions' (Hirst, 1994: 33). Now, in one sense, this argument is entirely defensible. The constitutional state, consisting of an elected legislature and an independent judiciary with autonomy to apply the rule of law provides certain of the necessary conditions of existence of associative governance. Yet, Hirst's view is overly governmental and insufficiently sociological. Though associationalism has the laudable aims of 'publicizing civil society' and 'pluralizing the state' (Hirst, 1994), there is little recognition that the state has already been pluralized – fragmented, stretched, hollowed-out, unravelled – under late modern conditions. This begs the question of whether a constitutional solution – however necessary – is a sufficient condition of good governance and, indeed, of whether authoritative public power may also reside outside the exclusive domain of the constitutional state. The remainder of this section considers some of these issues in the context of the governance of local security networks.

Governing local security networks

Diversity in policing is already evident in an increasing number of British towns and cities where a complex of agencies operates alongside public police. These include commercial security companies contracted by residents to undertake preventive patrols; commercial security companies contracted by local authorities to patrol streets and protect council properties; municipal security forces composed of unsworn personnel; municipal constabularies composed of sworn officers; and neighbourhood watch groups involved in preventive street patrol. In addition to that there are individuals and groups involved in spasmodic acts of vigilante activity. These may range from the benign (peaceful preventive street patrols) to the pathological (acts of violence and retribution committed against burglars, drug-dealers and, most recently, those accused of paedophile activity). The danger is, of course, that this diverse mixture of elements may degenerate into a disorganized and anarchic patchwork. Diversity, thus, poses a governmental problem: how to transform a disparate collection of security providers into what Shearing (1996) has termed a coherent 'security network'.

This governmental problem consists of three elements. The first of these concerns equity and justice. In a 'two-thirds one-third society', a fragmented 'patchwork' of security providers – including significant commercial elements – will exacerbate the problem of distributive injustice. Equity will not emerge naturally from a system combining structural inequality at the societal level and commercial provision at the network level. For that reason 'doing nothing' is hardly a viable governmental option since, left to its own devices, the market will determine the distribution of security and risk.

Bayley and Shearing (1996) have addressed this problem in a North American context suggesting that prosperous members of the community who pay most taxes are, already, aiming to withdraw resources from the public sector on the grounds that they pay twice for security – once to the government and once to the commercial sector. As they suggest, this exacerbates the unequal distribution of risk since 'the people who are most interested in reducing taxes are those who feel relatively secure and spend most of their time in privately protected places' (Bayley and Shearing, 1996: 594). What we have here is a direct parallel of the position of a century ago when those who were able to afford private protection objected to contributing taxes towards the establishment of the 'new police' (Johnston, 1992a). The problem is that the modern solution to this difficulty – the massive expansion of state policing in order to provide, at least in principle, a minimum level of security for all – is unfeasible under late modern conditions. The solution that Bayley and Shearing (1996) suggest is a very different one, its aim being to enable poor people 'to participate in markets for security' (Bayley and Shearing, 1996: 603). In order for this to happen, however, it would be necessary to develop mechanisms for reallocating public funding towards security. One way of achieving this, they suggest, is by the provision of block grants to communities, enabling them to purchase various mixtures of public and private policing. Such an approach, it is hoped, would level out inequities, encourage communities to develop security regimes appropriate to their needs and invest direct authority in the hands of the people most affected by existing inequities. Inevitably, redistributive initiatives of this sort depend upon governmental policies which confirm the indivisibility of security. As Bayley and Shearing (1996) suggest, however, the well-to-do already pay for crime but 'have not learned that they will save more by leveling up security than by ghettoising it' (Bayley and Shearing, 1996: 603). These proposals also affirm the principle of distanciation, the state bearing a fundamental responsibility for the government of security without having the necessary obligation to provide it. Finally, distanciated redistribution facilitates the making of social and economic gains through market-based efficiencies, individuals and groups within a security network being able to exercise 'voice and choice' (Hirst, 1994) over the services they consume.

A second governmental problem concerns the coordination of the elements in a security network. Here, two issues arise: what functions do the various elements (civil, commercial, municipal and state) fulfil? and how do these relate to one another? To date, discussion of this topic has been preoccupied either by purely pragmatic concerns or by attempts to secure a public police monopoly over security. Pragmatism undoubtedly dominated the Home Office's *Review of Police Core and Ancillary Tasks* (Home Office, 1995). The Review, set up by the previous Conservative government, had suggested that some £200 million per annum might be saved by 'hiving off' non-essential duties to non-police agencies (Travis, 1994). However, vigorous resistance by the police associations led to a report being produced which was far less radical than had been anticipated. Of the eventual 26 police tasks proposed for reallocation, the majority were, in fact, relatively uncontroversial. The Home Office's approach to this issue was driven mainly by technical and pragmatic considerations and although the Review did distinguish between categories of task ('inner core', 'outer core' and 'ancillary') the subsequent allocation was not linked, in any obvious way to these, distinctions. As Loader (1997a) suggests, the

Review's limitation was to dress up questions of principle in the language of cost-effectiveness. This meant that although one of the aims of the Review was to support the idea of an integrated, multifunctional public police service, there was little by way of coherent analysis of the principles lying behind that objective.

Like the Home Office Review, an earlier analysis by Bayley (1994) also subscribed to the idea of an integrated, multifunctional public police service which would maintain a monopoly over policing. Bayley began from a recognition that the police face a crisis due to their apparent inability to prevent crime and suggested a number of options which might be considered. The first of these, 'determined crime prevention' would turn the police into 'society's official criminologists' (Bayley, 1994: 124). This approach would require the police to identify both causes of and solutions to crime, though the danger might be 'maximal' and 'authoritarian' modes of policing. 'Efficient law enforcement', by contrast, would privatize or civilianize secondary police functions, enabling the police to focus on crime prevention. However, Bayley (1994) suggested that some of the items commonly defined as secondary functions, such as traffic regulation, remain fundamental to effective crime prevention. 'Stratified crime prevention' would involve allocating preventive responsibility to uniformed front-line officers, something which is already enshrined in community policing programmes. Drawing upon elements of these options Bayley (1994) proposed a three-pronged blueprint for police reform in which neighbourhood police officers would deliver crime prevention; 'basic police units' would develop operational strategies from the bottom-up; and police forces would provide resources, management and evaluation from the centre.

Bayley's (1994) provision of a police solution to the problem of policing is, however, unconvincing when considered alongside the process of late modern restructuring. Indeed, he rejected a further option which conformed most closely to some of the tendencies implicit in that restructuring. Under the 'honest law enforcement' option the police would give up all pretence of preventing crime and concentrate, instead, on what they do well, the provision of 'authoritative intervention, symbolic justice and traffic regulation' (Bayley, 1994: 128). Although Bayley accepted that this solution might benefit crime prevention in the long run since it would force people to recognize the police's limitations and, by so doing, increase the likelihood of alternative commercial and community provision, it was rejected on two major grounds. First, he suggested that commercial provision might produce inequity: private policing for the rich, coupled with 'a poor police policing the poor' (Bayley, 1994: 144). As our previous discussion suggests, Bayley has now qualified this position significantly (Bayley and Shearing, 1996). That qualification undermines the second objection – that it is impossible to separate the functions of law enforcement from those of crime prevention. Once that objection is called into question, however, it can no longer be claimed that the police have to retain a monopoly over security networks. This conclusion is developed in two other analyses.

The Independent Committee of Inquiry into the Role and Responsibilities of the Police (Police Foundation/Policy Studies Institute, 1996), which ran more or less concurrently with the Home Office Review, focused most of its attention on the issue of police patrol. Unlike the Home Office Review, however, the Committee considered the issue on grounds broader than mere cost-effectiveness, arguing that as there is unlikely to be any genuine expansion of community and problem-orientated policing in the foreseeable future diverse providers should be encouraged, subject to their effective governance. The approach adopted is expounded in a recent book by two members of the Committee who suggest that what is needed 'and what the government has so far resisted doing . . . is [defining] . . . the role and responsibilities of *other complementary actors* vital to policing and crime prevention' (Morgan and Newburn, 1997: 160: emphasis in original). The Committee made a number of recommendations in this regard: that the police – who should retain their monopoly of legal powers of arrest and coercion – should experiment to find new ways of patrolling; that municipal security organizations and regulated commercial security companies should have a legitimate role in patrol; and that police forces should recruit sworn auxiliaries to undertake dedicated patrol activities on the lines of the Dutch initiatives described in the last chapter.

Though the Committee's view that police functions can be diversified contrasts with Bayley's original insistence on their indivisibility, both positions differ markedly from Brogden and Shearing's (1993) demand that they be demarcated. Although this analysis is directed towards the reform of policing structures in post-apartheid South Africa, the authors consider that 'dual policing' is also applicable to other jurisdictions. Beginning from the premise that policing should be regarded as the product of a network of security institutions, the authors merely follow that argument to its logical conclusion. Since security networks are located mainly outside the state sphere it follows, they suggest, that the primary location of policing lies in civil society rather than in the state. Further to this, they add that the state police should be defined, not as the all-purpose problem-solvers of community policing, but as a body organized around its legitimate capacity to exercise force. This capacity, in turn, delimits the scope of their activity. The capacity to coerce is one resource, albeit a specific one, within a network of security encompassing civil society and the state. As such, it defines the state police's role: 'The police are seen as valuable, not because they are all-purpose problem-solvers, but because they are equipped in terms of legal authority, capacity and knowledge to be bandit-catchers . . .' (Brogden and Shearing, 1993: 174). The implication of this view is that, contrary to Bayley (1994), the law enforcement ('bandit-catching') role of state police has to be differentiated from the crime prevention/community safety functions of civil policing. Shearing expresses the implication of this view with admirable bluntness: 'we should be doing community policing by taking the police out of community policing' (Shearing, 1994: 143).

What do these different positions tell us about future functional relations within security networks? The Home Office's preoccupation with matters of cost-effectiveness, and its consequent failure to provide a principled defence of multifunctional public policing, is the least helpful since, as Loader (1997) suggests, 'it is likely, not least in the field of patrolling, simply to be overtaken by events' (Loader, 1997a: 149). Bayley's (1994) analysis, though providing a clear rationale for the maintenance of public police hegemony, is unconvincing. The indivisibility of the police function, if it ever existed, is long dead, something which his later analysis recognizes. Almost two decades ago, Shearing and Stenning (1981) had noted that, in North America, the Peelian dream of providing an 'unremitting watch' through preventive foot patrol was being effected through commercial, rather than public, police means. Far from being indivisible, then, preventive police functions have leaked across the sectoral divide. Are we to conclude from this that the long-term future is one of 'dual policing'; a bifurcated system in which sworn police officers control crime by the use of enforcement-led techniques, leaving prevention in the hands of commercial, municipal and civil institutions?

There is undoubtedly something to be said for this model, though it faces two immediate criticisms: that the crime-orientated ('bandit-catching') model of police work conflicts with empirical evidence of what police do; and that the separation of enforcement from community policing impacts negatively on the former due to its dependence on intelligence received through the latter. Though true, neither of these criticisms is, necessarily, telling. Empirical confirmation of what police do does not, necessarily, amount to a justification of what they should do. And the fact that 'bandit-catching' depends upon information gleaned from the public need not require the enforcing body to collect it. It merely requires the existence of a security network with sufficient support to gain information from the public and, having gained it, with sufficient internal coherence to manage it effectively.

This suggests that the bifurcated model might, under appropriate conditions, provide a coherent basis for the organization of local security networks. Having said that, there are factors which suggest that bifurcation may be a long time coming and that, if it does, it will involve more than a mere distinction between prevention and enforcement. One of these reasons is sheer practicality: the fact that there will be resistance to paring down the functions of large multifaceted police organizations. The other is the impact of risk: the fact that public police make increased use of proactive and anticipatory (risk-based) practices and, by so doing, come to think and act more like commercial security organizations. Though one should not overstate the impact of this tendency – public policing is still dominated by a mixture of arrest, deterrence, order maintenance and service – its consequence is to undermine the distinction between preventive (proactive) and enforcement-based (disciplinary) techniques upon which the bifurcated model hinges. In the light of these qualifications it is striking that the article by Bayley and Shearing (1996), proposing to combine community policing (by the police) with rights to commercial security (for the poor), involves a realignment of each of their views. On the one hand, Bayley's commitment to the redistributive benefits of commercial security contradicts his original emphasis on the indivisibility of the police function. On the other hand, Shearing's acceptance of police involvement in community policing conflicts with his earlier demand for their exclusion from that activity.

Yet, Shearing's apparent change of mind need not rule out a gradual and long-term transition to some form of bifurcation. At present, the police's level of commitment to preventive community policing is limited. Although the implementation of community approaches is repeatedly undermined by alternative organizational goals (Jones, 1980; Bennett, 1994), this does not reduce the police's desire to maintain leadership over community policing. (A cynic might say that while the police do not want to do community policing themselves, they do not want anybody else to do it either.) To that extent, whatever the real level of organizational commitment to programmes, the police will be difficult to dislodge from their hegemonic role in community policing. Yet, the logic of community policing – if it is more than mere empty rhetoric – is to create the means whereby 'communities of risk' (Johnston, 1997b) may 'develop . . . self-disciplining and crime preventive capacities' (Bayley and Shearing, 1996: 604) through civil, commercial and municipal means. Ultimately, the successful implementation of community policing might produce something similar to Shearing's original demand: community policing without the police. For, if the long-term objective of community policing is to engender communal self-policing, 'success' will be achieved when the police no longer have a leading role to play in that project.

If that happens, however, the result will be something more complex than the bifurcation suggested by Brogden and Shearing (1993). Civil institutions will bear the bulk of responsibility for preventive policing at the community level. But the public police will be more than a mere enforcement agency since risk changes the connections between discipline and enforcement. Public policing will continue to be dominated by the legally sanctioned practices of arrest and coercion, but those practices will run alongside others. The police will be concerned not only with reactive 'bandit-catching', but also with deploying alternative proactive means to anticipate prevent, pre-empt, destabilize, disrupt and disorganize the activities of bandits – and, sometimes, of others as well. To be sure, this is a dual model of policing, but one whose functional characteristics are variegated rather than bifurcated.

Finally, there is a third issue: the means by which dual security networks – albeit ones with variegated features – might be regulated. As is clear from the earlier discussion of associative democracy, one of the questions which

arises here is whether the state remains the exclusive source of authoritative public power or whether such power may also reside in civil society.
Connected to this is the question of whether policing, by its very nature,
should be excluded from the ambit of democratic governance as Hirst's
(1994) analysis implies. Undoubtedly, the application of democracy to
policing and crime control raises complex issues (Crawford, 1997). For
example, Jordan and Arnold (1995), rightly, point to the emergence
of repressive criminal justice policies in both Britain and the USA when
populist demands are voiced in a context of inter-group conflict and
social exclusion.

Both Morgan and Newburn (1997) and Brogden and Shearing (1993)
address the issue of the democratic governance of local security networks.
Morgan and Newburn (1997), developing their earlier work as members
of the *Independent Committee*, draw particular attention to the absence of a
civic culture in Britain following two decades of local government decline.
It is no accident, they suggest, that the consequent erosion of 'civic dignity'
has coincided with widespread public insecurity. In addressing this latter
issue they affirm the Morgan Committee's (Home Office, 1991) recommendation that local authorities, working with the police, should be given
a statutory responsibility for the development of community safety and
crime prevention programmes. Adapting this proposal to the situation
following PMCA (which requires police authorities to produce annual
Policing Plans), they suggest that a statutory obligation should be placed
upon local authorities to prepare an annual draft Community Safety
Plan for presentation to police authorities. In order to facilitate this, they
propose that the Police Consultative Committees set up under PACE
should be placed under local authority control and deployed as a means
of maximizing public consultation on community safety matters. One of
the main aims of this exercise would be to ensure that Policing Plans
would be informed by the Community Safety Plans of their constituent
local authorities. The rationale of this argument is that 'civic dignity' will
be regenerated through the development of consultative processes which,
subsequently, feed into local democratic structures, the local authority
then interacting with the police in the formation of policing and community safety policy. Interestingly, Morgan and Newburn (1997) leave
open the question of how consultative groups should be constituted (and
how many of them there should be), suggesting that 'the existence of
PCCGs [police community consultative groups], or Community Safety
Groups, based on district council boundaries would in no way preclude
the . . . operation of . . . groups designed to address the problems . . . of
particular sections of the population' (Morgan and Newburn, 1997: 190–
1). That raises the question, of course, of whether consultation is restricted
to territorially defined communities or is also open to those organized
on a non-territorial basis.

Morgan and Newburn's (1997) analysis aims to empower civil society
by means of integrating civil institutions into local democratic political

structures. In that respect, it accords with Hirst's (1994) dual objective of 'politicizing civil society' and 'civilizing the state'. Brogden and Shearing's (1993) analysis, though very different in form and content from Morgan and Newburn's (1997), addresses similar issues. Like them, Brogden and Shearing (1993) maintain that legal powers of coercion should reside solely with the state police. They insist, however, that those powers delimit the police role, coercive police power being defined as one element within a wider institutional network of security. Within this network community policing involves civil institutions 'in taking direct responsibility for policing as part of a radical process of democratization', thereby leading to the wider 'resurrection of civil society' (Brogden and Shearing, 1993: 181). According to this model, policing is most effective where the coercive and authoritative resources of state policing are deployed in combination with the peace-keeping institutions of civil society. One of the challenges which this raises is to find ways of doing policing so as to 'ensure that civil institutions will have a say in the definition of local orders' (Brogden and Shearing, 1993: 186). The aim here is to enable communities – whether defined territorially or not – to influence, within lawful parameters, the dimensions of security and peace-keeping. This 'empowering . . . [of] those who are directly affected by an order to take primary responsibility for its definition and promotion' (Brogden and Shearing, 1993: 186) is, in one sense, nothing new. After all, commercial security has applied those principles since its inception. In that context, however, empowerment has not always coincided with equity. Thus, in North America, Europe and South Africa, it is middle and upper class 'orders' rather than lower class ones which, traditionally, have been protected by the commercial policing sector. Empowerment may liberate but it also may harm.

This tension between empowerment and equity was one of the problems addressed by a Panel established under the Goldstone Commission in post-apartheid South Africa whose findings are drawn upon by Brogden and Shearing (1993). The Panel recognized that any system aiming to exploit the benefits of civil [and, for that matter, commercial: LJ] policing must recognize the potential for harm that goes with such initiatives. At the same time, however, the potential benefits accruing to such initiatives suggested that rather than merely seeking to reimpose a public police monopoly over security, effective means should be found to minimize those potential harms. In order to do this the Panel made three suggestions. First, that physical force should, with strictly limited exceptions, be monopolized by the state police. Second, that national criteria be put in place to regulate the relationship between civil policing and state policing thereby putting effective limits on local definitions of order. Third, that local authorities be defined as the locus of police accountability with judicial appeal mechanisms being put in place to challenge its specific decisions. By these means primary responsibility for policing would rest with civil institutions rather than with the central state, local excesses being challengeable through the judicial process.

Such a dual system of policing, the authors propose, would maximize civil empowerment while avoiding some of the injustices associated with commercial and populist policing. Though these recommendations are very different from those of Morgan and Newburn (1997), the principle at stake, the integration of authoritative civil power into democratic political institutions – 'civilizing politics and politicizing civil society' – is similar. The dual policing model maintains that security networks operate most effectively when responsibilities and obligations are shared by all parties, thereby confirming that 'government is a civil as well as a state responsibility and that an acceptance of this should guide policing policy' (Brogden and Shearing, 1993: 190).

Embracing diversity: towards optimal policing

In this book policing has been equated with security, security consisting of intentional strategies aimed at the promotion of safety and the minimization of risk. Since the promotion of security is undertaken, not merely by public police but also by a plurality of other agencies, our concern has been with the growth of diverse security networks under late modernity, rather than merely with policing in its narrow institutional sense. In the Introduction it was suggested that this approach to policing raises two issues. First, it makes no assumptions about whose security is being promoted by policing agencies. Our earlier discussion of community policing (and of 'policing communities of risk') indicated that policing may have the effect of promoting one person's security at the expense of another's, and it is for this reason that the just and democratic governance of security networks is crucial. The second problem – the one to be addressed here – concerns the balance that needs to be struck between the promotion of security and the promotion of other social objectives. This problem has two aspects to it. The first is a quantitative one: the unlimited and unconditional promotion of security giving rise to a dangerous situation of 'too much policing'. The second is a qualitative one: the increased efficiencies associated with risk-based proaction encouraging an over-invasive style of policing which threatens to undermine public freedoms. Both of these maximal tendencies have to be addressed if, in the future, a model of optimal policing is to be developed.

Too much policing?

As to the first of these, it is necessary to distinguish three aspects of security; its effective promotion (something which, I have argued, demands good governance and efficient coordination of networks); the extent to which that promotion actually enhances safety; and the level of public demand which exists at any particular time for security services. It is the third of these issues which concerns us here though, inevitably, when discussing it, reference has to be made to the other two. Further complication arises from the fact that all three aspects of security, though connected, are also relatively independent of each other.

Loader's (1997a) recent analysis bears directly on the problem of the overproduction of policing since he, rightly, questions the conventional view that the public's demand for visible police protection can and should be met. Instead, Loader contends that 'the demand for protection ... might not be capable of being satisfied while it is couched in terms of more policing' (Loader, 1997a: 151). This claim rests upon three arguments.

First, he suggests that the public's demand for protection may be a demand for more police rather than for more (diverse) patrol. This argument is connected to his view that the expansion of private security should be challenged, an issue to which I return below. Second, he argues that powerful agencies like the police and private security have a say in defining the risks from which people demand protection. The fact that these agencies have such a role means that they also have a stake in public fear and, therefore, in maximizing the provision of policing. Undoubtedly, this argument is true since, as I have suggested earlier, the commodification of policing encourages both commercial and public police alike, to generate demand for security. Third, he contends, rightly, that the public's demand for protection may, in any case, be insatiable because policing has symbolic and affective components attached to it. The product of these three processes, Loader (1997a) suggests, is a ratchet effect which raises demand for protection, in general, and for patrol, in particular. However, the fact that the patrolling solution to crime has repeatedly failed suggests that there is 'no purely *policing* solution to problems of crime and "fear of crime"' (Loader, 1997a: 155: emphasis in original). If this is the case, he suggests, the policy question which faces us is not that of finding new ways of meeting demand for a visible police presence but, rather, of 'figuring out how to dissolve that demand' (Loader, 1997a: 155). Dissolution of demand rests, he argues, on security being constituted as a public good. This, he believes, is incompatible with the widespread commodification of security services since private security may not only increase protection but may also generate insecurity, displace crime, increase social and spatial inequalities in the distribution of crime and hollow out public space. Undoubtedly, this analysis is accurate. Private security, if left to its own devices, will give rise to the pathological effects described. Moreover, policing cannot, exclusively, provide a solution to the problem of insecurity, policing initiatives needing to be integrated with those from other areas of public policy if they are, genuinely, to enhance safety.

It is useful to contrast Loader's (1997a) position with that of Bayley and Shearing (1996). Where the former, like Spitzer (1987), observes that the escalation in demand for security may, paradoxically, generate further insecurity, Bayley and Shearing claim that the pluralization of security 'has made communities safer' (Bayley and Shearing, 1996: 592). Here, they reason that the growth of commercial security has been accompanied by an increase in public police provision, the effect being an absolute growth in the quantity of policing. In fact, Bayley and Shearing's (1996) position is rather more complex than this initial assertion would suggest, since they maintain that enhanced safety requires not merely the quantitative provision of security but also the dual reforms (community policing plus block grants) referred to previously. Nevertheless, their argument assumes that once these reforms are put into effect the result will be safer communities. In fact, each of these arguments is true in a different way. Bayley and Shearing (1996) are right to predict that the police's adoption of risk-orientated techniques, coupled with the effective integration of security networks, will eventually lead to better provision of security and, with the right social conditions, to greater safety. Yet, Loader (1997a) is also right to maintain that, under present (unreformed) conditions, the demand for security will continue to outstrip its supply. Part of the difference lies, then, in the prescriptive content of the former (commercial security as part of the solution) compared to the prescriptive content of the latter (commercial security as part of the problem).

A further complication is that the relationship between the provision of security, enhanced safety and demand for security services is a contingent one. Security is not a zero-sum game in which the provision of security reduces insecurity. It may be possible to design perfectly modulated security networks which embody democratic governance (accountability), good organization and management (effectiveness) and equitable systems of delivery (justice). And they may, with the right social and political conditions, genuinely enhance people's safety. Yet, those same people may also experience levels of anxiety which cause them to demand further security provision. This is an ever-present danger in a society orientated around risk. Moreover, as Loader's (1997a) analysis implies, under conditions where those who provide security have a stake in the enlargement of public fear, there is a real danger that the result may be a dangerous excess of policing.

Under these conditions it is unlikely that demand can ever be 'dissolved' (Loader, 1997a: 155), but it needs to be managed so as to provide an optimum level of policing rather than a maximal one. For that reason, one of the main tasks in the governance of security networks is to negotiate the appropriate balance which should exist between security and alternative values (democracy, free speech, rights of assembly, free association, free movement, etc.). In risk-orientated societies it will also require us to question the assumption that every risk justifies a security response. This, in turn, will demand an end to the dominant assumption – shared by police and their academic critics alike – that risks are, invariably, 'bad things'.

Too much invasive policing?

If, in the future, an optimal model of policing is to be developed it is necessary, not just to focus on the quantity of policing, but also on its quality. In Chapter 4 we looked at police functions in the broader context of risk-induced transformations in policing focusing, in particular, on the relationship between disciplinary and risk-based modes of engagement. One of the implications of this discussion was that new combinations of discipline and risk cut across the categories found in the matrix of police action outlined in Chapter 3. Thus, police use of 'techniques of disorganization' – methods having their basis in the 'informal justice' exercised by commercial and state security – undermines the traditional equation of 'discipline' with 'reactive enforcement' and 'proaction' with 'prevention'. The result is the emergence of specifically *proactive* forms of disciplinary policing. These developments raise two issues. First, in the light of such new combinations, it will be necessary to reassess some of the conventional distinctions – including those contained in the matrix – by which police action is analysed. In particular, the idea that policing constitutes a combination of 'force' and 'service', while true, becomes less and less helpful. Second, risk-orientated thinking makes policing more and more proactive and, by implication, more and more invasive. In Chapter 3 it was suggested that the vacant cell in the matrix (Cell D: minimal-proactive policing), though an impossible mode of *police* action, nevertheless poses a critical problem for the future of *policing*: whether it is possible to minimize the scope of proactive engagement. In the same chapter it was also argued that proaction cannot be limited through minimal policing (Kinsey *et al.*, 1986). The minimalist project rests upon levels of control of police discretion which are unfeasible and which, even if they were not, would almost certainly be counter-productive. Apart from that, rigorous control of police discretion – even if it were possible or desirable – would fail to address the issue of proactive engagement by non-police participants in security networks. Proaction is an inevitable component of late modern policing and it cannot be eradicated by minimalist solutions.

Does this mean that the future of policing is, inevitably, a maximal-proactive one? Marx (1988) argues that the proactive thrust of surveillance-based policing, backed by the unlimited potential contained in sophisticated new technologies, may in the future give rise to a 'maximum security society' (Marx, 1988). Such a society has five characteristic features. It is a dossier society in which computerized records play a vital role; an actuarial or predictive society where the focus of control is on anticipated behaviours; an engineered society where choices are limited by the physical and social environment; a porous society in which the boundaries protecting privacy are weakened; and a self-monitored society where auto-surveillance dominates (Marx, 1988: 221). Many of the technologies which Marx (1988) describes here reflect developments discussed in earlier chapters of this book. They are risk-based, involuntary, of low visibility and capital, rather than labour, intensive. They involve decentralized self-policing. They transcend time and space, enabling data to be collected, collated, stored, retrieved, combined, analysed, communicated, reconstituted and recomposed. They involve a shift from targeting specific subjects to 'categorical suspicion of everyone' (Marx, 1988: 219). They are both more intensive than previous technologies, invading new social and psychic spaces, and more extensive in their scope.

The dangers which Marx (1988) associates with a future maximum security society are, undoubtedly, real. However, it is necessary to be clear about what the term implies. If it is being suggested that a maximum security society is one in which the sovereign state retains a capacity to manipulate and control diverse security technologies for purposes of public domination, then the prognosis is unduly pessimistic. Such an image would be subject to many of the criticisms identified in Cohen's (1989) 'auto-critique' of the concept of social control. Not only does that image overestimate the power of the sovereign state, it assumes a degree of coherence between – and, for that matter, within – security agencies which is rarely achieved. One has only to consider the intra-organizational obstacles to intelligence-led policing for confirmation of this fact. After all, police culture defines information as a commodity to be stored for future personal career advancement, rather than as one to be shared with colleagues for the collective good of the intelligence-led organization. The presence of such obstacles does not undermine the significance of risk-based policing techniques in the construction of a maximum security society, but it reminds us that their implementation is no simple matter. If, however, it is being suggested that the future maximum security society comprises a diversity of proactive security technologies which are subject to greater or lesser degrees of state and non-state governance (from 'governance by government' at one extreme, to unrestricted market anarchy at the other), and in which there may be little or no systematic protection of public interests, then the concept is a useful one. What this second reading of the concept implies, however, is that under late modern conditions the protection of public interests cannot be achieved by the mere reimposition of state sovereignty. Rather, the diverse and invasive policing techniques which constitute the maximum security society will require diverse governance.

Embracing diversity

I am suggesting that diversity is both a precondition of various policing problems (over-policing, invasive policing, unjust, ineffective and unaccountable policing) and a necessary means of their resolution. The dysfunctional consequences of diverse policing will, in the absence of any sovereign solution, demand resolution by diverse means. Diversity has, in other words, to be embraced as a guiding principle of governance. In order to explore this view further, let us consider Loader's (1997a; 1997b) recent analysis.

Optimal policing, as I have described it here, may be defined as a system of security which is neither quantitatively excessive (to the detriment of alternative social values and objectives) nor qualitatively invasive (to the detriment of public freedoms) and which satisfies conditions of public accountability, effectiveness and justice for all. The aim of optimal policing is to secure public interests under conditions in which security is diversified. That objective is consistent with Loader's demand for the development of security as 'a *public good*, available to all citizens within a political community on account simply of their membership of that community' (Loader, 1997a: 159: emphasis in original). However, the concept of public good poses a problem. Hitherto, the sovereign state ('the public sphere') has been conceived as the locus of public interests. Yet, under late modern conditions, the increased fragility of state sovereignty, coupled with its penetration by commercial interests, make it unreasonable to define the state as the exclusive preserve of the public good. The challenge for democratic government is to ensure that the actions of those commercial and civil bodies which participate in democratic decision-making accord with the public good. Though that challenge may be difficult to meet, it is predicated upon the assumption that there is no *immutable* contradiction between public and commercial interests.

It is useful to compare this view with Loader's claim that private security is a contradiction in terms, 'an oxymoronic way of thinking about and delivering community safety' (Loader, 1997a: 155). Loader has three grounds for this contention. First, he suggests that by virtue of its coercive content and/or its exercise of surveillance, policing involves the exercise of political authority and, therefore, requires legitimation. For that reason, private security may be interpreted as a form of 'illegitimate power' (Loader, 1997b: 393, note 76). Second, he maintains that the widespread market distribution of security offends against the principle of policing as an indivisible social good. In consequence, the product of commercial and civil provision is the generation of 'private orders' (Loader, 1997b: 386). Third, he maintains that security is, in essence, a 'shared, collectively generated state-of-affairs [arising] from an overall basis of economic and social well-being' (Loader, 1997a: 155). Each of these arguments has considerable justification though, in each case, a qualification has to be added. Loader's (1997b) first suggestion, that the exercise of the security function demands legitimation, is undoubtedly, true. Yet, it does not follow that commercial security must, invariably, involve the exercise of illegitimate power. My decision to employ a security guard to prevent youths from gathering outside my house may be illegitimate. A decision made by a democratic body to employ a commercial security company to operate, with police and others, under the aegis of an optimal policing plan would be a different matter. Loader's (1997b) second argument, that widespread market distribution of security gives rise to 'private orders', is also true, though the critical issue, surely, is whether democratic intervention can minimize or eradicate those dysfunctions? Loader's (1997a) third point, that security is inseparable from wider considerations of collective well-being, is also incontestable. Yet, there is no inherent reason why, in a market economy, governmental mechanisms should not be put in place to ensure that public interests are effectively represented in security networks composed, in part, of commercial elements. Nor is there any reason why the security policies arising should not be informed by, and integrated with, wider economic and social considerations. To sum up, the term *private* security may well, as Loader (1997a; 1997b) suggests, be a (linguistic) oxymoron, but this does not preclude the involvement of commercial security companies (and other civil bodies) in democratically governed security networks. Once the diversity of policing is accepted that conclusion is inevitable. The only alternative – some implicit demand for the resocialization of security by means of the reimposition of a state monopoly over policing – is an impossible one.

The critical factor for the future, as Loader suggests, is that all forms of security provision which impact on public space should be 'located within some kind of framework of democratic deliberation and decision-making' (Loader, 1997b: 388). It is not the task of this book to consider what that framework should look like, though Loader's (1996; 1997b) own analysis provides a good account of the main issues at stake. Principal among these is that democracy should concern itself not just with how to exert legal controls over those who police, but should also 'develop institutional forms in which considerations of justice and legitimacy can be sustained' (Loader, 1997b: 388). That approach, he suggests, needs to be grounded in certain fundamental principles: that all issues and interests are accorded an equal place in the process of democratic deliberation; that such deliberation proceeds by reference to the common good, participants being required to justify their claims in that light; and that any putative democratic body combines both procedural principles of justice (so maximizing rights of participation) with substantive ones (so ensuring that 'good' outcomes are achieved without prejudicing the rights of minorities or other affected groups). By these means, Loader suggests, it will be possible to defend the idea of security as a public good rather than as a mere 'tradeable commodity' (Loader, 1997b: 389). Undoubtedly, the development of such mechanisms will be a major task for the future, though it will not be an easy one. Crawford (1997) reminds us of two things in this regard. First, we should not delude ourselves that the development of effective democratic mechanisms in the governance of security will eradicate community conflicts. Indeed, under conditions of diversity, conflicts may be a sign of normality rather than an indicator of social pathology (Johnston, 1997b). Second, crime and policing are particularly difficult areas around which to organize 'open, tolerant and inclusive communities' (Crawford, 1997: 312). Under those circumstances, it is particularly important that policing policies are integrated with wider debates about social and economic security, rather than ghettoized under the rhetorical banner of 'law and order'.

Suggestions for further reading

This Guide is divided into six sections. The first two sections cover, respectively, 'General texts and articles' and 'Recent edited collections'. The next three sections follow the thematic structure of the book. Section 3 ('Processes') recommends key texts in three areas 'modern society and the police', 'risk and late modern society' and 'late modernity and governance'. Section 4 ('Functions') outlines important books and articles on the functional dimensions of modern and late modern policing. Section 5 ('Forms') recommends key works on public, commercial, municipal and civil policing. Finally, Section 6 suggests some useful reading on the important theme of 'Policing futures'.

1. General texts and articles

Though originally written in the mid-1980s and revised in the early 1990s, the best single-authored text on British policing remains R. Reiner's *The Politics of the Police*, Hemel Hempstead: Harvester Wheatsheaf, 2nd edn (1992). Though the sections of Reiner's book dealing with police account-ability now need to be read in the light of the recent legislation discussed in Chapter 5 of this book, the text provides an invaluable analysis/synthesis of important debates in a number of fields including police history, police culture, the sociology of police work, crime, police and the media, police effectiveness and the nature and scope of the police function. Another useful text which may be used in conjunction with Reiner's – and is probably best read before embarking on the latter – is *Introducing Policework* by M. Brogden, T. Jefferson and S. Walklate, London: Unwin Hyman (1988). Again, though written a decade ago, the book provides a good analysis of historical and contemporary issues in the field of police work. Two articles written by Reiner during the 1990s provide a good review of past and present research on policing and the police: 'Police research in the United Kingdom: a critical review', in Morris, N. and Tonry, M. (eds) *Modern Policing*, Chicago Illinois: Chicago University Press (1992); and 'Policing and the police', in Maguire, M., Morgan, R. and Reiner, R. (eds) *The Oxford Handbook of Criminology*, Oxford: Clarendon Press (1997): 997–1049.

2. Recent edited collections

Several good edited collections have appeared in the last few years. R. Reiner's collection *Policing*, Aldershot: Dartmouth, two volumes (1996) is part of a multi-volume series (The International Library of Criminology, Criminal Justice and Penology) whose aim is to 'bring together the most significant journal essays' in the field. That aim is, undoubtedly, achieved in the policing volumes, the first alone containing key articles from British and European criminologists as well as papers from North American writers such as Robert Storch, Egon Bittner, Herman Goldstein, George Kelling and James Q. Wilson. *Core Issues in Policing*, edited by F. Leishman, B. Loveday and S. Savage, London: Longman (1996) provides good coverage of contemporary issues in British policing (including management, crime control, crime prevention, public order and police use of force), locating them in the context of recent legislative changes and taking into account debates about globalization and governance. A second edition of this volume will be published in 1999. Another useful collection, *Themes in Contemporary Policing* collated and edited by W. Saulsbury, J. Mott and T. Newburn, London: Independent Inquiry into the Roles and Responsibilities of the Police (1996) grew out of the Police Foundation/Policy Studies Institute inquiry into British policing. The collection consists of papers by a number of British and North American writers whose expertise was drawn upon during the course of the inquiry. The volume covers core themes such as police patrol, the role of private police and the future of police accountability. The best edited volume from North America is *Thinking About Police: Contemporary Readings*, edited by C.B. Klockars and S.D. Mastrofski, New York: McGraw Hill (1991). This is an imaginative collection of papers including extracts from crime fiction (Joseph Wambaugh, Arthur Conan Doyle), coverage of vigilante policing (Richard Maxwell Brown), empirical studies of the efficacy of police patrol (Kelling *et al.*), accounts of undercover police work (Marx), debates about problem-orientated and community policing (Goldstein, Mastrofski) and a discussion about the moral hazards of policing (including Klockars's fascinating discussion of the 'Dirty Harry Problem').

3. Processes

(i) Modern society and the police

C.D. Robinson, R. Scaglion and J.M. Olivero explore anthropological debates on the evolution of social control mechanisms in the transition from pre-state to state formations in their book *Police in Contradiction: The Evolution of the Police Function in Society*, Westport, Connecticut: Greenwood Press (1994). C. Dandeker's *Surveillance, Power and Modernity*, Cambridge: Polity Press (1990) includes a thoughtful analysis of the development of state (especially police and military) power under modern conditions. A good analysis of the emergence of the new police is contained in C. Emsley's *The English Police: A Political and Social History*, 2nd edn, London: Longman (1996). Two papers by Robert Storch 'The plague of blue locusts: police reform and popular resistance in Northern England, 1840–1857, *International Review of Social History* (1975) 20: 61–90 and 'The policeman as domestic missionary: urban discipline and popular culture in Northern England, 1850–1880, *Journal of Social History* (1976), 9, 4: 481–509 provide classic revisionist interpretations of the new police. The first of these articles is reproduced in M. Fitzgerald, G. McLennan and J. Pawson (eds) *Crime and Society: Readings in History and Social Theory*, London: Routledge and Kegan Paul (1981): 86–115, the second in R. Reiner (ed.) *Policing*, Volume 1, Aldershot: Dartmouth (1996): 49–77. The colonial dimension of modern policing, an aspect often ignored in mainstream accounts, is examined in D.M. Anderson and D. Killingray (eds) *Policing the Empire: Government, Authority and Control 1830–1940*, Manchester: Manchester University Press (1991): 1–15 and in M. Brogden 'The emergence of the police – the colonial dimension', *British Journal of Criminology*, (1987) 27, 1: 4–14. Both of these studies draw attention to the critical importance of Irish events in the development of policing in the United Kingdom. Those interested in pursuing that issue should look at S.H. Palmer's monumental work *Police and Protest in Ireland 1780–1850*, Cambridge: Cambridge University Press. A useful comparative study of modern police systems is R. Mawby's *Comparative Policing Issues*, London: Unwin Hyman (1990).

(ii) Risk and late modern society

The definitive account of risk society is contained in U. Beck *Risk Society: Towards a New Modernity*, London: Sage (1992). This may be read in conjunction with A. Giddens *The Consequences of Modernity*, Cambridge: Polity (1990) which covers a number of themes including risk, trust and time–space distanciation. Two excellent texts dealing with the themes of globalization and modernity are S. Crook, J. Pakulski and M. Waters *Postmodernization: Change in Advanced Society*, London: Sage (1993) and M. Waters *Globalization*, London: Routledge (1995). For articles relating late modern themes to criminology see, D. Nelken (ed.) *The Futures of Criminology*, London: Sage (1994) – especially the papers by Ericson and Carriere and Feely and Simon.

(iii) Late modernity and governance

Though both Rose and O'Malley eschew the concept of late modernity, preferring to adopt a 'genealogical' approach to governance, their analyses have had a direct bearing on the arguments contained in this book. Rose's analysis of 'advanced liberalism', N. Rose, 'The death of the social? refiguring the territory of government', *Economy and Society* (1996), 25, 3: 327–56, locates the problem of governance in the context of contemporary societal change. Two papers by O'Malley (J. O'Malley 'Risk, power and crime prevention', *Economy and Society* (1992), 21, 3: 252–75; and J. O'Malley and D. Palmer 'Post-Keynesian policing', *Economy and Society* (1996), 25, 2: 137–55) consider crime prevention and policing as governmental practices. Further interesting applications of the governance debate to crime and policing may be found in K. Stenson, 'Community policing as governmental technology', *Economy and Society* (1993), 22, 3: 373–99 and in D. Garland, 'The limits of the sovereign state: strategies of crime control in contemporary society', *British Journal of Criminology* (1996), 36, 4: 445–71. A useful examination of debates about state fragmentation is contained in A. Crawford, *The Local Governance of Crime: Appeals to Community and Partnerships*, Oxford: Clarendon (1997), Chapter 6. A full exposition of the principles of associationalism may be found in P. Hirst, *Associative Democracy: New Forms of Economic and Social Governance*, Cambridge: Polity (1994). A recent application of Hirst's argument to the reform of the Australian system of criminal justice is contained in R. Hogg and D. Brown, *Rethinking Law and Order*, Annandale, NSW: Pluto Press, (1998): 211–17.

4. Functions

The standard analysis of the modern police function is E. Bittner's *The Functions of the Police in Modern Society*, Chevy Chase: National Institute of Mental Health (1970). An extract from the 1980 edition of this book (published in Cambridge Massachusetts by Olegeschlager, Gunn & Hain) is contained in C.B. Klockars and S.D. Mastrofski (eds) *Thinking About Police*, New York: McGraw Hill (1992): 35–51. An equally influential study is J.Q. Wilson's *Varieties of Police Behaviour*, Cambridge, Massachusetts: Harvard University Press (1968). A recent paper by D.H. Bayley 'What do police do'? in W. Saulsbury *et al.* (eds) *Themes in Contemporary Policing*, London: Independent Inquiry into the Roles and Responsibilities of the Police (1996): 29–41 provides an illuminating account of the realities of police work, while M. Punch and T. Naylor's 'The police: a social service',

New Society, 24, (1973): 358–61, though somewhat dated, gives a useful empirical account of the various dimensions of the modern police function in Britain. Police functions under late modern conditions are, increasingly, orientated towards the management and minimization of risk. In addition to O'Malley's writings (cited in Section 3 (iii) above), Ericson's recent work on risk provides a solid basis for understanding these developments. Three sources are particularly relevant: R. Ericson, 'The division of expert knowledge in policing and security', *British Journal of Sociology* (1994), 45, 2: 149–75; R. Ericson and K. Carriere 'The fragmentation of criminology', in D. Nelken (ed.) *The Futures of Criminology*, London: Sage (1994): 89–109; and R. Ericson and K. Haggerty *Policing the Risk Society*, Oxford: Clarendon (1997). For an application of the concept of risk-based policing to the practice of community policing see L. Johnston, 'Policing communities of risk', in Francis, P., Davies, P. and Jupp, V. (eds) *Policing Futures: The Police, Law Enforcement and the Twenty-First Century*, London: Macmillan (1997): 186–207. Finally, the left realist attempt to subject the modern police function to democratic control by means of the imposition of 'minimal policing', though flawed, remains one of the few serious attempts to address this important issue. The argument is a stimulating one and may be found in R. Kinsey, J. Lea and J. Young, *Losing the Fight Against Crime*, Oxford: Blackwell (1986).

5. Forms

(i) Public police

T. Jefferson and R. Grimshaw's *Controlling the Constable*, London: Muller (1984) provides a thought-provoking analysis of the problem of democratic police governance. L. Lustgarten's *The Governance of Police*, London: Sweet and Maxwell (1986) offers a rigorous analysis of the issues surrounding police accountability. Ian Loader's *Youth, Policing and Democracy*, London: Macmillan (1996) draws upon Jefferson and Grimshaw's analysis to construct a model of democratic policing relevant to the managerialist conditions pertaining under PMCA. The first empirical study of the effects of PMCA is contained in T. Jones and T. Newburn's *Policing After the Act*, London: Policy Studies Institute (1997). An excellent book on police governance in a European context is M. Anderson, M. Den Boer, P. Cullen, W.C. Raab and N. Walker's *Policing the European Union*, Oxford: Clarendon Press (1995) while J. Sheptycki's 'Transnational policing and the making of the modern state' *British Journal of Criminology* (1995), 35, 4: 613–35 offers a valuable analysis of the governmental implications of transnationalism. Though now ten years old J.R. Green and S.D. Mastrofski's (eds) *Community Policing Rhetoric or Reality?* New York: Praeger (1988) contains many useful articles on the pros and cons of community policing.

A forceful critique of community policing in Britain is contained in P. Gordons's 'Community policing: towards the local police state'? *Critical Social Policy* (1984), 10: 39–58. This article is reproduced in P. Scraton (ed.) *Law, Order and the Authoritarian State*, Milton Keynes: Open University (1987). A good collection of articles on public order policing in Britain may be found in C. Critcher and D. Waddington (eds) *Policing Public Order: Theoretical and Practical Issues*, Aldershot: Avebury (1996) while two valuable, though contrasting, perspectives on public order policing are T. Jefferson's *The Case Against Paramilitary Policing*, Milton Keynes: Open University (1990) and P.A.J. Waddington's *Liberty and Order: Public Order Policing in a Capital City*, London: UCL Press (1994).

(ii) Commercial policing

Literature on commercial policing – like that on municipal and civil policing – remains relatively sparse, though it has begun to grow in recent years. The books by N. South *Policing for Profit*, London: Sage (1988) and L. Johnston, *The Rebirth of Private Policing*, London: Routledge (1992) combine discussion of the growth of the private sector with consideration of its impact on governance, the state and the public sphere. T. Jones and T. Newburn's *Private Security and Public Policing*, Oxford: Clarendon Press (1998) provides the most reliable estimate yet of the British commercial security sector's size, as well as an analysis of its structure and. function. The edited collection by C.D. Shearing and P.C. Stenning (eds) *Private Policing*, California: Sage (1987) contains a number of important papers (not least the editors' own contribution) while Shearing and Stenning's 'Modern private security: its growth and implications' in M. Tonry and N. Morris (eds) *Crime and Justice: An Annual Review of Research*, Vol. 3, Chicago: University of Chicago Press (1981): 193–245 remains a seminal article.

(iii) Municipal policing

L. Johnston's 'Privatization and protection: spatial and sectoral ideologies in British policing and crime prevention', *Modern Law Review* (1993), 56, 6: 771–92 contains an analysis of recent developments in municipal policing together with a discussion of their legal and political significance. Jones and Newburn's *Private Security and Public Policing* (see, Section 5 (ii) above) includes a detailed empirical study of municipal initiatives in one London borough. The article by A. Hauba, B. Hofstra, L. Toornvliet and A. Zandbergen 'Some new forms of functional social control in the Netherlands and their effects', *British Journal of Criminology* (1996), 36, 2: 199–219 outlines developments in the Netherlands, while an earlier article by R. Kania 'The French municipal police experiment', *Police Studies* (1989), 12, 3: 125–31 does the same for France.

(iv) Civil policing

R.M. Brown's *Strain of Violence*, New York: Oxford University Press (1975) rightly remains the definitive work on American vigilantism. A conceptual discussion of vigilantism and civil policing may be found in L. Johnston 'What is vigilantism'? *British Journal of Criminology* (1996), 36, 2: 220–36. A new book by R. Abrahams, *Vigilant Citizens: Vigilantism and the State*, Cambridge: Polity Press (1998) explores the anthropological, historical and contemporary evidence on vigilantism and discusses its political implications. M. Brogden and C.D. Shearing's *Policing for a New South Africa*, London: Routledge (1993) provides a thoughtful discussion of civil policing in South Africa and its relationship to public and commercial modes.

6. Policing futures

Reiner's article 'Policing a postmodern society', *Modern Law Review* (1992), 55, 6: 761–81 gives a perceptive analysis of the impact of contemporary social change on policing. P. Francis *et al.* (eds) *Policing Futures* (full reference in Section 4 above) contains an interesting collection of papers on various futuristic themes ranging from crime control to the policing of cyberspace. D.H. Bayley's *Police for the Future*, New York: Oxford University Press (1994) draws upon the author's lengthy experience of comparative research to contemplate the future of public policing while R. Morgan and T. Newburn, *The Future of Policing*, Oxford: Clarendon (1997) address a number of issues including, privatization, nationalization and the future of police patrol. D.H. Bayley and C.D. Shearing 'The future of policing', *Law and Society Review* (1996), 30, 3: 585–606 make some radical proposals for the effective governance of pluralistic policing systems while I. Loader 'Thinking normatively about private security', *Journal of Law and Society* (1997), 24, 3: 377–94 considers the normative implications of having policing systems in which commercial security plays an increasing role. Finally, for those who regard pluralistic policing as inherently divisive and oppressive – or for those eternal pessimists who take pleasure in nightmare scenarios – M. Davis's account of policing in Los Angeles *Beyond Blade Runner: Urban Control: The Ecology of Fear*, Westfield N.J.: Open Magazine Pamphlet Series (1992) provides fascinating reading.

Bibliography

Abrahams, R. (1987) 'Sungusungu: Village Vigilante Groups in Tanzania', *African Affairs*, 86, 343: 179–96.

Ackroyd, C., Margolis, K., Rosenhead, J. and Shallice, T. (1977) *The Technology of Political Control*, Harmondsworth: Penguin.

ACPO (1988) *A Review of the Private Security Industry*, North Wales Police.

ACPO (1990) *Strategic Policy Document: Setting the Standards for Policing: Meeting Community Expectation*, London: New Scotland Yard.

Alderson, J. (1979) *Policing Freedom*, Plymouth: McDonald & Evans.

Alderson, J. (1982) 'Policing the Eighties', *Marxism Today*, April: 9–14.

Anderson, D.M. and Killingray, D. (1991) 'Consent, Coercion and Colonial Control: Policing the Empire, 1830–1940', in Anderson, D.M. and Killingray, D. (eds) *Policing the Empire: Government, Authority and Control 1830–1940*, Manchester: Manchester University Press: 1–15.

Anderson, M. (1994) 'The Agenda for Police Cooperation', in Anderson, M. and Den Boer, M. (eds) *Policing Across National Boundaries*, London: Pinter: 3–21.

Anderson, M., Den Boer, M., Cullen, P., Gilmore, W.C., Raab, C. and Walker, N. (1995) *Policing the European Union*, Oxford: Clarendon Press.

Ascoli, D. (1979) *The Queen's Peace*, London: Hamish Hamilton.

Audit Commission (1990) *Effective Policing. Performance Review in Police Forces. Police Paper No. 8*, London: Audit Commission.

Audit Commission (1993) *Helping With Enquiries: Tackling Crime Effectively*, London: Audit Commission.

Audit Commission (1994) *Cheques and Balances: A Framework for Improving Police Accountability*, London: Audit Commission.

Audit Commission (1996) *Streetwise: Effective Police Patrol*, London: Audit Commission.

Bagguley, P., Mark-Lawson, J., Shapiro, D., Urry, J., Walby, S. and Warde, A. (1990) *Restructuring: Place, Class and Gender*, London: Sage.

Ballantyne, R. (1998) 'Pushbutton Terrors', *The Guardian Online*, 29 January: 12.

Barbalet, R.M. (1988) *Citizenship*, Milton Keynes: Open University Press.

Bayley, D.H. (1988) 'Community Policing: A Report From the Devil's Advocate', in Greene, J.R. and Mastrofski. S.D. (eds) *Community Policing Rhetoric or Reality?* New York: Praeger: 225–37.

Bayley, D.H. (1994) *Police for the Future*, New York: Oxford University Press.

Bayley, D.H. (1996) 'What Do Police Do'? in Saulsbury, W., Mott, J. and Newburn, T. (eds) *Themes in Contemporary Policing*, London: Independent Inquiry into the Roles and Responsibilities of the Police: 29–41.

Bayley, D.H. and Shearing, C.D. (1996) 'The Future of Policing', *Law and Society Review*, 30, 3: 585–606.

Beck, U. (1992) *Risk Society: Towards a New Modernity*, London: Sage.

Beck, U. (1996) 'Risk Society and the Provident State', in Lash, S., Szerszynski, B. and Wynne, B. (eds) *Risk, Environment and Modernity*, London: Sage: 27–43.

Bennett, T. (1994) 'Recent Developments in Community Policing', in Stephens, M. and Becker, S. (eds) *Police Force, Police Service*, London: Macmillan: 107–29.

Bennett, T. (1995) 'Evaluating Police and Public Performance in the Delivery of Community Policing', in *Workshop on Evaluating Police Service Delivery: Report*. Ministry of the Solicitor General of Canada/International Centre for Comparative Criminology, University of Montreal: 316–47.

Benyon, J. (1994) 'Policing the European Union: The Changing Basis of Cooperation on Law Enforcement', *International Affairs*, 70, 497–517.

Benyon, J. (1996) 'The Politics of Police Co-operation in the European Union', *International Journal of the Sociology of Law*, 24, 4: 353–79.

Benyon, J., Turnbull, L., Willis, A., Woodward, R. and Beck, A. (1993) *Police Co-operation in Europe: An Investigation*. Leicester: Centre for the Study of Public Order, University of Leicester.

Bigo, D. (1994) 'The European Internal Security Field: Stakes and Rivalries in a Newly Developing Area of Police Intervention', in Anderson, M. and Den Boer, M. (eds) *Policing Across National Boundaries*, London: Pinter: 161–73.

Bittner, E. (1991) 'The Function of Police in Modern Society', in Klockars, C.D. and Mastrofski, S.D. (eds) *Thinking About Police*, New York: McGraw Hill: 35–51.

Blair, I (1994) 'Let the Police Fund Their Own Expansion' *The Times*, 1 October.

Boothroyd, J. (1989) 'Nibbling Away at the Bobby's Patch', *Police Review*, 13 January: 64–5.

Bottoms, A. and Wiles, P. (1996) 'Understanding Crime Prevention in Late Modern Societies', in Bennett, T. (ed.) *Preventing Crime and Disorder: Targeting Strategies and Responsibilities*, Cambridge: Institute of Criminology: 1–42.

Bowden, T. (1978) *Beyond the Limits of the Law*, Harmondsworth: Penguin.

Brearley, N. and King, M. (1996) 'Policing, Social Protest: Some Indicators of Change', in Critcher, C. and Waddington, D. (eds) *Policing Public Order: Theoretical and Practical Issues*, Aldershot: Avebury: 101–16.

Brewer, J. and Styles, J. (1980) *An Ungovernable People*, London: Hutchinson.

Brewer, J.D. (1996) 'Police–Society Relations in Northern Ireland', in Critcher, C. and Waddington, D. (eds) *Policing Public Order: Theoretical and Practical Issues*, Aldershot: Avebury: 147–56.

Brewer, J.D., Guelke, A., Hume, I., Moxon-Browne, and Wilford, R. (1996) *The Police, Public Order and the State*, London: Macmillan.

Brewer, J.D. with Magee, K. (1991) *Inside the RUC: Routine Policing in a Divided Society*, Oxford: Clarendon.

Brodeur, J.P. (1983) 'High Policing and Low Policing: Remarks About the Policing of Political Activities', *Social Problems*, 30: 507–20.

Brogden, M. (1987) 'The Emergence of the Police – the Colonial Dimension', *British Journal of Criminology*, 27, 1: 4–14.

Brogden, M., Jefferson, T. and Walklate, S. (1988) *Introducing Policework*, London: Unwin Hyman.

Brogden, M. and Shearing, C.D. (1993) *Policing For a New South Africa*, London: Routledge.

Brown, R.M. (1975) *Strain of Violence*, New York: Oxford University Press.

Bunyan, T. (1977) *The History and Practice of the Political Police in Britain*, London: Quartet.

Bunyan, T. (1991) 'Towards an Authoritarian European State', *Race and Class*, 32, 3: 19–27.

Bunyan, T. (1993) *Statewatching the New Europe*, London: Statewatch.

Burrows, W.E. (1976) *Vigilante*, New York: Harcourt Brace Jovanovich.

Butler, A.J.P. (1984) *Police Management*, London: Gower.

Butler, A.J.P. (1996) 'Managing the Future: A Chief Constable's View', in Leishman, F., Loveday, B. and Savage, S. (eds) *Core Issues in Policing*, London: Longman: 218–30.

Button, M. (1998) 'Under-researched, Under-utilized and Underestimated: Private Security and its Contribution to Policing', *Institute of Police and Criminological Studies Occasional Paper No. 8*, Portsmouth: University of Portsmouth.

Caddle, D. (1995) *A Survey of the Prisoner Escort and Custody Service Provided By Group 4 and By Securicor Custodial Services*, London: Home Office Research and Planning Unit Paper 93.

Cain, M. (1996) 'Policing There and Here: Reflections on an international Comparison', *International Journal of the Sociology of Law*, 24, 4: 399–426.

Campbell, D. (1996) 'Drug Dealers in Crime Phonelines War', *The Guardian*, 3 September.

Carr, F. (1996) 'The New Security Politics in Europe', *International Journal of the Sociology of Law*, 24, 4: 381–398.

Castel, R. (1991) 'From Dangerousness to Risk', in Burchall, G., Gordon, C. and Miller, P. (eds) *The Foucault Effect*, London: Harvester Wheatsheaf: 251–80.

CIPFA (1989) *Financial Information Service, Vol. 24, Law and Order*, London: Chartered Institute of Public Finance.

Clarke, M. (1989) 'Insurance Fraud', *British Journal of Criminology*, 29, 1: 1–20.

Cohen, J.L. and Arato, A. (1992) *Civil Society and Political Theory*, Cambridge Massachusetts: MIT Press.

Cohen, S. (1983) 'Social Control Talk: Telling Stories About Correctional Change', in Garland, D. and Young, P. (eds) *The Power to Punish*, London: Heinemann.

Cohen, S. (1985) *Visions of Social Control*, Cambridge: Polity Press.

Cohen, S. (1989) 'The Critical Discourse on "Social Control": Note on the Concept as a Hammer', *International Journal of the Sociology of Law*, 17: 347–57.

Coleman, R. and Sim, J. (1996) 'From the Dockyards to the Disney Store: Surveillance, Risk and Security in Liverpool City Centre', paper presented to *Joint Meeting of the American Law and Society Association and the Research Committee on the Sociology of Law of the International Sociological Association*, Glasgow, 10–13 July.

Conway, P. (1993) 'The Informal Justice system in N. Ireland', paper presented to the British Criminology Conference, University of Cardiff, July.

Cope, S., Leishman, F. and Starie, P. (1995) 'Hollowing-out and Hiving-off: Reinventing Policing in Britain', in Lovenduski, J. and Stanyer, J. (eds) *Contemporary Political Studies*, Vol. 2, Belfast: Political Studies Association of the United Kingdom: 552–65.

Crawford, A. (1995) 'Appeals to Community and Crime Prevention', *Crime, Law and Social Change*, 22: 97–126.

Crawford, A. (1997) *The Local Governance of Crime: Appeals to Community and Partnerships*, Oxford: Clarendon Press.

Critchley, T.A. (1978) *A History of the Police in England and Wales*, London: Constable.

Crook, S., Pakulski, J. and Waters, M. (eds) (1993) *Postmodernization: Change in Advanced Society*, London: Sage.

Cunningham, W.C., Strauchs, J.J. and Van Meter, C.W. (1990) *Private Security Trends 1970 to 2000: The Hallcrest Report II*, Boston: Butterworth-Heinemann.

Cunningham, W.C. and Taylor, T. (1985) *Private Security and Police in America: The Hallcrest Report I*, Boston: Butterworth-Heinemann.

Dandeker, C. (1990) *Surveillance, Power and Modernity*, Cambridge: Polity Press.

Davey, B.J. (1983) *Lawless and Immoral*, Leicester: Leicester University Press.

Davies, S. (1989) 'Streets Ahead', *Police Review*, 10 November: 2277.

Dean, J. (1997a) 'Mallon's Law', *Police Review*, 18 April: 22–3.

Dean, J. (1997b) 'Combined Tactics', *Police Review*, 18 April: 22–3.

Den Boer, M. (1994) 'The Quest for European Policing: Rhetoric and Justification in a Disorderly Debate', in Anderson, M. and Den Boer, M. (eds) *Policing Across National Boundaries*, London: Pinter: 174–96.

Dennis, N. and Erdos, G. (1992) *Families Without Fatherhood*, London: IEA Health and Welfare Unit.

Dennis, N. and Mallon, R. (1997) 'Confident Policing in Hartlepool', in Dennis, N. (ed.) *Zero Tolerance: Policing a Free Society*, London: IEA Health and Welfare Unit: 61–86.

de Waard, J. (1993) 'The Private Security Sector in Fifteen European Countries: Size, Rules and Legislation', *Security Journal*, 4, 2: 58–63.

de Waard, J.J. and van der Hoek, J. (1991) *Private Security: Size of Sector and Legislation in the Netherlands and Europe*, The Hague: Dept. of Crime Prevention, Ministry of Justice.

Donovan, E.J. and Walsh, W.F. (1986) *An Evaluation of Starrett City Security Services*, Pennsylvania: Pennsylvania State University.

Donzelot, J. (1979) *The Policing of Families*, London: Hutchinson.

Dorn, N., Murji, K. and South, N. (1992) *Traffickers: Drug Markets and Law Enforcement*, London: Routledge.

Downes, D. and Morgan, R. (1997) 'Dumping the "Hostages to Fortune"? The Politics of Law and Order in Post-war Britain', in Maguire, M., Morgan, R. and Reiner, R. (eds) *The Oxford Handbook of Criminology*, Oxford: Clarendon: 87–134.

Drucker, H.M. (ed. 1979) *Multi-Party Britain*, London: Macmillan.

Dunleavy, P. (1980) *Urban Political Analysis*, London: Macmillan.

Dunnighan, C. and Norris, C. (1997) 'Subterranean Blues: Conflict as an Unintended Consequence of the Police Use of Informers', paper presented to *British Criminology Conference*, The Queens University Belfast, July.

Durkheim, E. (1964) *The Division of Labour in Society*, New York: Free Press.

Dyson, K. (1994) *Elusive Union*, London: Longman.

Eck, J.E. and Spelman, W. (1987) 'Who Ya Gonna call? The Police as Problem Busters', *Crime and Delinquency*, 33: 31–52.

Edgell, S., Walklate, S. and Williams, G. (eds 1994) *Debating the Future of the Public Sphere*, Aldershot: Avebury.

Edwards, A. (1994) 'Thatcherism, Authoritarian Statism and the Dispersal of Discipline: Problems in Conceptualising Law and Order in the 1980s', paper presented to the Politics of Law and Order Group Panel, *Political Studies Association Annual Conference*, University of Swansea, March: 1–16.

Elliott, N. (1989) *Streets Ahead*, London: Adam Smith Institute.

Ericson, R. (1994) 'The Division of Expert Knowledge in Policing and Security', *British Journal of Sociology*, 45, 2: 149–75.

Ericson, R. and Carriere, K. (1994) 'The Fragmentation of Criminology', in Nelken, D. (ed.) *The Futures of Criminology*, London: Sage: 89–109.

Ericson, R. and Haggerty, K. (1996) 'The Population of Police', paper presented to the *Joint Meeting of the American Law and Society Association and the Research Committee on the Sociology of Law of the International Sociological Association*, Glasgow, 10–13 July.

Ethington, P.J. (1987) 'Vigilantes and the Police: The Creation of a Professional Police Bureaucracy in San Francisco 1847–1900', *Journal of Social History*, 21, 2: 197–227.

Etzioni, A. (1993) *The Spirit of Community: The Reinvention of American Society*, New York: Simon & Schuster.

Ewald, F. (1991) 'Insurance and Risk', in Burchall, G., Gordon, C. and Miller, P. (eds) *The Foucault Effect*, London: Harvester Wheatsheaf: 197–210.

Factor, F. and Stenson, K. (1987) 'At the End of the Line', *Youth in Society*, January: 18–19.

Factor, F. and Stenson, K. (1989) 'Community Control and the Policing of Jewish Youth', paper presented to British Criminology Conference, Bristol Polytechnic, July.

Featherstone, M. (1991) *Consumer Culture and Postmodernism*, London: Sage.

Feeley, M. and Simon, J. (1994) 'Actuarial Justice: The Emerging New Criminal Law', in Nelken, D. (ed.) *The Futures of Criminology*, London: Sage: 173–201.

Field, J. (1981) 'Police, Power and Community in a Provincial English Town: Portsmouth 1815–75', in Bailey, V. (ed.) *Policing and Punishment in Nineteenth Century Britain*, London: Croom Helm: 42–64.

Fielding, N. (1996) 'Enforcement, Service and Community Models of Policing', in Saulsbury, W., Mott, J. and Newburn, T. (eds) *Themes in Contemporary Policing*, London: Independent Inquiry into the Roles and Responsibilities of the Police: 42–59.

Fielding, N., Kemp, C. and Norris, C. (1989) 'Constraints on the Practice of Community Policing', in Morgan, R. and Smith, D.J. (eds) *Coming to Terms with Policing*, London: Routledge: 49–63.

Foucault, M. (1977) *Discipline and Punish: The Birth of the Prison*, London: Allen Lane.

Foucault, M. (1991) 'Governmentality', in Burchell, G., Gordon, C. and Miller, P. (eds) *The Foucault Effect*, London: Harvester Wheatsheaf: 87–104.

Garland, D. (1996) 'The Limits of the Sovereign State: Strategies of Crime Control in Contemporary Society', *British Journal of Criminology*, 36, 4: 445–71.

Garrett, A. (1997) 'When Rising Crime Equals Rising Profits', *The Observer*, 8 June.

Gaylord, M.S. and Traver, H. (1995) 'Colonial Policing and the Demise of British Rule in Hong Kong', *International Journal of the Sociology of Law*, 23, 1: 23–43.

George, B. and Button, M. (1998) 'Too Little too Late? An Assessment of Recent Proposals for the Private Security Industry in the United Kingdom' *Security Journal*, 10: 1–7.

Gibbons, S. (1996a) 'Change to Criminal Investigation Planned to Save Time and Money', *Police Review*, 23 August: 4.

Gibbons, S. (1996b) 'Private Function', *Police Review*, 9 February; 15–17.

Gibbons, S. (1996c) 'Problem Solved'? *Police Review*, 29 November: 22–4.

Gibbons, S. (1997a) 'Euro "Feds"' *Police Review*, 3 January: 14–15.

Gibbons, S. (1997b) 'Bugging Tactics', *Police Review*, 31 January: 25–6.

Gibbons, S. and Hyder, K. (1996) 'MI5 Crime-fighting Role Needs Tighter Control Says Sharples', *Police Review*, 19 January: 5.

Giddens, A. (1990) *The Consequences of Modernity*, Cambridge: Polity.

Gill, M. and Thrasher, M. (eds 1985) 'Problems in Implementing Community Policing', *Policy and Politics*, 13, 1: 37–52.

Gill, P. (1994) *Policing Politics: Security Intelligence and the Liberal Democratic State*, London: Frank Cass.

GLC (1983) *A New Police Authority for London*, London: Greater London Council.

Goldstein, H. (1979) 'Policing: A Problem-oriented Approach', *Crime and Delinquency*, 25: 236–58.

Gordon, P. (1984) 'Community Policing: Towards the Local Police State'? *Critical Social Policy*, 10: 39–58.

Grabosky, P. (1996) 'Telecommunications and Crime: Dimensions and Dilemmas', Paper presented at the Annual Meeting of the Law and Society Association, Glasgow, July.

Graham, V. (1996) 'Warning on Russian Mafia Threat', *Police Review*, 24 May.

Green, P. (1989) *Private Sector Involvement in the Immigration Detention Centres*, London: The Howard League for Penal Reform.

Greene, J.R. and Klockars, C.B. (1991) 'What Police Do', in Klockars, C.B. and Mastrofski, S.D. (eds) *Thinking About Police*, New York: McGraw-Hill: 273–84.

Griffiths, W. (1997) 'Zero Tolerance – A View from London', paper presented to the *IEA Zero-Tolerance Policing Conference*, London, 12 June.

Hall, S. (1979) *Drifting into a Law and Order Society*, London: Cobden Trust.

Hall, S., Critcher, C., Jefferson, T., Clarke, J. and Roberts, B. (1978) *Policing the Crisis: Mugging, the State and Law and Order*, London: Macmillan.

Hauber, A., Hofstra, B., Toornvliet, L. and Zandbergen, A. (1996) 'Some New Forms of Functional Social Control in the Netherlands and their Effects' *British Journal of Criminology*, 36, 2: 199–219.

Hawkins, R. (1991) 'The "Irish Model" and the Empire: A Case for Reassessment', in Anderson, M. and Killingray, D. (eds) *Policing The Empire: Government, Authority and Control, 1830–1940*, Manchester: Manchester University Press: 18–32.

Heald, S. (1986) 'Mafias in Africa: The Rise of Drinking Companies and Vigilante Groups in Bugisu District, Uganda', *Africa*, 56, 4: 446–66.

Hebenton, B. and Thomas, T. (1995) *Policing Europe: Co-operation, Conflict and Control*, London: Macmillan.

Hebenton, W. and Thomas, T. (1996) 'Sexual Offenders in the Community: Reflections on Problems of Law, Community and Risk Management in the USA and England', *International Journal of the Sociology of Law*, 24, 4: 427–43.

Heidensohn, F. (1991) 'Introduction: Convergence, Diversity and Change', in Heidensohn, F. and Farrell, M. (eds) *Crime in Europe*, London: Routledge: 3–13.

Held, D. and McGrew, A. (1993) 'Globalization and the Liberal Democratic State', *Government and Opposition*, 28, 2: 261–88.

Hesselling, R.B.P. (1995) 'Functional Surveillance in the Netherlands: Exemplary Projects', *Security Journal*, 6, 1: 21–5.

Hills, A. (1995) 'Militant Tendencies: "Paramilitarism" in the British Police', *British Journal of Criminology*, 35, 3: 450–8.

Hillyard, P. (1997) 'Policing Divided Societies: Trends and Prospects in Northern Ireland and Britain', in Francis, P., Davies, P. and Jupp, V. (eds) *Policing Futures; The Police, Law Enforcement and the Twenty-First Century*, London: Macmillan: 163–85.

Hindess, B. (1982) 'Power, Interests and the Outcome of Struggles', *Sociology*, 16, 4: 498–511.

Hirst, P. (ed.) (1989) *The Pluralist Theory of the State*, London: Routledge.

Hirst, P. (1993) 'Associational Democracy', in Held, D. (ed.) *Prospects for Democracy*, Cambridge: Polity: 112–35.

Hirst, P. (1994) *Associative Democracy: New Forms of Economic and Social Governance*, Cambridge: Polity.

Hirst, P. (1996) 'Democracy and Civil Society', in Hirst, P. and Khilnani, S. (eds) *Reinventing Democracy*, Oxford: Blackwell: 97–116.

Hirst, P. and Thompson, G. (1995) 'Globalization and the Future of the Nation State', *Economy and Society*, 24, 3: 408–42.

HMSO (1962) *Royal Commission on the Police*, London: HMSO. Cmnd. 1728.

HMSO (1993) *Inquiry into Police Responsibilities and Rewards. Final Report*, London: HMSO.

Home Office (1979) *The Private Security Industry: A Discussion Paper*, London: HMSO.

Home Office (1984) *Crime Prevention*, Home Office Circular 8/84, London: Home Office.

Home Office (1991) *Safer Communities: The Local Delivery of Crime Prevention Through the Partnership Approach*, London: Home Office.

Home Office (1993) *Police Reform: A Police Service for the Twenty-First Century*, London: HMSO.

Home Office (1995) *Review of Police Core and Ancillary Tasks*, London: HMSO.

Hood, C. (1991) 'A Public Management for all Seasons'? *Public Administration*, 69, 1: 3–19.

Hoogenboom, A.B. (1989) 'The Privatization of Social Control', in Hood, R. (ed.) *Crime and Criminal Policy in Europe: Proceedings of a European Colloquium, 3–6 July 1988*, Oxford: University of Oxford Centre for Criminological Research: 121–4.

Hough, M. (1985) 'Organization and Resource Management in the Uniformed Police', in Heal, K., Tarling, R. and Burrows, J. (eds) *Policing Today*, London: HMSO.

Hough, M. (1996) 'The Police Patrol Function: What Research Can Tell Us', in Saulsbury, W., Mott, J. and Newburn, T. (eds) *Themes in Contemporary Policing*, London: Independent Inquiry into the Roles and Responsibilities of the Police: 60–71.

House of Commons (1995) 'First Report of the Home Affairs Committee Session 1994–5' *The Private Security Industry*, Vol. 1, HC 17–1, London: HMSO.

Hudson, B. (1996) *Understanding Justice*, Buckingham: Open University Press.

Hughes, G. (1996) 'Communitarianism and Law and Order', *Critical Social Policy*, 49: 17–41.

Hyder, K. (1996) 'Customs Aim to Take on the Mobs', *The Observer*, 12 May.

I'Anson, J. and Wiles, P. (1995) *The Sedgefield Community Force*, Centre for Criminological and Legal Research, University of Sheffield.

Illich, I. (1975) *Medical Nemesis: The Expropriation of Health*, London: Marion Boyars.

Jacobs, J. (1961) *The Death and Life of Great American Cities*, New York: Vintage.

James, A.L. Bottomley, A.K., Clare, E. and Liebling, A. (1997) *Privatizing Prisons: Rhetoric and Reality*, London: Sage.

JCC (Joint Consultative Committee) (1990) *Operational Policing Review. Policing in the Nineties*, Avon & Somerset Constabulary.

Jefferson, T. (1987) 'Beyond Paramilitarism', *British Journal of Criminology*, 27, 1: 47–53.

Jefferson, T. (1990) *The Case Against Paramilitary Policing*, Milton Keynes: Open University.

Jefferson, T. (1993) 'Pondering Paramilitarism', *British Journal of Criminology*, 33, 3: 374–81.

Jefferson, T. and Grimshaw, R. (1984) *Controlling the Constable*, London: Muller.

Jeffries, Sir Charles (1952) *The Colonial Police*, London: Max Parrish.

Jessop, B. (1993) 'Towards a Schumpeterian Workfare State? Preliminary Remarks on Post-Fordist Political Economy', *Studies in Political Economy*, 40: 7–39.

Johnston, L. (1986) *Marxism, Class Analysis and Socialist Pluralism*, London: Allen & Unwin.

Johnston, L. (1988) 'Controlling Police Work: Problems of Organisational Reform in Large Public Bureaucracies', *Work, Employment and Society*, 2, 1: 51–70.

Johnston, L. (1992a) *The Rebirth of Private Policing*, London: Routledge.

Johnston, L. (1992b) 'An Unseen Force: The Ministry of Defence Police in the UK', *Policing and Society*, 3, 4: 23–40.

Johnston, L. (1993a) 'Privatization and Protection: Spatial and Sectoral Ideologies in British Policing and Crime Prevention', *Modern Law Review*, 56, 6: 771–92.

Johnston, L. (1993b) 'Vigilantism and Informal Justice in the United Kingdom', paper presented to British Criminology Conference, University of Cardiff, 28–31 July.

Johnston, L. (1994) 'Policing Plutonium: Issues in the Provision of Policing Services and Security Systems at Nuclear Facilities and for Related Materials in Transit', *Policing and Society*, 4: 53–72.

Johnston, L. (1996a) 'Policing Diversity: The Impact of the Public-Private Complex in Policing', in Leishman, F., Loveday, B. and Savage, S. (eds) *Core Issues in Policing*, London: Longman: 54–70.

Johnston, L. (1996b) 'What is Vigilantism'? *British Journal of Criminology*, 36, 2: 220–36.

Johnston, L. (1997a) 'New Labour and the Usual Suspects', *The Chartist*, March–April: 14–15.

Johnston, L. (1997b) 'Policing Communities of Risk', in Francis, P., Davies, P. and Jupp, V. (eds) *Policing Futures. The Police, Law Enforcement and the Twenty-First Century*, London: Macmillan: 186–207.

Johnston, L. (forthcoming) 'Transnational Private Policing'.

Jones, J.M. (1980) *Organisational Aspects of Police Behaviour*, Aldershot: Gower.

Jones, T. and Newburn, T. (1995) 'How Big is the Private Security Sector'? *Policing and Society*, 5: 221–32.

Jones, T. and Newburn, T. (1997) *Policing After the Act*, London: Policy Studies Institute.

Jones, T. and Newburn, T. (1998) *Private Security and Public Policing*, Oxford: Clarendon Press.

Jones, T., MacLean, B. and Young, J. (eds) (1986) *The Islington Crime Survey: Crime, Victimization and Policy in Inner City London*, Aldershot: Gower.

Jordan, B. and Arnold, J. (1995) 'Democracy and Criminal Justice', *Critical Social Policy*, 44/45: 170–82.

Jordan & Sons Ltd. (1987) *Britain's Security Industry*, London: Jordan & Sons Ltd.

Jordan & Sons Ltd. (1989) *Britain's Security Industry*, London: Jordan & Sons Ltd.

Jordan & Sons Ltd. (1991) *Britain's Security Industry*, London: Jordan & Sons Ltd.

Judge, T. (1988) 'Is There a Profit to be Made Out of Policing', *Police*, December: 12–16.

Kakalik, J.S. and Wildhorn, S. (1972) *Private Police in the United States*, National Institute of Law Enforcement and Criminal Justice: US Dept. of Justice. 4 volumes.

Kania, R.E. (1989) 'The French Municipal Police Experiment', *Police Studies*, 12, 3: 125–31.

Kelling, G., Pate, T., Dieckman, D. and Brown, C. (1974) *The Kansas City Preventive Patrol Experiment: A Summary Report*, Washington DC: Police Foundation.

Kenny, D.J. (1986) *Examining the Role of Active Citizen Participation in the Law Enforcement Process*, unpublished PhD. Thesis, Rutgers University.

Kettle, M. (1985) 'The National Reporting Centre and the 1984 Miners' Strike, in Fine, B. and Millar, R. (eds) *Policing the Miners' Strike*, London: Lawrence & Wishart: 23–33.

King, P. (1989) 'Prosecution Associations and Their Impact in Eighteenth Century Essex', in Hay, D. and Snyder, F. (eds) *Policing and Prosecution in Britain 1750–1850*, Oxford: Clarendon Press: 171–207.

Kinsey, R., Lea, J. and Young, J. (1986) *Losing the Fight Against Crime*, Oxford: Blackwell.

Klockars, C.B. (1980) 'The Dirty Harry Problem', *The Annals*, 452: 33–47.

Klockars, C.B. (1991) 'The Rhetoric of Community Policing', in Klockars, C.B. and Mastrofski, S.D. (eds) *Thinking About Policing*, New York: McGraw-Hill: 530–42.

Kraska, P.B. and Kappeler, V.E. (1997) 'Militarizing American Police: The Rise and Normalization of Paramiltary Units', *Social Problems*, 44, 1: 1–17.

Labour Party (1986) *Protecting Our People: Labour's Policy on Crime Prevention*, London: Labour Party.

Lash, S. and Urry, J. (1987) *The End of Organized Capitalism*, Cambridge: Polity.

Lea, J. and Young, J. (1984) *What Is To Be Done About Law And Order?* Harmondsworth: Penguin.

Leishman, F., Cope, S. and Starie, P. (1996) 'Re-inventing and Restructuring: Towards a "new policing order", in Leishman, F., Loveday, B. and Savage, S. (eds) *Core Issues in Policing*, London: Longman: 9–25.

Liang, Hsi-Huey (1992) *The Rise of the Modern Police and the European State System from Metternich to the Second World War*, Cambridge: Cambridge University Press.

Lilley, J.R. and Knepper, P. (1992) 'An International Perspective on the Privatization of Corrections', *The Howard Journal*, 31, 3: 174–91.

Lipschutz, R.D. (1992) 'Reconstructing World Politics: The Emergence of Global Civil Society', *Millennium: Journal of International Studies*, 21, 3: 389–420.

Lipset, S.M. (1960) *Political Man*, London: Heinemann.

Loader, I. (1996) *Youth, Policing and Democracy*, London: Macmillan.

Loader, I. (1997a) 'Private Security and the Demand for Protection in Contemporary Britain', *Policing and Society*, 7: 143–62.

Loader, I. (1997b) 'Thinking Normatively About Private Security', *Journal of Law and Society*, 24, 3: 377–94.

Logan, C.H. (1990) *Private Prisons and Penal Purpose*, Oxford: Oxford University Press.

Loveday, B. (1996a) 'Business as Usual? The New Police Authorities and the Police and Magistrates' Courts Act', *Local Government Studies*, Summer: 22–39.

Loveday, B. (1996b) 'Crime at the Core'? in Leishman, F., Loveday, B. and Savage, S. (eds) *Core Issues in Policing*, London: Longman: 73–100.

Lubans, V. and Edgar, J. (1979) *Policing By Objectives*, Hartford Connecticut: Social Development Corporation.

Lustgarten, L. (1986) *The Governance of Police*, London: Sweet & Maxwell.

McCorry, J. and Morrisey, M. (1989) 'Community, Crime and Punishment in West Belfast', *The Howard Journal of Criminal Justice*, 28, 4: 282–90.

McElroy, J.E., Cosgrove, C. and Sadd, S. (1993) *Community Policing: The CPOP in New York*, Newbury Park: Sage.

McLaughlin, E. (1994) *Community Policing and Accountability: The Politics of Policing in Manchester in the 1980s*, Aldershot: Avebury.

McLaughlin, E. and Murji, K. (1997) 'The Future Lasts a Long Time: Public Policework and the Managerialist Paradox', in Francis, P., Davies, P. and Jupp, V. (eds) *Policing Futures. The Police, Law Enforcement and the Twenty-First Century*, London: Macmillan: 80–103.

McMullan, J.L. (1987) 'Policing the Criminal Underworld: State Power and Decentralized Social Control in London 1550–1700', in Lowman, J., Menzies, R.J. and Palys, T.S. (eds) *Transcarceration: Essays in the Sociology of Social Control*, Aldershot: Gower: 119–38.

Magee, K. (1988) 'The Dual Role of the Royal Ulster Constabulary in Northern Ireland, in Reiner, R. and Cross, M. (eds) *Beyond Law and Order: Criminal Justice Policy and Politics in the 1990s*, London: Macmillan: 78–90.

Mair, G. and Mortimer, E. (1996) *Curfew Orders with Electronic Monitoring*, London: Home Office Research Study 163.

Manning, P. (1979) 'The Social Control of Police Work', in Holdaway, S. (ed.) *The British Police*, London: Arnold: 41–65.

Manning, P. (1988) 'Community Policing as Drama of Control', in Greene, J.R. and Mastrofski, S.D. (eds) *Community Policing Rhetoric or Reality?* New York: Praeger: 27–45.

Manwaring-Wright, S. (1983) *The Policing Revolution*, Brighton: Harvester.

Marshall, G. (1965) *Police and Government*, London: Methuen.

Marshall, G. (1978) 'Police Accountability Revisited', in Butler, D. and Halsey, A. (eds) *Policy and Politics*, London: Macmillan:

Marshall, T.H. (1963) *Sociology at the Crossroads and Other Essays*, London: Heinemann.

Marx, G. (1987) 'The Interweaving of Public and Private Police in Undercover Work', in Shearing, C.D. and Stenning, P.C. (eds) *Private Policing*, California: Sage: 172–93.

Marx, G. (1988) *Undercover: Police Surveillance in America*, Berkeley: University of California Press.

Mastrofski, S.D. (1991) 'Community Policing as Reform: A Cautionary Tale', in Klockars, C.B. and Mastrofski, S.D. (eds) *Thinking About Policing*, New York: McGraw-Hill: 515–29.

Mawby, R. (1990) *Comparative Policing Issues: The British and American Experience in International Perspective*, London: Unwin Hyman.

Ministerie van Justitie (1985) *Society and Crime: A Policy Plan for the Netherlands*, The Hague: Ministerie van Justitie.

Miyazawa, S. (1991) 'The Private Sector and Law Enforcement in Japan', in Gormley, W.T. (ed.) *Privatization and Its Alternative*, Madison: University of Wisconsin Press: 241–57.

Morgan, R. (1987) 'Consultation and Police Accountability', in Mawby, R. (ed.) *Policing Britain: Proceedings of a Conference in the South West Social Issues Series*, Plymouth Polytechnic, 28 April: 5–30.

Morgan, R. and Maggs, C. (1985) *Setting the PACE: Police Community Consultation in England and Wales*, University of Bath: Centre for the Analysis of Social Policy, Bath Social Policy Papers No. 4.

Morgan, R. and Newburn, T. (1997) *The Future of Policing*, Oxford: Clarendon Press.

Morn, F. (1982) *The Eye That Never Sleeps*, Bloomington: Indiana University Press.

Morris, T. (1985) 'The Case for a Riot Squad', *New Society*, 29 November: 363–4.

Munck, R. (1988) 'The Lads and the Hoods: Alternative Justice in the Irish Context', in Tomlinson, M., Varley, T. and McCullagh, C. (eds) *Whose Law and Order? Aspects of Crime and Social Control in Irish Society*, Belfast: Sociological Association of Ireland: 41–53.

Murray, C. (1996) 'The Underclass', in Muncie, J. and McLaughlin, E. (eds) *Criminological Perspectives*, London: Sage.

Murray, R. (1991) 'The State after Henry', *Marxism Today*, May: 22–7.

Nalla, M. and Newman, G. (1990) *A Primer in Private Security*, New York: Harrow and Heston.

Narayan, S. (1994) 'The West European Market for Security Products and Services', *International Security Review*, Winter: 28–9.

National Police Agency (1994) *White Paper on Police 1994 (Excerpt)*, Tokyo: National Police Agency, Government of Japan.

Newburn, T. (1995) *Crime and Criminal Justice Policy*, London: Longman.

Newburn, T. and Jones, T. (1996) 'Police Accountability', in Saulsbury, W., Mott, J. and Newburn, T. (eds) *Themes in Contemporary Policing*, London: Independent Committee of Inquiry into the Roles and Responsibilities of the Police: 120–32.

Norris, C.A. (1996) *The Role of the Informant in the Criminal Justice System*, Economic and Social Research Council.

Northam, G. (1988) *Shooting in the Dark: Riot Police in Britain*, London: Faber and Faber.

Northern Eye (1995) *The Thin Blue Line*, Broadcast 16 March.

Norton-Taylor, R. (1997) 'EU Guards its Secrets', *The Guardian*, 24 March.

O'Connor, J. (1973) *The Fiscal Crisis of the State*, New York: St. James Press.

O'Malley, J. (1992) 'Risk, Power and Crime Prevention', *Economy and Society*, 21, 3: 252–75.

O'Malley, P. and Palmer, D. (1996) 'Post-Keynesian Policing', *Economy and Society*, 25, 2: 137–55.

Osborne, D. and Gaebler, T. (1993) *Reinventing Government*, New York: Plume.

O'Toole, G. (1978) *The Private Sector: Private Spies, Rent-a-Cops, and the Police-Industrial Complex*, New York: Norton & Company.

Palmer, A. (1997) 'Global Crusade That Can Never Be Won', *The Sunday Telegraph*, 31 August: 17.

Palmer, S.H. (1988) *Police and Protest in England and Ireland 1780–1850*, Cambridge: Cambridge University Press.

PANI [Police Authority for Northern Ireland] (1997) *Listening to the Community Working with the RUC*, Belfast: PANI.

Parsons, T. (1964) 'Evolutionary Universals in Society', *American Sociological Review*, 29, 3: 339–57.

Parsons, T. (1966) *Societies: Evolutionary and Comparative Perspectives*, Englewood Cliffs, New Jersey: Prentice-Hall.

Parsons, T. and Smelser, N. (1957) *Economy and Society*, London: Routledge.

Pennell, S., Curtis, C. and Henderson, J. (1985) *Guardian Angels: An Assessment of Citizen Response to Crime*. US Dept. of Justice, Washington: Government Printing Office.

Perry, J.B. (1989) 'Public Support of the Guardian Angels: Vigilante Protection Against Crime', *Sociology and Social Research*, 73, 3: 129–31.

Philips, D. (1989) 'Good Men to Associate and Bad Men to Conspire: Associations for the Prosecution of Felons in England 1760–1860', in Gattrell, V.A.C., Lenman, B. and Parker, G. (eds) *Crime and the Law: The Social History of Crime in Western Europe Since 1500*, London: Europa: 155–89.

Police Foundation (1981) *The Newark Foot Patrol Experiment*, Washington DC: Police Foundation.

Police Foundation/Policy Studies Institute (1996) *The Independent Committee of Inquiry into the Role and Responsibilities of the Police*, London: Police Foundation/Policy Studies Institute.

Police Review (1996) 'Survey Shows Discrepancy in Police and Public Views on Tackling Crime', 2 August.

Pollard, C. (1997) 'Zero Tolerance: Short-term Fix, Long-term Liability?' in Dennis, N. (ed.) *Zero Tolerance: Policing a Free Society*, London: IEA Health and Welfare Unit: 43–60.

Punch, M. and Naylor, T. (1973) 'The Police: A Social Service', *New Society*, 24: 358–61.

Rainey, S. (1996) 'Dangerous Liaisons'? *Security Gazette*, April: 12–14.

Randall, W.E. and Hamilton, P. (1972) 'The Security Industry in the United Kingdom', in Wiles, P. and McClintock, F.H. (eds) *The Security Industry in the United Kingdom: papers presented to the Cropwood Round-Table Conference, July 1971*, Cambridge: Institute of Criminology: 67–72.

Rawlings, P. (1995) 'The Idea of Policing: a History', *Policing and Society*, 5: 129–49.

Read, S. (1997) 'Below Zero', *Police Review*, 17 January: 16–17.

Reiner, R. (1992a) 'Policing a Postmodern Society', *Modern Law Review*, 55, 6: 761–81.

Reiner, R. (1992b) *The Politics of the Police*, Hemel Hempstead: Harvester Wheatsheaf.

Reiner, R. (1997) 'Policing and the Police', in Maguire, M., Morgan, R. and Reiner, R. (eds) *The Oxford Handbook of Criminology*, Oxford: Clarendon Press: 997–1049.

Reiner, R. and Spencer, S. (1993) 'Conclusions and Recommendations', in Reiner, R. and Spencer, S. (eds) *Accountable Policing. Effectiveness, Empowerment and Equity*, London: Institute for Public Policy Research: 172–91.

Reiss, A.J. (1988) *Private Employment of Public Police*, Washington: US Dept. of Justice, Government Printing Office.

Reith, C. (1952) *The Blind Eye of History*, London: Faber & Faber.

Rhodes, R. (1994) 'The Hollowing Out of the State: The Changing Nature of the Public Services in Britain', *Political Quarterly*, 65, 2: 138–51.

Rhodes, R. (1995) *The New Governance: Governing Without Government*, ESRC State of Britain Seminar, Swindon: ESRC.

Robertson, K. (1994) 'Practical Police Cooperation in Europe: The Intelligence Dimension', in Anderson, M. and Den Boer, M. (eds) *Policing Across National Boundaries*, London: Pinter: 106–18.

Robinson, C.D., Scaglion, R. with Olivero, J.M. (1994) *Police in Contradiction: The Evolution of the Police Function in Society*, Westport, Connecticut: Greenwood Press.

Romeanes, T.J. (1996) *Problem Oriented Policing. The Cleveland Approach,* Cleveland Constabulary.

Rose, N. (1996) 'The Death of the Social? Re-figuring the Territory of Government', *Economy and Society*, 25, 3: 327–56.

Rose, R. (1979) 'Ungovernability: Is There Fire Behind the Smoke'? *Political Studies*, 27: 351–70.

Rosenbaum, D. (1995) 'The Changing Role of the Police in North America: Assessing the Current Transition to Community Policing', in *Workshop on Evaluating Police Service Delivery: Report*. Ministry of the Solicitor General of Canada/International Centre for Comparative Criminology, University of Montreal: 29–68.

Rosenbaum, H.J. and Sedeberg, P.C. (eds) (1976) *Vigilante Politics*, Pennsylvania: University of Pennsylvania Press.

Routledge, P. (1993) ' "Citizens" Army Will Fight Crime', *The Independent*, 5 December.

Royal Borough of Kensington & Chelsea (1992) *Holland Park Police* (pamphlet).

Royal Borough of Kensington & Chelsea (n.d.) *Parks, Gardens and Open Spaces By-Laws*.

Savage, S. and Charman, S. (1996) 'Managing Change', in Leishman, F. et al. (eds) *Core Issues in Policing*, London: Longman: 39–53.

Savage, S. and Wilson, C. (1987) 'Ask a policeman? Community consultation in practice', *Social Policy and Administration*, 21, 3: 252–63.

Scarman, L. (1981) *The Brixton Disorders: 10–12 April 1981*, Cmnd 8427, London: HMSO.

Schwartz, R.T. and Miller, J.C. (1964) 'Legal evolution and social complexity', *American Journal of Sociology*, 70, 1: 159–69.

Scraton, P. (ed.) (1987) *Law, Order and the Authoritarian State*, Milton Keynes: Open University.

Scull, A. (1977) *Decarceration: Community Treatment and the Deviant. A Radical View*, Englewood Cliffs, New Jersey: Prentice Hall.

Shapland, J. and Vagg, J. (1988) *Policing By The Public*, London: Routledge.

Shearing, C.D. (1992) 'The Relation Between Public and Private Policing', in Tonry, M. and Morris, N. (eds) *Modern Policing: Crime and Justice: A Review of Research*, Vol. 15, Chicago: University of Chicago Press: 399–434.

Shearing, C.D. (1994) 'Discussant's Comments' to *Workshop on the Evaluation of Police Service Deliver: Transcription*. Solicitor General of Canada/International Centre for Comparative Criminology, 2–4 November.

Shearing, C.D. (1996) 'Public and Private Policing', in Saulsbury, W., Mott, J. and Newburn, T. (eds) *Themes in Contemporary Policing*, London: Independent Committee of Inquiry into the Roles and Responsibilities of the Police: 83–95.

Shearing, C.D. (forthcoming) 'Violence and the Changing Face of Governance: Privatization and its Implications', in Einstein, S. and Amin, M. (eds) *Police, Security and Democracy*, Vol. 2, The Uncertainty Series, Hampshire: Ashgate Publishing Co.

Shearing, C.D. and Stenning, P.C. (1981) 'Modern Private Security: Its Growth and Implications', in Tonry, M. and Norris, N. (eds) *Crime and Justice: An Annual Review of Research*, Vol. 3, Chicago: University of Chicago Press: 193–245.

Shearing, C.D. and Stenning, P.C. (eds) (1987) *Private Policing*, California: Sage.

Sheptycki, J. (1995a) 'Transnational Policing and the Makings of a Modern State', *British Journal of Criminology*, 35, 4: 613–35.

Sheptycki, J. (1995b) Review of books on transnational policing [Benyon, J. *et al.* (1993) 'Police Co-operation in Europe'; Fijnaut, C. (ed.) (1993) The Internationalization of Police Co-operation in Western Europe', and Nadelmann, E.A. (1993) 'Cops Across Borders'] *British Journal of Criminology*, 35, 2: 302–6.

Sheptycki, J. (1996) 'Law Enforcement, Justice and Democracy in the Transnational Arena: Reflections on the War on Drugs', *International Journal of the Sociology of Law*, 24: 61–75.

Sheptycki, J. (1997) 'Transnationalism, Crime Control and the European State System: A Review of the Literature, *International Criminal Justice Review*, Vol. 7.

Sherman, L.W. (1991) 'Police Crackdowns', in Klockars, C.B. and Mastrofski, S.D. (eds) *Thinking About Police*, New York: McGraw-Hill: 188–210.

Sherman, L.W. (1992) 'Attacking Crime: Policing and Crime Control', in Tonry, M. and Norris, N. (eds) *Modern Policing. Crime and Justice. A Review of Research. Volume 15*, Chicago: University of Chicago Press.

Shotland, R.L. and Goodstein, L.I. (1984) 'The Role of Bystanders in Crime Control', *Journal of Social Issues*, 40, 1: 9–26.

Shubert, A. (1981) 'Private Initiative in Law Enforcement: Associations for the Prosecution of Felons', in Bailey, V. (ed.) *Policing and Punishment in Nineteenth Century Britain*, London: Croom Helm: 25–41.

Simon, J. (1988) 'The Ideological Effects of Actuarial Practices', *Law and Society Review*, 22, 772.

South, N. (1987) 'Law, profit and "private persons"', in Shearing, C.D. and Stenning, P.C. (eds) *Private Policing*, California: Sage: 72–109.

South, N. (1988) *Policing for Profit*, London: Sage.

Sparks, R. (1995) 'Are Prisons Part of the Public Sphere'? in Edgell, S., Walklate, S. and Williams, G. (eds) *Debating the Future of the Public Sphere*, Aldershot: Avebury: 79–98.

Spencer, S. (1985) *Called to Account*, London: NCCL.

Spitzer, S. (1987) 'Security and Control in Capitalist Societies: The Fetishism of Security and the Secret Thereof', in Lowman, J., Menzies, R.J. and Palys, T.S. (eds) *Transcarceration: Essays in the Sociology of Social Control*, Aldershot: Gower: 43–58.

Spitzer, S. and Scull, A. (1977) 'Privatization and Capitalist Development: The Case of the Private Police', *Social Problems*, 25, 1: 18–29.

Steedman, C. (1984) *Policing the Victorian Community: The Formation of English Provincial Police Forces 1856–80*, London: Routledge & Kegan Paul.

Stenning, P.C. and Shearing, C.D. (1980) 'The Quiet Revolution: The Nature, Development and General Legal Implications of Private Security in Canada', *Criminal Law Quarterly*, 22: 220–48.

Stephens, M. and Becker, S. (eds) (1994) *Police Force Police Service*, London: Macmillan.

Storch, R. (1975) 'The Plague of Blue Locusts: Police Reform and Popular Resistance in Northern England 1840–57', *International Review of Social History*, 20: 61–90.

Storch, R. (1976) 'The Policeman as Domestic Missionary: Urban Discipline and Popular Culture in Northern England 1850–1880', *Journal of Social History*, 9, 4: 481–509.

Swift, R. (1988) 'Urban Policing in Early Victorian England, 1835–86: A Reappraisal', *History* 73, 238: 211–37.

Taylor, L. (1976) 'Vigilantes – Why Not'? *New Society*, 4 November: 259–60.

Taylor, M. and Pease, K. (1989) 'Private Prisons and Penal Purpose', in Matthews, R. (ed.) *Privatizing Criminal Justice*, London: Sage: 178–94.

Therborn, G. (1995) *European Modernity and Beyond: The Trajectory of European Societies 1945–2000*, London: Sage.

Tilley, N. and Brooks, S. (1996) 'Popular Coppers', *Police Review*, 2 February: 24–5.

Todd, R. and Elsworth, C. (1997) 'Stalkers Pay Private Eyes to do Dirty Work', *The Sunday Telegraph*, 26 January.

Travis, A. (1994) 'Treasury Touts Police Carve-up', *The Guardian*, 7 April.

Traynor, I. and Smith, H. (1998) 'EU Passport-free Regime Buckles', *The Guardian*, 6 January.

Troyer, R.J. and Wright, R.D. (1985) 'Community Response to Crime: Two Middle Class Anti-crime Patrols', *Journal of Criminal Justice*, 13, 3: 227–41.

Tucker, W. (1985) *Vigilante: The Backlash Against Crime in America*, New York: Stein & Day.

Uglow, S. with Telford, V. (1997) *The Police Act 1997*, London: Jordans.

UK Equities Direct (1996) *UK Equities Direct*, Hemmington Scott Publishers.

Van Dijk J.J.M. and Junger-Tas, M. (1988) 'Trends in Crime Prevention in the Netherlands', in Hope, T. and Shaw, M. (eds) *Communities and Crime Reduction*, London: Home Office Research and Planning Unit: 260–76.

Van Reenen, P. (1989) 'Policing Europe after 1992: Co-operation and Competition', *European Affairs*, 3 (2): 45–53.

Vidal, J. (1996) 'The Bypass of Justice', *The Guardian*, 9 April.

Vogler, R. (1991) *Reading the Riot Act: The Magistracy, the Police and the Army in Civil Disorder*, Milton Keynes: Open University.

Wackenhut Corporation (1995) *Annual Report*, March.

Waddington, D. (1996) 'Key issues and Controversies', in Critcher, C. and Waddington, D. (eds) *Policing Public Order: Theoretical and Practical Issues*, Avebury: Aldershot: 1–36.

Waddington, P.A.J. (1989) 'A National Police Force is the Safeguard of Civil Liberty', *The Independent*, 7 July.

Waddington, P.A.J. (1993) 'The Case Against Paramilitary Policing Considered', *British Journal of Criminology*, 33, 3: 352–66.

Waddington P.A.J. (1994) *Liberty and Order: Public Order Policing in a Capital City*, London: UCL Press.

Waddington, P.A.J. (1996a) 'The Politics of Public Order Policing: A "Typographical Analysis"' in Critcher, C. and Waddington, D. (eds) *Policing Public Order: Theoretical and Practical Issues*, Avebury: Aldershot: 129–44.

Waddington, P.A.J. (1996b) 'Public Order Policing: Citizenship and Moral Ambiguity', in Leishman, F., Loveday, B. and Savage, S. (eds) *Core Issues in Policing*, London: Longman: 114–30.

Waddington, P.A.J. (1996c) 'Stop and Search', *Police Review*, 19 April: 16–17.

Waddington, P.A.J. (1997) 'Policing with the Gloves Off', *Police Review*, 25 April: 26–7.

Wall, D. (1997) 'Policing the Virtual Community': The Internet, Cyberspace and Cybercrime', in Francis, P., Davies, P. and Jupp, V. (eds) *Policing Futures: The Police, Law Enforcement and the Twenty-First Century*, London: Macmillan: 208–36.

Wall, D. (1998) *The Chief Constables of England and Wales: The Socio-Legal History of a Criminal Justice Elite*, Aldershot: Dartmouth.

Wall, D. (forthcoming) 'Policing Cybercrimes: The Virtual Community and the Policing of Cyberspace'.

Walsh, W.F. and Donovan, E.J. (1989) 'Private Security and Community Policing: Evaluation and Comment', *Journal of Criminal Justice*, 17: 187–97.

Wandsworth Parks Constabulary (n.d.) 'What Can They Do For You'? (pamphlet).

Waters, I. (1996) 'Quality of Service: Politics or Paradigm Shift'? in Leishman, F., Loveday, B. and Savage, S. (eds) *Core Issues in Policing*, London: Longman: 205–17.

Waters, M. (1995) *Globalization*, London: Routledge.

Weatheritt, M. (1988) 'Community Policing: Rhetoric or Reality'? in Greene, J.R. and Mastrofski, S.D. (eds) *Community Policing Rhetoric or Reality?* New York: Praeger: 153–75.

Weber, M. (1964) *The Theory of Social and Economic Organization*, New York: Free Press.

Weitzer, R. (1995) *Policing Under Fire: Ethnic Conflict and Police-Community Relations in Northern Ireland*, Albany: State University of New York Press.

West, M.L. (1993) 'Get a Piece of the Privatization Pie', *Security Management*, March: 58–60.

Wiggs, S. (1990) *Re The Constitutional Position of Bodies Such As the 'Wandsworth Parks Constabulary'*, London: New Scotland Yard.

Wilson, J.Q. (1968) *Varieties of Police Behaviour*, Cambridge Massachusetts: Harvard University Press.

Wilson, J.Q. and Kelling, G.L. (1982) 'Broken Windows: The Police and Neighbourhood Safety', *The Atlantic Monthly*, March: 29–38.

Woolf, M. (1996) 'British Firms Cash in on Crime', *The Observer*, 14 July.

Index